THE
BOND

THE
BOND

THE
BOND

TWO EPIC CLIMBS IN ALASKA AND A LIFETIME'S CONNECTION BETWEEN CLIMBERS

SIMON McCARTNEY

Published by Vertebrate Publishing, Sheffield.
www.v-publishing.co.uk

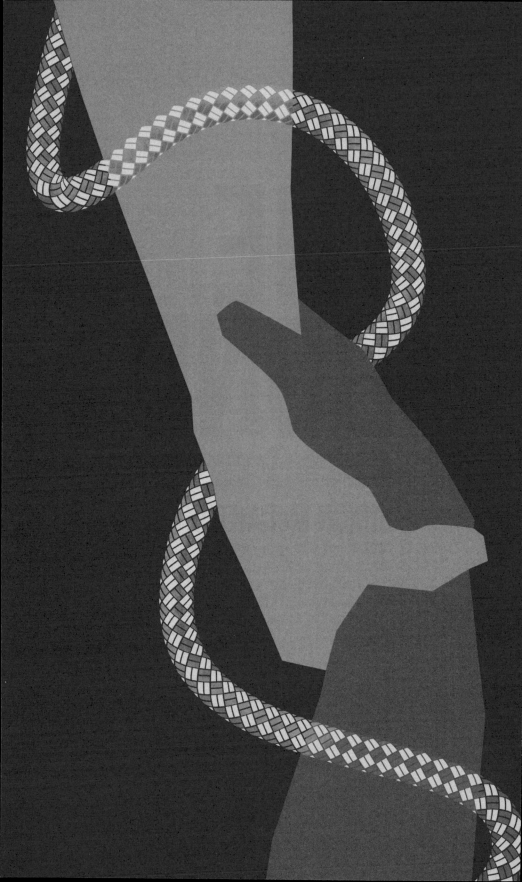

For Mac

This book is dedicated to the memory of my father – a fine and lovely man. He introduced me to the wonder of the mountains and made sure I grew up with the belief that you can always do better if you have the will to try.

THE BOND

SIMON McCARTNEY

First published in 2016 by Vertebrate Publishing.

Vertebrate Publishing
Crescent House, 228 Psalter Lane, Sheffield S11 8UT, UK.
www.v-publishing.co.uk

This book is a work of non-fiction based on the life of Simon McCartney. The author has stated to
the publishers that, except in such minor respects not affecting the substantial accuracy of
the work, the contents of the book are true.

A CIP catalogue record for this book is available from the British Library.

ISBN: 978-1-910240-66-3 (Hardback)
ISBN: 978-1-910240-67-0 (Ebook)

10 9 8 7 6 5 4 3 2 1

Design and production by Nathan Ryder.
Vertebrate Publishing. www.v-publishing.co.uk

Vertebrate Publishing is committed to printing on paper from sustainable sources.

MIX
Paper from
responsible sources
FSC® C013056

Printed and bound in the UK by T.J. International Ltd, Padstow, Cornwall.

CONTENTS

FOREWORD

MARK WESTMAN

In 1977, Jack Roberts, a California 'Stonemaster' and experienced young alpinist, teamed up with Simon McCartney, a highly motivated twenty-two-year-old Brit who had cut his teeth climbing in Europe with some of the most respected mountaineers of the time. Over the next three years the pair enjoyed a magical partnership during which they completed two of the boldest and most audacious climbs in the history of Alaskan alpinism.

The north face of Mount Huntington is one of the most dangerous walls in the Alaska Range, and Denali's south-west face is one of the largest and most technically difficult. Roberts and McCartney made the first ascents of both, pushing the boundaries of boldness, risk, commitment and difficulty, utilising a style and attitude that was on the cutting edge for its time. Eschewing any notion of fixed ropes or siege tactics, and with success as their only option, they walked to the foot of these faces with the bare minimum of gear and simply started climbing.

The tale of these two legendary climbs, and of the 'Too Loose' expedition (as the duo came to refer to themselves), was only ever documented enough to arouse curiosity, leaving decades of mystery surrounding the ascents of these savage mountain faces and an absence of appreciation for one of the strongest climbing partnerships of its time. I was one of those captivated by these enigmatic ascents, intrigued by the cryptic accounts that accompanied them, and inspired by the climbers' vision.

In the mid 1990s, as I made my first of many visits to Alaska, I endeavoured to consume every piece of local mountaineering literature and history I could find. At this time, most information was largely found in the *American Alpine Journal* and in Jonathan Waterman's book *High Alaska*, the latter of which became my personal holy scripture. As a novice alpinist with grand ambitions, I found that the colourful history of Alaskan ascents fired my imagination as much as the mountains themselves. The big faces and ridges of the range held heart-stopping tales of bravery, boldness, commitment and vision.

Pervading these stories almost universally was a spirit of teamwork and camaraderie that is seldom witnessed in ordinary pursuits. I wanted to be like the people in these stories – to meet the challenges of these beautiful mountains in the company of my closest friends, to learn, to progress, and to create my own unique experiences. I admired climbers who let their actions and skills speak for them, those who used alpinism as a vehicle for personal challenge and self-discovery rather than for a vacant pursuit of fame or attention.

I wanted to be like Jack and Simon.

Mount Huntington was one of my earliest mountain obsessions. It looks like a mountain should look: steep, forbidding and with a perfect symmetry of razor-sharp ridges rising to a pointed summit. There is no easy way up the mountain and the difficulties are varied and continuous. In 1995, en route to Denali's south buttress, I skied directly beneath Huntington's perilous, 5,500-foot-tall north face. It would be hard to imagine a more dangerous wall. A steep and difficult rock band guards the base, and above that the face is stacked with multi-tiered hanging glaciers and séracs. The complete length of the summit ridge is a continuous mass of large cornices, and the face is generally angled such that any snowfall will trigger an immediate barrage of spindrift avalanches. There is no line which could be considered remotely safe to climb, and camping in the valley of the Ruth Glacier's west fork, beneath the face, provides an intimidating and humbling experience as avalanches roar from the wall on a regular basis, with colossal blast clouds sweeping the entire width of the valley. It was hard for my inexperienced mind to imagine that the face had been climbed when I was eight years old.

But I knew there were two climbers who had ignored conventional wisdom and believed, however naively, that their skills and the strength of their partnership were powerful enough that they could create their own luck. Jack Roberts and Simon McCartney were not only very skilled climbers, they were also bold and brash, and any ascent of Huntington's north face required such an attitude, if not outright arrogance, to believe one could survive it.

Roberts submitted a report to the 1979 *American Alpine Journal* which was an entertaining read, written as a stream of consciousness, a metaphorical style which wryly and eloquently alluded to how serious and dangerous the ascent had been. More specifically, his report focused less on the details of the climb and more on the situations, his connection with Simon, and dreamy ruminations on what drives him to seek such experiences. The article was in fact a brilliant essay on difficult alpine climbing which made a strong impression upon my youthful and ambitious mind.

One line succinctly captured the essence of the ascent:

We were definitely bluffing our way up this mountain without a clue where we were going. The only thing that was certain was that the correct way off was up. Uninterested in anything except survival, Simon and I fled from one sheltered spot to another.

There is often a raw simplicity that characterises hardcore alpinism, which is also one of its greatest attractions. I would allow these words to guide me into and through many intense situations of my own in the future.

Roberts continued:

On again and, moving higher, I was puzzled, a trifle alarmed. The belay stance was supposed to be here; it must have moved! Deciding not to sound panic-stricken, I yelled down to Simon. 'No belay here. Move the belay up fifteen feet more.' Simon didn't understand. 'Here I come. Got me on?' For a while we climbed roped together without belays.

Simply being on a glacier was serious to me at the time I read this passage and I was in complete awe of people who climbed technical ground in the mountains. This sort of boldness, described in casual, humorous and low-key terms, left me dumbstruck. It revealed attitudes and options which up until then I had not considered possible.

Roberts reflected further during one of Simon's leads:

Climbers who choose to pioneer first ascents up difficult and dangerous faces on high mountains have chosen to be crazy – people such as Simon and I. For my part I have chosen to be crazy in order to cope with a crazy world and have adopted craziness as a lifestyle. Only on becoming convinced that the world I left behind in Los Angeles is sane, could I give up my craziness. And that cannot be done. A climber entering the subculture of a climbing community accepts his alienation from larger society and proclaims he is a full-fledged 'normal' person – that it is others who are abnormal. Simon meanwhile is gripped speechless above me, unaware that his faithful belayer is spacing out on crystals of ice and snow. There is some comfort to know that I am tied into somebody who is also crazy.

The words resonated in my consciousness as I read them. I, too, was raised in southern California; I was twenty-five years old, three years out of school and freshly laid off from an office job that was deeply dissatisfying compared to the life of mountain adventure I dreamed of and which consumed every one of my weekends. I was at the headwaters of the life I truly wanted to lead and Jack's words strengthened my resolve to take the 'proper' path. I was also in the early stages of one of my greatest alpine partnerships, that with my friend Joe Puryear, and aspiring to the biggest routes. In our long apprenticeship, one of our frequent comical refrains while climbing was to quote the 'no belay here' exchange between Simon and Jack. We didn't have the precocious skills of those two, but we jokingly adopted their attitude to break the tension of the stressful situations in which we frequently found ourselves. And happily, we each thought the other was crazy.

Their successful 1978 ascent of Huntington only emboldened Simon and Jack, and they returned to Alaska in 1980 with a much bigger and more serious project in mind: Denali's unclimbed, 8,000-foot-tall south-west face, by way of a line tackling the precipitous rock wall rising to the left of the hallowed Cassin Ridge. True to form, Jack and Simon boldly made their ascent in alpine style, which was only just coming into vogue in Alaska. The style was in its infancy and had yet to develop – and benefit from – the extreme speed tactics or the lightweight gear utilised by modern ascents. Attacking committing routes in Alaska in such a manner, with no fixed lines and planning for six to ten days of climbing, was extremely risky given that fine weather in Alaska seldom lasts longer than three or four days. The Infinite Spur on Mount Foraker, climbed in 1977 by George Lowe and Michael Kennedy, was at that time the most difficult and committing route accomplished in Alaska. As of 1980, it was still the only ascent in the Alaska Range of comparable size and difficulty to Denali's south-west face which had been undertaken and completed without the use of fixed ropes or multiple carries. While the Infinite Spur is more remote and committing than the south-west face of Denali, the technical difficulties on Denali are considerably harder, and the mountain's additional 3,000 feet of altitude make the south-west face a far more demanding undertaking.

Unfortunately, altitude illness was less understood in 1980 than it is now. Jack and Simon did not acclimatise prior to their ascent, believing they could do so during the climb. Far above all the technical difficulties, in a veritable no man's land at 19,000 feet, Simon was stricken and immobilised with high altitude cerebral oedema. Both men survived the ensuing ordeal but Simon McCartney would never climb again and Jack Roberts would carry the weight of these events for the remainder of his life.

The epic rescue of Simon McCartney involved the assistance of the park service and many independent teams. Jack had made the agonising decision, while suffering from starvation and frostbitten feet, to leave his completely incapacitated partner high on the Cassin Ridge in order to go for help. These facts, along with a slew of conflicting accounts and a letter to a magazine written by someone impersonating McCartney, helped to generate a great deal of post-climb controversy and criticism in the ensuing months. The fallout from the ascent surely contributed to the fact that no official written account of the climb was ever published.

After leaving Alaska, Simon and Jack met and spent time together only once more, in 1981 in London. Soon afterwards, Simon 'disappeared' without explanation and his status amongst the climbing community became 'whereabouts unknown'. Many people thought Simon had died.

The controversy surrounding the Denali ascent would also lead to questions being asked about the actions of Jack and Simon on Huntington. Years later, some credible sources in the community openly speculated that the ascent of Huntington had been an elaborate hoax. With Simon out of the picture, Jack was the only one left to answer to these allegations. When asked for proof, he would reportedly answer, dismissively, 'Go climb the route and then get back to me'. Jack's complex personality off the mountain had perhaps helped to drive some of these questions, and it is indeed odd that producing a single photo could have silenced his critics in an instant. Instead, I suspect that Huntington had been hard enough to climb and survive that Jack simply felt no obligation to revisit it, much less defend it.

It would not be hard to imagine, also, Jack's private sense of disappointment and isolation at having lost all contact with Simon, the only other person in the world who knew and could relate to the innermost substance of these life-altering achievements.

The objective hazards of Huntington's north face always kept it out of consideration for me as a climb, but in 2007 I finally consummated my own appointment with the south-west face of Denali. During an ascent of the

Cassin Ridge in 2000, I had been captivated by the up-close views of the face. Its difficulties were beyond my capabilities at the time, but I diligently worked my way towards it for the next seven years. With Colin Haley, I climbed the Denali Diamond, a route established in 1983 and which, I later confirmed, actually follows the Roberts-McCartney route for the first two-thirds of the lower rock wall. The Diamond finishes by way of an obvious and very difficult upper dihedral. Jack and Simon had intended to climb this same dihedral but upon reaching it did not believe they could climb the overhanging ice it contained, leading them to forge an also-difficult finish on steep rock several hundred feet to the left.

In the years leading up to my ascent, I had the opportunity to befriend Jack Roberts at Kahiltna Base Camp on Denali. Jack regularly guided ice routes on the lower peaks around the area and was a frequent presence in camp over many seasons. Jack was in his fifties when we met, and he typically sported a 1920s-style newsboy hat and lots of gold jewellery. I tried to imagine what a character he must have been thirty years earlier. I always enjoyed his casual demeanour and could sense his comfort and ease in the mountain environment, provided by his years of experience. He was friendly and helpful as I prodded him for information about the south-west face, and he provided me with a topo drawing he had created many years earlier. At the same time, I could tell he was holding something back. I knew a summarised version of his epic ascent and of Simon's rescue, but I was reluctant to press further, sensing that it might be a touchy subject.

When Colin and I eventually succeeded in climbing the south-west face in a forty-five-hour effort, Jack emailed to congratulate me on the ascent, which was a humbling moment. He told me that his ascent of the south-west face was perhaps his proudest achievement.

During this same period I made a discovery that got me thinking about Jack and Simon's 1978 ascent of Mount Huntington. Was it a hoax? I personally had never doubted the legitimacy of their climb, but those who had raised doubts were trusted people in the community. And with Simon gone, no photos published, and Jack seemingly not looking back, the climb had taken on mythical proportions.

I wanted the story to be true. In Jack's 1979 report he had noted that, while descending the Harvard route after the ascent, their climbing ropes had become hopelessly stuck while rappelling over a prominent feature, a roof named the Nose. This forced the pair to continue descending with what rope they could cut free and some old fixed line they discovered. In 2005, I made one of my many attempts on the Harvard route. Conditions were very dry that season, and at the foot of the Nose there was far more rock exposed than in prior attempts. Here I found a very old, faded, purple and gold climbing rope snagged on a flake at the foot of the wall and extending downhill into the snow … very much the appearance and arrangement one might expect of a rope which had been stuck and abandoned on a rappel pull. On my prior attempts this rope had evidently been buried by deep snows. Later, I checked my photos from a 1998 attempt, and noticed an additional length of this same climbing rope hooked in a flake seventy feet above this point, atop the Nose pitch, and hanging part way down the upper portion of this very steep wall. I suspected, of course, that the rope could be Jack and Simon's.

I mentioned my find to Jack the following season. He simply shrugged and said, with a faraway look, 'Yeah … probably ours … ' He otherwise seemed unsurprised. Out of respect, and because I only knew him casually, I never raised the subject of the doubts surrounding the ascent with him, but I could only imagine how it would feel to have accomplished – to have survived – an ascent of that face, and then have it questioned publicly.

In January of 2012, I was scheduled as a featured slide-show presenter for the annual ice festival in Ouray, Colorado. By this time, I had spent enough seasons hanging around Jack in Alaska that he began to feel like an old friend. We sat together and had a light-hearted conversation during the first evening of the festival's social events. The following evening, Jack came to my slide presentation, and I was filled with pride that one of my Alaska climbing heroes was sitting in the audience to watch my own show about Alaskan alpinism. Afterwards, Jack and I had drinks at the Mexican restaurant down the street. At fifty-nine years old, Jack was clearly in his element, holding court as one of the elder statesmen of the American climbing community. He carried the relaxed aura of a man who had followed his dreams.

Perhaps one month later, an email from an internet forum appeared in my inbox.

Simon McCartney has sent you a message.

I could scarcely believe my eyes. Simon was alive! I was soon to discover that a magnificent journey was about to begin for us both.

Two years have passed since that message arrived. During this time, Simon and I have spent long hours gathered around a virtual campfire and I listened in rapture as he began to recount the greatest story never told in the annals of

Alaskan climbing literature. It is a very personal and human tale that carries one from the Bernese Oberland and the glaciated spires of Chamonix to the walls of Yosemite and the faces of Alaska, and which showcases the development and progression of two young and inspired alpinists who followed a shared dream to its ultimate and inescapable conclusion.

During the course of this journey, Simon has taken me, in my mind's eye and in his photos, to where I know I will never go: up Huntington's north face. I thanked him for climbing that face so that no one else has to do it. We have discussed our respective and extremely contrasting adventures on Denali's enormous south-western wall. The whole experience has been akin to a visit with a man who has returned from the dead – but Simon is very much alive, and he carries the gleam in his eye of one who has seen, of one who knows, and of one who survived, just barely, to tell the tale. His story is a celebration, a remembrance, a tribute to Jack and their partnership, and is told with the objectivity of a man softened by age and decades of detachment from the addiction of alpine pursuits.

It has been humbling to witness Simon unload thirty years of suppressed memories in the writing of this book. It has been my privilege to be the first to hear his whole story, one I have spent decades waiting to hear, and to help Simon bridge the gap across the several generations of his absence from the community.

What gets buried in alpinism does not stay buried forever. Such pursuits, no matter how we may try to escape them, come to shape who we are as people and to define the essence of our lives and our spirit, even long after the deeds are done. In the compelling pages ahead, Simon McCartney has assembled input from the entire surviving cast of characters who contributed to these gripping adventures. Over thirty years have passed, but the vivid precision with which Simon illustrates the relationships, emotions and the forbidding mountain landscapes that combined to create these stories is a testimony to their everlasting imprint upon his life.

Oh, and he showed me a photo of himself and Jack, taken in 1978, standing beneath Huntington's north face. In it, they hold a shiny, new purple and gold climbing rope.

I hope his timeless story inspires and instructs you in your own journeys, wherever they might lead.

MARK WESTMAN
Talkeetna, Alaska – January 2014

How he comes o'er us with our wilder days.
Not measuring what use we made of them.
Henry V
WILLIAM SHAKESPEARE

PROLOGUE

It has been a long, pointless, frustrating day and my mood should be worse. I have been giving advice to a committee of the local tourism and cultural development company, in a disgusting smoky room, via a translator who looks bored, to an audience that looks confused.

Luckily I am not alone in this part of rural China; Al Chambers is with me. At least I have his dry sense of humour to keep me sane. Almost.

Al and I have worked all over the world together. It is my role as a design director for the company Laservision to visualise new high-tech multimedia shows for customers – most of whom are theme parks or governments – and persuade them to part with their cash, lots of it. Al's great talent is building whatever I think of and, incredibly, it works. We share a mutual respect and trust for one another, and while many projects have been a challenge, so far all of them have ended well.

Unfortunately, this time we are on a fool's errand. We are designing an attraction for the 'historical' tourist development that is being hastily built on the banks of the Grand Canal that runs from Hangzhou to Beijing. This ancient canal became a major transport artery after it was constructed by hand and by oxen hundreds of years ago; it brought the prosperity that spawned the little Qing dynasty town where we are treading water today.

It is a fool's errand because the government-owned enterprise we are dealing with does not have the money to build the show we are designing. We are actors in a pointless farce. If I am honest, I am not even convinced that they *should* build a multimedia show, even if money were no object. A show like this seems somewhat out of place in this little old town. It would be a bit like putting a laser show in the Alamo or in the Forbidden Palace. Come to think of it, there was a laser show in front of the Forbidden Palace in Tiananmen Square a few years back. It looked terrible.

The previous year, in Hong Kong, we helped to put together the largest permanent light and sound show in the world. Twenty-four buildings on Victoria Harbour light up every night at eight o'clock in a music-synchronised show called 'A Symphony of Lights'. It was the most stressful project the pair of us had ever worked on. It made us sick, tired and a bit cynical. But it was this project that brought us to the attention of the local Chinese government in Wuzhen.

And so here we are, in an ancient water village that is charming but which has been largely neglected until now. The notion that there might be money to be made from tourism is a recent concept for the local government and now they are suddenly on fire, developing the idea as quickly as possible and frantically rebuilding a desecrated part of the village in 'traditional style'. They are, allegedly, even paying old people to pretend to be living in it.

But as fascinating as the villages of Dong Zha and Xi Zha might be, the little 'modern' satellite town we are staying in lacks any vestige of charm. It is dirty and noisy and garbage is strewn everywhere. To make things worse, the airborne pollution is all-pervasive and smog hangs over the town. Combined with the flat light from an overcast sky, it is a depressing place.

I do not mind that the hotel we are staying in only has hot water after 2 p.m., or that it is actually a 'love hotel' you can rent by the hour. No, that just explains why the wall between the bedroom and the bathroom is glass. I don't really care that the food is awful or that the mice outnumber us at the breakfast buffet because we can buy fruit from the roadside stalls. Besides, Al and I could both lose a little weight. What is irritating is that it is now nearly dark and we cannot find anywhere even vaguely nice to drink a few beers and relax. But we are not giving in easily; we are on a mission.

I sometimes play the 'if you were marooned on a tropical island, who would you take with you?' game. Well, Al would be on my list: intelligent, funny, sarcastic, resourceful and just at this minute, determined. The locals in Wuzhen must surely like fun, so where do they hide it?

We have slipped away, disappointed, from the main street into a maze of dark alleyways that lie brooding behind it. We are on a military exercise now and this has become a systematic search, block by tiny block. Turning a corner we see a splash of red neon above a small doorway, beyond which is a set of dimly lit and greasy stairs. Horrid music issues forth, accompanied by the off-key screeching of a tone-deaf singer. We must have reached a cultural hub of Wuzhen: the karaoke bar. We will not go inside, but we know that if there is another bar, it must be close.

Al sees it first and I follow his gaze through the grimy window. I can make out the figure of a skinny girl behind a counter, her features ghostlike in the dreary glow of a television.

The bottom edge of the door groans wearily on the dirty floor as I pull it open and the girl looks up with a start.

'Ni hao,' Al says.

I let Al do the talking because my Putonghua is appalling. I have seen Al successfully order beer in China before, so I am content to study our tiny surroundings while he organises the liquids.

There is only one table, which is bounded on both sides by two 'love seats' – swing seats made of woven bamboo suspended precariously by ropes. If that were not enough, someone has added to the romance by weaving blooms of plastic ivy around the edges of the seats and up the ropes that support them.

There is beer but it is warm. There is a fridge but it is not working. This is a problem because we are Australians, albeit one of us adopted, and warm beer is anathema to us. The local beer is not that good anyway, even when it is cold. As an alternative there are two dust-covered bottles of Chinese red wine, standing unloved and forgotten on a dusty shelf like two terracotta warriors. Al turns to me:

'OK, McCartney, the bottle of Great Wall or the bottle of Die-Nasty?'

Perhaps the careful storage has improved these great appellations. I choose the one from the sunny side of the vineyard (nearest to the window).

'Take the Die-Nasty.'

'Aha, I was born to have adventure.'

He is quoting to me from one of his favourite Frank Zappa songs, 'Camarillo Brillo'.

Al is a musical encyclopaedia; I shared a house with him on Lamma Island in Hong Kong last year. Thanks to Al, we had the blues for breakfast, lunch and dinner, often to the dismay of our neighbours.

The girl sells us the wine and even has two washed glasses – but no bottle opener. No problem for the desert-island team because Al has a Swiss army knife with a corkscrew in it. Of course he does.

We settle into our romantic nook. He makes a comedy out of pouring a splash for me. I hold it up to the light to examine the 'legs' like a connoisseur might and take a sniff before I drink it in one gulp.

'Merde!'

'But are you going to drink it, Monsieur?'

'Immédiatement!'

Somehow the awful surroundings have made the evening all the more amusing and the undrinkable wine has just made us thirstier.

Despite the fact that I had spent a lot of time with Al, all our conversations have been mostly work related. For the first time we talk about our families and our early years.

Al grew up in Mosman, a well-to-do and now very expensive suburb on the north shore of Sydney Harbour. He spent his youth as many young Aussies do, surfing and sailing in one of the most idyllic places on earth.

I created a picture for him of my teens and early twenties spent in the UK. I tell him how walking in the mountains of Scotland with my dad had developed into a passion for rock and ice climbing as a teenager.

'Climb anything famous?' he asks.

It has been many years since I have discussed climbing with anybody. I have to think about the reply, but one obvious milestone suggests itself.

'Well, yes I did actually. Have you heard of the north face of the Eiger?'

'Who hasn't? Clint Eastwood even made a film about it.'

'Sort of … well, I climbed that face in winter 1979.'

Al is impressed.

'It was OK actually. Hard, but I enjoyed it. But the biggest two climbs I ever did were in Alaska. I made two first ascents with an American climber called Jack Roberts, before I quit.'

'Why did you stop, Si?'

Now I really have to stop and think. I locked all this away long ago. Al is watching me intently as my face clouds; he immediately senses that he has touched a nerve.

'Sorry, mate, if I have pried … '

'No, it's fine. I just haven't been to that drawer in my memory for a while.'

'How long has it been?'

I have to work it out.

'Twenty-five years, give or take.'

Al has always been a good friend but, I have to say, he is the bluntest person I know. Now he is holding out a hand, an opportunity to talk about something I have put away. He makes light of it, buys the other bottle of wine and plonks it down on the table.

'There are chemicals in here that will make you talk or die trying.'

Ha ha. But true.

So I tell him a little about the two climbs I did with Jack.

'In 1978 we made the first ascent of the north face of Mount Huntington, a very dangerous climb. We were on the mountain for almost ten days, which was a problem because we only took four days' food. In 1980 we went back to Alaska and made the first ascent of the south-west face of Mount McKinley – Denali – the hardest route on the biggest mountain in North America at the time, I guess.'

I tell him what little I can about the climbs before I am swept away in an avalanche of emotion that I thought I had tamed more than two decades ago. I cannot go on. Al does not press me further, but I can see he is thinking.

The bottle of Great Wall is actually not as bad as the first one. Not a significant accolade, but it helps my mood recover. The past is put away and we pass the evening plotting to escape Wuzhen as quickly as we can and head for the comforts of our adopted homes in Hong Kong.

A few years later, in March 2009, Al visits me for a hike on Lantau Island, where I live. The hills on Lantau remind me of Scotland in proportion and it is easy to have a long, rugged day out with great views. There are some fascinating temples and old villages to visit along the way. The main difference to Scotland is that it does not get unexpectedly wet or suddenly very cold here, so you can travel light. A lot of people think that Hong Kong is just a concrete jungle and, without visiting, never realise that most of it is just the opposite. I have chosen to live in the little village of Mui Wo, where the peace is disturbed only by birdsong in the mornings as there are no roads – often the case in traditional villages. I ride my bicycle to catch the ferry into the city each day and that is a pleasure. Even when it rains, I do not regret my choice.

It is a sunny but cool day. The walk is going to be glorious. Starting from Tung Chung, the new metropolis on the north side of the island, we take a taxi to the little fishing village of Pak Mong, where the trail starts.

The path is surprisingly vague and steep, and we have to scramble in a few places. We have set out to climb Lantau's third peak, Lin Fa Shan, which gets very little traffic because there is no trail all the way to the summit. The majority of local hikers are generally not very adventurous and so give it a miss.

We reach a ridge, from where the views are as magnificent as they are contrasting. We are standing on the spine of the island, which runs east to west. To our north we look down on the dense cluster of high-rise apartments in Tung Chung. To the south, all is peaceful; the mountains roll down to the sea, colliding at the margin with golden sandy beaches. We scramble up the final steep rocky slope, knee-deep in prickly vegetation.

The view from the summit of Lin Fa Shan is wonderful for two reasons. The slope that faces south-east is spectacularly steep and breathtaking and we can look down on my home village. Secondly, in the distance, we can just see the food market we have picked out for lunch.

The market we have in our sights is actually a gaggle of half-outdoor restaurants housed by the government for local islanders to operate. We always eat at the restaurant nearest the ferry pier. It is run by a very noisy but friendly woman, Ah Ying, who has endless energy. A lifetime of shouting over the din in her restaurant has given her a booming, gravelly voice. Cantonese is the loudest language in the world to begin with, but Ah Ying has had to compete with the kitchen gas cooker, tended by her husband, which sounds like a jet engine.

Al and I have been to her restaurant so many times that it would seem like an act of betrayal to go to any of the other dozen establishments that are clustered under the one leaky roof. Ah Ying's restaurant is now our only target.

We are hungry and decide to take a shortcut marked on the map, which will drop us straight down, very steeply, into the back of the village. I have seen trails like this on the Hong Kong maps before: thin brown dotted lines. Mostly they are fine, but it seems the guy who draws the dots is no hiker and now and then you find one that is so steep that a safety rope would not be out of place.

It is very steep and, if we fall, we might tumble hundreds of metres, so we slither down the worst bits on our arses, hanging on to handfuls of the tough and prickly undergrowth. We get dirty and scratched but we love it, eventually tumbling out of the bushes on to the highest of the concrete village paths among the hillside grave sites found everywhere on Lantau.

'Damn fine that!' Al says. 'But not a patch on your epic on Denali.'

At first I cannot take it in. What's he talking about? He has even used the traditional name for Mount McKinley. Then I am shocked; I hadn't told Al any of the details about what happened all those years ago, just that I had climbed a new route. I don't mind but am surprised he mentions it, even in fun.

'How did you know about the epic bit?' I ask.

'I googled you, mate. Some guy called Waterman wrote about you in a book called *Surviving Denali*. Amazing stuff! Why didn't you say?'

I am taken aback.

'I had no idea anybody wrote about that … '

After I quit climbing, I shut it out totally. It was like grieving for a lost lover – best ignored as if it had never happened.

We walk down the steep village paths in silence, passing by the old school and along the river to the market where we are treated to one of Ah Ying's raucous greetings. She had seen us coming and two bottles of ice-cold beer arrive at our table in perfect synchronisation with our need for them.

'Veeeeery cold. You like, ah?'

As usual, lunch is as cheap as it is wonderful; the freshest ingredients are treated momentarily in the furnace of the kitchen and served to us just seconds later. Two beers become many as we eat and joke our way through a sunny afternoon on the shores of Silvermine Bay. Al is curious about the Denali climb. My mood has been loosened by exercise and beer. And for the first time in almost thirty years, I tell a friend a little of what really happened on those climbs with Jack. I am pleased he thinks they are interesting and, actually, it is cathartic for me.

'What happened to Jack?'

I cannot answer at once; I am swept into the shadows that pervaded my twenties.

'Al, I am afraid that if Jack went on climbing in the vein that we did, I fear he may be dead now. I really don't know what happened to him.'

How had it come to this, why had I just put my memories away so suddenly all those years ago?

We are not always truthful to ourselves. I think the mind will attempt to lie to itself to avoid things that are difficult. I don't know if this is weakness or self-defence. Whichever it is, in truth, I have been guilty of it, because never has a month gone by when I have not strayed, in my mind, back to Alaska and the emotion of *that* climb.

How had I come to be there? How had that begun?

Three decades ago ...

1
FIRST TIME LUCKY

1977, BERNESE OBERLAND

I can see why this part of the face had not been climbed before. It is difficult terrain, but that is not the main reason other suitors have stayed away. I am staring up at the real reason: a continuous wall of séracs that line the ridge between the rocky Ochs peak and the main summit of the Fiescherhorn Nordwand. Séracs are ice cliffs, hanging glaciers that result from snow being compacted into ice, and then pulled at by gravity, which causes them to creep ever downward until they 'calve' – a euphemism meaning 'very big bits break off' – simply because they have grown too heavy or crept over a change in angle in the underlying rock. Huge pieces of ice collapse; tens, hundreds, *thousands* of tons of ice can avalanche unpredictably. I am currently climbing the wall of rock and ice that connects the two summits, a wall directly under those séracs.

Climbing below séracs is a lottery. We have chosen to gamble with our lives for the sake of a little glory amongst our tribal peers, flying in the face of the wisdom of alpine tradition. We have chosen a line up a face where sensible climbers have stayed away.

We have been under the threat of the séracs all day and I doubt that we will be entirely out of the firing line tonight at the bivouac. The séracs get smaller on the left-hand side of the wall towards the Ochs peak, where we are heading, but they are still there. And they are looking at me. Looking on with rotten pockmarked faces and threatening at any moment to disintegrate and crush me with the weight of their decomposing mass. We will be forced to sleep under the random chaos of hanging ice.

◀ We started in the dark, and dawn revealed the enormity of our situation. I gaze up at the séracs above us on the first day of our Ochs climb. **Photo:** Dave Wilkinson.

Dave 'Wilco' Wilkinson, my climbing partner, has been fixated by this unclimbed wall and he insists on climbing it before we go and try the north face of the Eiger at nearby Grindelwald. How I wish we had gone there directly, but no, I am the sorcerer's apprentice this summer, I will do as I am bidden. A 'warm-up climb' made perfect sense in the car when he explained it to me in those terms. But now, on the wall, our first ascent does not feel like an easy start. I suspect the Eiger Nordwand is less dangerous, but there shall be no dissent in the ranks. The new Wilkinson-McCartney route beckoned and, as the weather was fine, must be climbed.

I never asked and he never said, but I guess Dave Wilkinson is at least ten years my senior, which is a lot when you are just twenty-one. We met in North Wales. He was part of a group of climbers who grew up around the Midlands town of Wolverhampton. Snowdonia, the climber's soggy paradise of North Wales, was their favoured climbing destination most weekends. Wilco and I got on immediately, I could not help but like him. He was a very experienced alpine climber and yet he treated me as an equal, which was kind considering my disposition: an arrogant young man in a big hurry. He was a teacher at a technical college, no doubt a lifestyle choice, for his career afforded long holidays to the Alps. I think he was only truly at home in the company of climbers; he made absolutely no effort to dress or groom for life away from the mountains. His clothes were of two types: climbing apparel or the attire of somebody that cared only enough to keep himself warm. Rips and tears would be repaired by darning and worn like badges of merit. This was his eccentric statement to the world. 'I am a climber and I don't care.' He had me in stitches one rainy afternoon in the Padarn Lake Hotel, an adopted climbers' pub in the heart of Snowdonia, explaining his views on society and, in particular, how he thought shampoo was an 'utterly pointless affectation of a world that had lost its way'.

I was a suitable partner for a summer in the Alps. I was extremely fit, climbing at the highest standard I had ever done and had one alpine season behind me; I was able and up for absolutely anything. This suited him well. There would be no argument about what we climbed; he had the plan and the experience – anything he aspired to climb would be good enough for me.

Dave has been to the Bernese Oberland before, so I just follow dutifully along behind the expert, awed by adventure, stricken by trust. We flogged up the Zasenberg valley in a morning and found a good bivouac site on the glacier from which we could study the face. All of it looked dangerous but we picked out a line just to the right of the rocky summit of the Ochs peak, which seemed least threatened by séracs. Dave's plan was to force a new line directly up the wall to the saddle that lies just to the right of the rocky triangular headwall of the Ochs.

Today has gone well: we started in the pre-dawn glowering and are now more than halfway up. The bottom of the wall had been time-consuming mixed rock and ice climbing, and I hated spending so much time down there. If the séracs at the summit ridge were not enough to worry me, the hanging glacier, which lies roughly in the middle of the climb, looked dangerous too. We skirted that on the right.

Wilco hadn't said much about the climb and I had not seen a picture of the face, so the objective dangers were a complete surprise to me when I first looked up at them. He had seemed unperturbed as he settled down for a good night's sleep in our comfortable bivouac at the foot of the face. I figured that, with all his alpine experience, he knew better than me so I just switched my worry gland off. However, ever since the sun came up I have found myself staring again up at the séracs when I've been stationary on the belays. The movement of climbing feels much better because it keeps me busy, but standing still minding the ropes gives me ample time to look up and worry.

Climbing is a cerebral sport, if indeed it is a sport at all, which I personally question. As a result you rarely meet stupid climbers, but you do meet silly ones who let ambition get the better of them. Are we being silly?

The sun will set soon, so there will be only two more pitches today. I took the last lead on easy sixty-degree ice and I managed to stretch it so that I belayed just below a little rock band on good anchors. Dave is now above me – it is his turn to swing into the lead, front pointing with his crampons and probing with his axes, scratching his way through the steep icy rocks for the next rope length. It is hard to watch every move because he is showering me with debris. Since I saw that he had a solid running belay in place I have been hiding under my helmet. Without looking I can anticipate each shower of ice particles from the noise his ice picks make as he places them. If his first swing is good, the pick enters the ice with a simple 'snick' sound and he strikes only once. If the placement is bad, he will strike more than once, which means wrenching the pick out of the ice and releasing a little debris. The sound I most dislike is when he hits hollow or fractured ice and the noise is 'pock'. This often causes a dinner plate of ice to break away like an icy discus, rattling its way in my direction and gaining speed with every second. 'Below!' he will shout, confirming what I can already hear as I hide, neckless like a beetle, a rucksack for a shell and a Joe Brown lightweight helmet for a shiny head. In these cases I really have to keep my head down because a plate of ice could break a bone.

Happily for me he finally traverses away to the right. I am no longer directly below him and therefore no longer being pelted with his detritus. I can watch, hypnotically, the droppings created by his progress being swallowed by gravity, sucked earthwards, accelerating away from me into the gloom below.

I tend the ropes diligently, which includes measuring how they are being used up.

'Thirty feet, Dave.' I want him to know that he should think about his next belay. The rope is still for a minute; he is thinking and searching. He makes a decision and the rope runs out quickly for twenty feet and stops. I hear his hammer as he places a piton, and then hear the metallic sound again – a second piton. The sound of his ice axe follows, not climbing, but chopping out a ledge to stand on. Showers of ice debris rattle down the mountain.

In the middle of his excavations there is a pause and some strong profanities – this is out of character for Wilco. Something has annoyed him. His cursing was a considered expletive, not the sort of noise you might make if you accidentally hit yourself. Eventually I get the terse call:

'Climb when ready.'

It is my turn. I slacken the knots in my belay.

'Take in, Dave.' The ropes go taut immediately and I set about removing the nuts and ice screws I have used for my anchors.

'Climbing.'

Two swings of my axes and two kicks with the front points of my crampons and I am on my way. It is a nice pitch – not easy but not hard and, despite the temptation to savour it, I do not tarry. It will be dusk soon and we need to find a place to sleep. I climb as quickly as safety allows. Dave has belayed under a rock atop a small ice arête between two runnels – ditches in the ice carved by the abrasion of avalanches. The arête is a ridge in the ice that parts the endless passing of debris like a snowplough. He has chopped the top of the icy ridge away to make a ledge big enough to sit on. I move close. He has found a position that is at least safe from the small falls of the mountain's ammunition.

'Si, I reckon this spot is as good as it will get today, especially because of this.'

He points to his ice axe. The pick is broken off near the shaft. It failed during his excavation of the ice ledge. The axe was a good one, a beautifully crafted Chouinard with a bamboo shaft. Dave had his axe modified in the metalwork shop of his college so that the angle of the pick was steeper and it had failed at the point of the new bend. Now, without a pick, it is a walking stick, dead weight and no longer any use. The four paws of a cat work well in unison when it climbs, but they must all have claws. Wilco has lost those on his left hand –

Our new route climbs directly to the col immediately to the right of the obvious triangular rock wall of the Ochs peak. We strayed under the séracs on the ridgeline.

a major blow because now only one of us can climb ice properly. The upside for me is that with two good ice picks, I will get much of the leading.

I agree with the plan to stop and we chop out an extension of the ledge, wide enough for us both to sit and cook. We are still exposed to avalanches but will not be able to improve our position now. We must sit here and pretend we are not concerned, or else admit to ourselves that we are tense (at the very least) and entirely to blame for our own predicament. This would spoil a lovely evening high in the Alps – from our little ledge we can see sweeping vistas of the face and our earlier work today – and so we resort to the sort of blithering and stoical British behaviour that has been the precursor to many unlucky turns of fate. We make ourselves as comfortable as we can and I brew up, melting ice for our dinner of dehydrated soup and rye bread. Neither of us removes his helmet, I notice.

Over dinner we discuss the route above. We will start early so we can definitely get off the climb in the morning, or by noon at worst. Neither of us wants to be on the face for another afternoon, when the sun destabilises the ice holding the rocky debris and creates missile-like stone fall. Worse still, the diurnal warmth could cause the rotting séracs above to expand, loosen and collapse on our heads, ruining an otherwise splendid outing.

We might not be back in the pub, but we pass the time congratulating ourselves on the best leads of the day when an almighty explosion echoes around the valley, followed immediately by a huge crash and a noise like concrete poured from a great height. A sérac just to the right of our position has collapsed and hundreds, no, *thousands* of tons of ice are tumbling and exploding down the route we climbed earlier today.

The shock makes us both grab the nylon slings connecting us to our anchors in fright. As if they would be any help! All we can manage is a barrage of expletives.

The avalanche seems to go on interminably, finally smashing into the glacier below in one last mighty explosion, which is repeated over and over in echoes from the mountains around us like morbid applause. We are briefly enveloped in a cloud of snow and the stove is blown out by the force of the airborne ice particles, swept along by the avalanche's backdraught.

Neither of us speaks. Frosted with ice, we look like two slapstick comedians, coated white from a pie in the face.

I cannot blame Dave for leading me on to this face although I consider it for a moment. I am not stupid, I could see what I was getting into, but I now feel puny in the face of such an attack from nature. This is the real deal; a first ascent to be wrung from the mountain in the face of danger. Mixed emotions flow through me: enlightenment and stimulation. Oh, and worry, because the mountain clearly has plenty of ammunition left.

Neither of us can sleep. The slightest noise startles us, even if it is just the other shuffling from one frozen arse cheek to the other. I pass the time by making tea. At 4.30 I can stand it no longer.

'Wilco, let's go, let's get out of here, we can climb the next few ice pitches in the dark with the light of our head torches.'

He has obviously been thinking the same thing and we are packed and ready to go in fifteen minutes. We are only delayed by waiting for the stove to cool down enough to pack.

We are carrying two types of ice piton. The best is the tubular screw-in type that has recently become available from an American company founded by Yvon Chouinard. These make better anchors but don't make good ice daggers. Luckily we have a few warthogs – the older type of ice piton, designed to be hammered directly into the ice then screwed out. They look like the love child of a serrated knife and a corkscrew, and it's one of these that Wilco will use, gripped in his fist like a dagger, in place of his broken axe.

At first the climbing is easy and we quickly reach the top of a little snowfield. From here we can see the crux of the climb, consisting of steep mixed rock and ice. We can also see the horrifyingly unstable nature of the séracs. There is enough ice to enable us to weave a path through the rocks, connecting narrow gullies and streaks of ice webs together – winter spiders. The climbing some-times reaches Scottish grade V, so the leads are absorbing. We climb several pitches each, the last of which is Dave's.

When I stick my head above the last rocky bulge below his stance, I find him brooding, belayed on ice screws underneath a steep wall of ice. We are close to the summit ridge. Although this is the shortest part of the sérac wall vertically, it is more difficult than we had expected. We had hoped to avoid the séracs by threading the eye of the needle, passing just at the point the séracs petered out. It seems that we were dreaming. We have arrived at the point where the ice cliffs are smaller, but they are still here and, in parts, very steep. I climb past Dave rapidly to become the new leader.

'Take it easy, Si.'

I think about leaving my pack with him, but it doesn't weigh much so I decide to save time and get on with the last pitch while wearing it. I take all of the ice screws and leave Dave with all the rock anchors to save weight; I will not need them again today, as there is no more rock above us. I climb just ten feet and place the first ice screw. Forty feet higher I can see that the wall steepens to almost vertical for perhaps twenty feet before relenting. I decide to place two of our best ice screws just below this bulge because I won't want to stop and place another on the really steep ground. I clip one of my two ropes into each of the screws to spread the load if I should fall. Dave is watching my every move.

'How good are those screws, Si?'

'Solid … Watch me here.'

The request is unnecessary. I can feel Wilco's intense attention flowing up the ropes like electricity. I take a few deep breaths and place my picks as high above my head as I can and step up on my front points. It is very steep but I can just keep my weight on my feet. This is no place to get tired.

I climb without a pause until the angle relents. Then I chop out a single step, allowing me to place my boot flat and sideways. This enables me to rest my calf muscles while I place one more screw. Wilco is going to find that last bit hard work when he follows with only one axe, but I can help him by giving him some tight rope from my belay above.

'Well done, Si, can you see the top?'

I can. Just fifty feet of ice that is no more than sixty degrees and I shall be free of this wall. No time to lose concentration now. I climb with careful and deliberate movements up to a little three-foot-wide cornice that has formed a wind-blown snow meringue on the very edge of the summit ridge. I chop an opening and cut two big steps for my feet, as the granular ice is not firm enough for the front points of my crampons to support my weight. I reach over the lip, ram the shafts of my ice axes into the snow and grovel on to the plateau on my knees. I can now stand on almost level ground for the first time in two days.

There is no ice or rock to provide an anchor so I must improvise. I wade as far as I can down the back slope of the plateau and dig a hole to sit in, bracing my feet against the edge of my pit. I drive my axes, which are clipped into my harness, into the snow and sit on them so that my weight will help anchor them. If Dave falls, the rope will cut into the snow, creating friction and easing the load on me. Anyway, he won't fall. This is Wilco after all.

'Climb when ready!' I shout as loudly as I can. I don't hear the reply but I feel the rope go slack and I take in like a fisherman tending the line of a fish that has taken the bait. The slack is Wilco undoing his belay knots. Soon he is moving steadily towards me and I gather in my invisible catch. There is a halt as he removes my ice-screw runners below the bulge. As expected there is a period of slow progress as he tackles the bulge and then the rope comes to me quickly again. He is over the crux. A minute later, Wilco's bearded face pops into view. It is smiling.

'Hey Si, you have just put up your first new route in the Alps!'

Part of me is happy just to see a new day, but the feeling I have of being the first climber to set foot on unclimbed territory is, I suspect, addictive. I had put up a few new rock climbs in the UK but this is another step entirely and as we walk the long walk back to the valley I imagine myself on other first ascents. The Eiger would always entice me, but at that moment I realise that first ascents are what I now long for.

2
DELIVERANCE

We did try the Eiger, and raced up to the Swallow's Nest bivouac but the weather was far too warm. The face was running with water and volleys of falling stones raked the ice fields incessantly. Reluctantly, I let go of my dream and we retreated, all the way back to Chamonix.

Wilco and I have climbed a lot of ice this season and now a big rock climb beckons to us. Using Terrordactyl ice axes has given me sore knuckles, so a break from the bashing I had given my fists on hard ice climbs would be welcome. Our last climb was a rapid ascent of the north face of Les Droites, the benchmark hard ice climb in the Haute Savoie. That was a thrill and we had even managed to make it back to the haunt of most British climbers, the Bar National, by lunchtime the next day.

After that we needed a new adventure and I was not sure what to suggest. I need not have worried, of course; Wilco had already made a list of climbs to cover any circumstance. Like a scribe, he produced a manila folder from his pack and carefully arranged the selected contents on the gingham tablecloth in our regular corner of the Bar National. A serious discussion about the choices began, only pausing so we could dispose of some steak-frites. Wilco declared that the next adventure of the summer should be the second ascent of the central pillar of Brouillard on Mont Blanc, a beautiful column of orange granite in the heart of the Brenva side of the mountain that leads, via a lofty ridge, to the Italian summit. Eric Jones, a remarkable British climber, had climbed the route solo and Wilco wanted to see what he had been up to.

We took the bus through the Mont Blanc tunnel early the next morning. Our climb would start in Italy and finish on the summit of Europe, from where we would descend into France. We had bought fresh food and managed to

◀ Wilco follows me on the first pitch of the central pillar of Brouillard.

hitch a lift up to the Val Veni to start our long approach march.

The weather is sunny but cool and the walk passes easily. We are both very fit after our long climbing holiday. The walk up to the Monzino hut is spectacular and we stop there for a beer and an opportunity to take in the view. This is my first time on the Italian side of Mont Blanc and the view is so much more interesting than that from Chamonix. The Aiguille Noire de Peuterey is a spectacular black fang of rock that would undoubtedly be fun, but it just doesn't seem big enough to lure me now and, crucially, it does not lead to the summit of Mont Blanc. Last year I would have found it interesting but my exposure to Dave the Sorcerer has changed my attitude as to the climbs that are important.

The approach to the Eccles bivouac on the Brouillard Glacier has only a few crevasses that need to be avoided and we reach the hut at a trot in the late afternoon. What a great place! Because the hut is located at the foot of such a challenging climb, we are the only people there. We are able to sleep indoors, alone and in comfort all night, which seems a luxury.

From below, the climb looks like it will be moderately difficult, but spectacular. The technical rock section of the pillar is not long, about 1,200 feet, but we will have to ascend both the Italian summit of Mont Blanc and the French summit to complete the route, making this one of the longer technical routes in Europe.

The weather seems stable so we won't have to turn this into a race, and the journey from the hut to the base of the climb is short. We feel relaxed. Wilco says he is happy to bivouac on the route if need be. We could probably tear up it in a day but instead have chosen to enjoy it.

The next morning I am awakened by the blue glow of the sky coming through the window next to my bunk. We have a breakfast of porridge with brown sugar and sit out on the steps of the hut, hardly speaking. It's a 'Gilbert and Sullivan' morning today; a climber's life for me is indeed a happy one. I am about to embark on what is by any measure a significant climb and we will be only the second party ever to attempt this route. I am confident and relaxed and as soon as I am no longer hungry, I become impatient. I am sure I irritate Wilco but he does not complain as I stand on the moraines near the hut, very obviously waiting for him, all but tapping my foot.

We rope up for the first broken mixed pitch that connects us to the pillar proper. The rock is excellent and the climbing hard enough to keep me fully occupied and enjoying the route finding at the same time. We make rapid and interesting progress as we put the pieces of Eric's fine climb together. We are following the handholds and footsteps of a brother, bonded by the touch of the rock. As I pass Wilco on each of his belays he passes me the remaining rack of

Wilco happy in his work on day one. Sometimes steep, sometimes less so,
Eric Jones's line is a classic rock climb.

equipment and nuts, which are already sorted by size, allowing me to efficiently lead past him with minimum fuss. We both get into the habit of studying the pitch above while taking in the ropes for the other. This allows us to give helpful advice and encouragement for the new leader. Wilco and I have become a well-oiled machine.

Particularly satisfying is the fact that we are not using pitons. We were not carrying many anyway, but have avoided using them all day. We are treating the Brouillard face with the same respect as a hallowed British crag. There is just a little aid required on the climb and we set ourselves the goal of trying to free-climb all of it. It is hard to tell where the original aid sections are, but we were tempted to pull on protection in a couple of places, so I guess we found them. Two Austrians, Germans or Swiss are climbing the Peuterey ridge to our right. We can guess at their nationality only because they yodel at us from time to time. Only a few European cultures actually yodel.

In the afternoon I pull up out of a little corner and arrive at a large 'five-star' ledge, easily big enough for two climbers to lie down on, and as I belay Wilco I set my mind on a lovely comfy bivouac here. Wilco, however, will have none of it and lectures me on the possibility of incoming dodgy weather. In a school-masterly tone he says, 'We must press on until dark'. It seems that the 'take it easy and enjoy it' approach has been replaced by a trigger in Wilco's mountain DNA and instinct has taken over. Of course I give in; Dave *is* a teacher and much as I love that big flat ledge, I do not argue. Much. We climb on in the red afternoon sun, but find no such comfortable accommodation higher up.

We eventually spend the night sitting in our packs 300 feet higher on an uncomfortable crease in the rock, entertained by a monster thunderstorm roaming up and down the Val d'Aosta in front of us. We beg it to stay away and are fortunate that it does. We would be crucified in a storm like that, out in the open and unprotected. Our anxiety only allows us to doze fitfully. My legs keep going numb, so I give up on trying to sleep and get the stove going long before dawn so we can make a very early start.

The conditions are still marginal at 6 a.m., and by the time we are a few pitches higher it's obvious that there will be a major change for the worse in the weather. Thin cloud has scudded across our entire horizon, replacing deep blue skies with pale grey. Below us, big clouds have begun to billow, hiding our view of the valley.

I have a sixth sense that Wilco is about to make a point about how right he was to press on last evening. My arse is still sore from the uncomfortable bivouac but I don't want to let him have the last word, so as he climbs up to my stance on an increasingly windy day I congratulate him on his planning.

When we reach the top of the rock pillar the weather is deteriorating rapidly. The wind is picking up, clouds are forming all around us and it has begun to snow. We put on all of our bad weather clothing and climb the Brouillard ridge as fast as safety permits, chased all the way by billowing clouds from below.

As we summit on the Italian peak of Mont Blanc, 'Monte Bianco', the storm is in full cry and visibility is reduced to perhaps thirty or forty squinty feet, even with our ski goggles on. The wind is howling and it is snowing heavily. Our challenge now is to navigate from the Italian summit to the French one, from which point we can set a course down the *voie normale* – the Goûter ridge. If we can find that we cannot get lost, no matter what the weather does.

On a good day the terrain between the Italian and French summits presents as a simple snow slope with a blunt saddle in the middle called Col Major. In a whiteout it is almost completely featureless. If you get disoriented in this place, it is possible to wander off the slope into some very unpleasant territory.

Wilco decides that I shall be the snowplough and he will hold the compass. We know exactly where we are and we have a detailed contour map. I will break a trail through the deep snow, on a compass bearing according to his instructions. I will lead out until he starts to lose sight of me, then I will stop and wait for him. The process will be repeated again and again, marching on a tight heading and counting steps to estimate the distance travelled and computing the subtle changes in terrain simultaneously. It is a familiar and automatic process, and despite the whiteout I still have some sense of where the sun is.

On the way towards the Col Major, I stumble across an unusual little mound in the snow. It does not look natural and as I look more closely I see a coil of rope. The shouting between Wilco and I has disturbed the resident of the snow mound and the snow crumbles away as a hand appears, followed by a human head frantically searching for the source of the voices it has heard. The head is joined quickly by a second. I have found two climbing gophers hiding from the storm in a snow hole. A few yards further to the west and I would have passed by without seeing them. These must be the Peuterey ridge yodellers from the day before. Unable to navigate in the foul conditions they have dug a hole to shelter from the storm and climbed inside their bivouac sack in such a way that there is little of them left above the drifting snow. They are a mixed team, a man and a woman, and are very glad to meet us, having sensed my presence at the last moment.

'Hello, hello, vere are you going?' asks the bearded one breathlessly.

'The Bar National,' I reply.

Without the language barrier it might have been funny, but I instantly regret my sarcasm. When I look into the face of his partner, the poor women is obviously frightened sick. She is confused by my smart-arse remark and gives me a look of tortured anxiety.

'OK, we go to Mont Blanc then the Goûter ridge and down to Chamonix.'

That was what they want to hear. They scramble out of the snow hole and start frantically to tighten the frozen laces on their boots, fumbling with cold, numb hands to put their crampons on.

'Vait please, please, vee come vith you please.'

Of course I will 'vait'. What else can I do? These two will surely perish if they stay where they are.

I pull in the rope that connects me to an almost invisible Wilco and turn my back to the wind, which is howling now, tugging and buffeting at my cagoule.

Wilco arrives looking like a snowman, his bushy beard thick with frost. He has already started to weigh the odds associated with our acquisition of two followers. I can sense his furrowed brow even if I cannot see it. While we were happy enough with just the two of us alone in the whiteout, the dynamic has changed; we now have two climbers of unknown mettle to guide out of the storm, both of whom look as if they are suffering from exposure and are obviously shaken.

'Si, don't hang about while they are sorting themselves out, lead out another rope.'

He squints at his compass and points the way like a command. I want to say 'Wilco, I can use a compass too, how about you do some snow-ploughing?', but I don't. He would just stand there pointing anyway. I plod away, up to my crotch in snow, and we repeat the slow but methodical dance, rope length by rope length. I am the puppet, Wilco is the puppeteer, now with two faithful followers. I seem to take only a few steps before I can no longer see them in the storm.

The terrain is now almost level so we are on track; this is what we expect from the geography at Col Major. I am anticipating the slope to flatten completely and then start to slowly climb to the French summit, which I know arises unseen on my left. Wilco joins me. Our eyes meet and he nods in approval. The terrain looks good and without a word I turn and set off. About halfway out I notice a tiny hint of bright colour and I stop to study it. I can just see a blurry anomaly in the snow. There is somebody else here on the moon!

I make a small detour to the left to discover another group of benighted climbers, four this time. They are sitting in a line astern in the snow with the hoods of their down jackets pulled tight over their heads, backs to the wind. Just sitting there. Hell!

Many people climb Mont Blanc well enough on a blue-sky day but the less able can have a very bad time if the weather decides to bite. At least the Austrian pair had some bivouac kit and had dug a hole to get out of the howling wind. This group are just sitting in a line, exposed to the wind and the snow, with no bivouac equipment to protect them from a now very angry mountain.

Not much of a plan here then. We are at an altitude in excess of 4,500 metres, a huge storm is setting in and they are completely exposed. The air is thin and the temperature is plummeting. I guess that it could be -30° Celsius or lower, but that does not take into account the wind-chill factor. Frostbite is on the menu for starters, and freezing to death is an option for the main course. I guess that they must have summited Mont Blanc, then walked off the wrong side in the ensuing whiteout. They are lucky we have bumped into them, as this storm is obviously going to be quite sporting. Perversely, it is hilarious for me as, wading through the snow up to the first of the group, he does not see or hear me coming, poor sod. I tap on his shoulder and he jumps out of his skin.

'Lost are we, mate?'

'Oh Mon Dieu! Quelle surprise! Où est le Mont Blanc? On est perdu et on a très froid!'

(What a surprise! Where is Mont Blanc? We are lost and very cold!)

These are four French then.

'I can see that, mate, best you come with us.'

'Où allez-vous?'

(Where are you going?)

'Mont Blanc and then Le Pub dans Chamonix.'

At least he got the message if not the sarcasm.

'Vous connaissez le chemin?'

(You know the way?)

'Yes, mate, it's on the map.'

'Pouvez-vous nous attendre s'il vous plait – on vient avec vous.'

(Please hang on a minute, we are coming with you.)

'Très vite, thanks pal or no beer for us ce soir.'

The poor guy had been startled in the midst of his final nightmare, only to be greeted by an adolescent Brit with an attitude and a drinking problem. Well, he'd have to put up with me – we are the total extent of the good news today. In the middle of this discussion Wilco arrives and we have a chat while the French group sort themselves out. He has already embraced our ever-increasing risk, but now we have a crowd to lead to safety and he points out that the odds have moved against us once again, just in case I didn't realise.

'Si, I need you to move really quickly now. I'm not sure how this mob will go but if you can bash down a trail I will try to drag them along. We will head for the Vallot hut.'

Wilco and I had spent enough time in Scotland's awful winter weather together that howling wind and total white-outs seemed almost normal and so we dressed for them. However, we are close to the summit of the highest mountain in Europe and it is getting very cold. Just the two of us would be no bother at all, but how would our six new companions fare? Collecting the first two had not troubled me. The ratio of us to them was 1:1 and if the situation got bad I felt sure that Wilco and I could get them to safety. But the addition of four more strays changed things dramatically. The group was big enough to create its own anxieties and they might be difficult to control.

Wilco pulls out his compass and squints, pointing a new bearing to walk on, shouting to me until I fade from view. He then pulls on the rope when he loses sight of me and I stop. He joins me and we repeat, with the six acquisitions flogging along behind in the crotch-deep snow trench I have made. Quickly, and as best we can, we will try to guide our six new companions to the Vallot refuge.

I locate the summit of Mont Blanc, but I continue to wander about trying to find anything higher, just to make sure. This is confusing to some of our new companions because it looks like indecision. I am just making absolutely sure that we're on the summit, and we are. As confirmation I scratch at the new snow to find the definitive evidence that we are on the top of Europe. I find the telltale orange peel and piss stains and there is no doubt. I do not know why people on the *voie normale* eat oranges and urinate on the summit, but they do.

Wilco does the pointing again, due north now. It makes me smile because he looks just like the famous statue of de Saussure and Balmat in the town square of Chamonix; Balmat is pointing the way to the summit. Dave is doing the exact opposite, pointing the way *from* the summit to the town square and the Bar National.

'OK, Balmat,' I offer as I start to swim down the west-trending ridge, now waist deep in new snow. I call him 'Balmat' all the way. He does not get the joke for an hour, but eventually it sinks in.

The Vallot hut is an emergency shelter located at the Bosses ridge just off the main climbing line on the Goûter route – the easiest way up Mont Blanc from the Chamonix side. For us it is normally just a walk and we only ever descend it, but today it has taken on an entirely more serious complexion. What is ordinarily an easy snow and ice ridge, with a trench cut by the passing of hundreds of crampon-clad feet, has become a hideous meringue-like sculpture of windblown snow. The light is so flat that I have to watch snow fall away from me, noting which way it rolls, to ensure I stay on the centre of the ridgeline. I am up to my waist and it is hard work. We also have to contend with some dissent in the ranks behind us because one of our new French companions has an anxiety attack about the location of Mont Blanc; had we actually crossed the correct summit? Dave has obviously been waiting for just this issue. He gives the panicking French climber short shrift in his Brummie accent and his best French:

'Attendez, this is absolutement le bonne voie.'

(Listen chum, this is definitely the way.)

I do not pause at all. Crunch, swim, crunch. I am determined to keep up the little pace we have. If I stop they will falter. I want to give them no choice. 'Follow me or I will leave you' is the physical language. It seems to be working and the group follows stumbling along behind Wilco, wading like drunks in the deepening snow trench in my wake.

I had been to the Vallot hut the year before, after climbing the Route Major, but that was in clear weather. This time I am depending on Wilco for wisdom and his direction in this impenetrable storm.

'Si, press on, but not so fast that this lot can't keep up. When you come to a piece of rock, stop.'

It is vital we do not pass by the emergency hut by accident. Our followers are getting very tired and we must find the shelter quickly. The French group in particular is not equipped to bivouac outside and there is no chance of continuing our descent below the hut in this weather without likely fatal consequences. I know that the Vallot hut is only a few hundred metres lower than the summit of Mont Blanc, but it is taking us hours to get there today. Close by the refuge are two 'bosses' – humps with small rocks. Eventually I bump into the first of these, a positive sign. Then, exactly where it should be, I find the second rock. The shivering and shambolic group gathers near the second 'petit rocher'. Wilco and I know we are safe now; we know the hut is just metres away. Not so our followers and they have to wait anxiously, cowering in the wind while I set about yet more snow swimming to try and locate the hut. Since we know exactly where we are on the ridge, we want to keep the group together in this position while I do the searching for the hut alone on the end of a rope.

The hut is literally a long stone's throw from our position at the bosses but it takes an age to find as the weather is now even worse and the light is failing. On Wilco's bearing I set out in chest-deep snow trailing the rope. After twenty minutes of failed stabs in the direction we believe the hut will be, I deliberately aim off and slightly high. I then trail to the left where the hut should be and bingo, I practically stumble into it. I tie the rope to the steps of the aluminium structure and give a mighty heave. Wilco has been like a diligent fisherman tending the line and he feels the bite and gives two tugs in reply.

My snow-swimming duties are concluded for the day and the seven of them can now follow the rope through the dark to safety. I cannot be bothered to take off my pack and fetch my head torch, so I crunch up the metal steps, hardly seeing the way. The door is missing, blown away perhaps, and instead there is a frozen sheet of canvas at the threshold. I push past it into the blackness inside, almost blind. My crampons grate on the metal floor – until I step on something soft. It wails in agony. I have stepped on somebody, and whoever it is is not happy at all. I stand still for fear of a repeat event as torch lights around the cabin start to flicker on. The refuge is completely full; the floor is covered with bodies in sleeping bags, all of them the same colour: khaki. The refuge has been taken over by a large team of British soldiers. I apologise to the poor sod I have stepped on and fortunately he is only slightly cut from my crampon and forgives me.

'Made me sleep near fookin door, t'bastards,' he complains.

'What have you guys been up to?' I ask.

'Ooh we've been at this lark fur fookin days, this is our advance camp.'

I think for a second about mentioning that the Vallot was intended as an emergency refuge, not a base camp, but never mind. This is hardly the moment or the audience and besides, the weather *has* declared an emergency.

A crash of crampons behind me on the steps heralds the arrival of abominable snowman Wilco. He does look a picture, his huge beard and his balaclava now a single helmet of ice. He pushes his snow goggles away with a mittened paw and surveys the crowded scene with a narrowed stare. We have obviously woken the infantry from an early night and they are slow to make a little floor space available. The six refugees behind Wilco arrive in one anxious bunch, exhausted and stressed and all desperate to get out of the storm.

There was now space for me and Wilco, but not for the other six, one of whom turns out to be a gendarme and is very upset that there is no room in the hut. Bad language in French is greeted with much the same in various British accents and a big argument breaks out between the irate Frenchman and the commanding officer of the British troops. The gendarme demands to see the Alpine Club cards of the army team (every alpinist is supposed to have one), then he tries to confiscate them. All hell breaks loose and a shouting match ensues.

'Just who do you think you are, coming in here so rudely?'

'You are a disgrace to the spirit of alpinism … you must make room for these people. Your men must make room. Immédiatement!'

I succumb to the giggles and get a stern look from Wilco as if to say 'don't make it worse'.

Eventually the fracas created by our arrival dies down and after much shuffling and grumbling, everybody has a spot on the smelly floor. Unfortunately, piss smells like piss regardless of the altitude. A few of the lads 'volunteer' to sit rather than lie down so that all of the new arrivals can stretch out. The girl in the French group is totally spent and is not so much asleep as unconscious. Wilco and I use the distraction to colonise a comfortable corner of the hut and I make soup while Wilco picks the more stubborn bits of ice from his beard.

It is squalid inside but we are happy to be out of the storm. We are especially happy to have delivered the six people intact as this means we can sleep the sleep of the guiltless. God knows how we would have felt if it had gone badly and we had lost any of them. This had occurred to Wilco of course from the outset, but it only dawns on me in the hut. Nothing had ever been a problem for me in the mountains so I have little empathy for others. This experience has been another step in my development and I consider the revelation of the potentially fatal storm quietly by myself.

We were free of the responsibility of the six followers. They could sit out the storm in the Vallot hut and make their way down by themselves when the weather was in a better mood. The army lads had a large quantity of food and equipment that they were happy to share, so we were all in good shape despite the very untidy conditions. For me, the day had now come to an almost perfect end. Wilco and I had made a splendid second ascent, we had been tested by some unhelpful weather and dealt with it like champions. I had also begun to realise that we had probably saved the lives of six people and that was a feeling I was not ready for. We chat quietly for a while even though we are knackered.

'What a great route, good lead in the big corner, well done!'

Wilco actually tells me that I did a fine job during the guiding of the six we had found and I am pleased to hear that from him.

For some reason the Austrian couple are standing up unsteadily and picking their way over uncaring khaki bodies towards Wilco and I. It would have been so easy for them just to surrender to sleep, but before doing so the pair must stagger over to our corner.

'Hello,' says Wilco. 'What's up?'

The couple look at each other and clear their throats. Wilco and I look at each other sheepishly. Haltingly, the guy starts to speak slowly and deliberately in German, a language we can follow well enough.

'Mein Freunden … danke dass sie so viel, zank you.'

The pair exchanges a glance and the Fräulein turns back to us. I can see in her exhausted eyes that tears are welling. She looks at both of us in turn, her voice is full of barely controlled emotion.

'Vielen Dank. Vielen Dank.'

Now it's Wilco's turn to clear his throat.

'Ahem well er … '

I try to save him with the best German I can muster:

'You are most willkommen too.'

Smiles all round ensue and a little exhausted laughter. We try to talk for a while but we are all too tired to keep it up. It was a moment of wonderful humanity. They were welcome; it had been great to help them and not so much bother really. What else could we have done? I was chuffed that they came over to thank us before they too collapsed on the dirty floor and passed out, safe after what, for them, must have seemed like a day in hell. How happily they had been yodelling to us the previous day on their sunny ridge climb. How desperate their plight had become today. But for the most unlikely piece of luck, the mountain would have claimed them. I think that confidence must be everything in situations like this. It is almost as if merely by forming the thought that you might actually die, death is allowed in the door.

3
THE WALKING ONE AND ONLY

Back in Chamonix, the elation of the climb is negated by the fact that the mountains are now in terrible condition, plastered with snow. I have the beginning of a sickening feeling that this might have been our last alpine climb of the summer.

The rock climbs are coated in ice and the ice climbs are dangerous until the mountains shed the deep layers of snow. There is nothing to do and the forecast is bad. So late in the season, it is unlikely that a sufficiently long fine spell of weather will arrive to clean up the mess left by the big storm.

Sadly, as the summer is winding down Wilco and I start to enjoy each other's company a little less. On the hill all is fine and we work well together, but sitting on our arses in a rainy Chamonix, we have started to get on each other's nerves. I am cocky and not very thoughtful and I am sure that I am to blame for most of the disharmony. We are like an odd couple with too great a gap in their ages. I am hyperactive and impatient while Wilco is patient but at times quite eccentric. He wants to go home and I do not. He has a job to go to and needs to prepare for the next term of teaching. I too have a job to go to, but two months later, so I decide to stay a little longer and see what fun can still be extracted before the autumn weather makes the mountains inhospitable. I will be one of the last to leave, as usual – the eternal impatient optimist. This decision is not a problem for Wilco – there are lots of Brits he knows in town looking to share a lift home. We agree to meet in North Wales later in the year and swap our photos, and we part on good terms, rejoicing in the great summer we've had together. We had missed out on the Eiger, but all in all had enjoyed a great season.

◀ Californians in Snowdonia. Jack Roberts is put to the test by the locals on a problem at Fachwen, as Rick Accomazzo looks on. Photo by Al Harris on Rick's camera. According to Rick, surviving Harris's hospitality at his house 'Bigle' was more hazardous than the climbing.

We tell ourselves the monster will still be standing in the same spot next year.

I am by myself in the Bar National, but I do not feel alone. The 'Nash' – run by charismatic Chamonix legend Maurice Simond – is possibly the world's best-known climbers' social destination and even though it is late in the season, today I have already met several climbers I know. Every summer afternoon, the coffee-sipping French locals and tourists are driven out of the bar by hordes of scruffy climbers from all over the world, though mostly Europe. The British are very heavily represented while those from the USA are rare, so when a group of four enters, their American lilt is immediately obvious amongst the background din of twenty different versions of the English accent.

Sitting at the bar, I am curious about these four Yanks, so I say hello to the first of them. His name is Jack. With his long blond hair he looks like a slightly scary version of the lead singer from Yes. He has a gold lightning-bolt earring in one ear. He is languid and approachable and has an irreverent sense of humour. Jack has a swagger about him, confident of himself amongst the tribe of climbers. He is followed into the bar by Steve Shea, Tobin Sorenson and Rick Accomazzo; they are here to set the standard as high as they can for Americans in Europe and have already made some impressive climbs, including an incredibly steep ice climb in the Dru Couloir. Steve, Jack, Mugs Stump and Randy Trover had begun a new direct line in the couloir. Rick and Tobin had come along second and reached Steve and Jack's high point. They then finished the direct route in impeccable style.

Jack and Rick had climbed the north face of Les Droites as Wilco and I had weeks ago, so we had something in common. Jack and I could both climb well enough evidently, and as the bond between climbers took hold, we began to enjoy the simple pleasure of talking about our climbs and ambitions in a beer-enhanced environment that is kind to one's ego. For both of us the summer in Cham is obviously over but we are reluctant to let go of its tail. It is time to move on, but like true hedonists we are only prepared to do so if it means the fun can continue unabated elsewhere. Jack still has weeks before he needs to be home in Santa Monica and I have time to kill for a month or so.

'Ever been climbing in the UK?' I ask.

'Yeah, we went to Snowdonia and the gritstone edges. The locals pointed us up some of the classics.'

'Fancy some more in the UK that is totally different?'

It is as simple as that. A week later we are in the West Country, in Cheddar Gorge, where we have a ball, climbing the spectacular 400-foot classic rock climb *Coronation Street*.

Later, we make our own Bar National in a friendly pub in the Mendip Hills. Jack reveals that he had been climbing in Alaska on the Kichatna Spires the previous summer. I have no plan for the next alpine season but this provocation reminds me that I need one.

Jack paints a picture of the Alaskan ranges by comparison with Chamonix. We have some common points of reference with Mont Blanc and he uses these to describe the scale of the Alaskan faces that interest him. The most important fact he imparts is that many of the harder faces are still virgin opportunities in Alaska; they have not yet been climbed. Moreover, expedition-style climbing with big teams and fixed ropes connecting forward camps is the common approach. Now is the time to apply simple alpine-style techniques to some grand new territory.

Unlike Europe and especially Chamonix, where almost every plausible – and sometimes implausible – line had been climbed, Alaska was little developed. Sure, all the peaks had been climbed, as had most of the ridges, but the big steep faces were relatively untouched. This really struck a chord with me. This year in the Alps I had found myself wishing I'd been born earlier. I might have had the chance to make the first ascent of the central pillar of Brouillard rather than the second, or all three of the Brouillard pillars for that matter. The thought of being the first to climb a big difficult face was intoxicating.

Jack explains that our climb would be approached by ski-plane and this impresses me greatly. 'We could fly to the base of the climb!' I loved the idea of approaching a mountain that way. It would save time, and the idea of living on a glacier was something new. The decision was made as simply as that.

Ordinarily, coming back to London after climbing would have depressed me, but this time I was energised because I had a plan for the next spring – a grand plan. A winter of drudgery would now seem different; it would be a winter of focused training and preparation. Nor was it difficult to see Jack off at the airport because I knew I would be at his home in Santa Monica six months later.

We wrote to each other often to exchange maps and other information. When we could we would call each other for a quick chat, but that was very expensive. We knew where we were going but had yet to develop a specific climbing objective. Then fate took a hand. Ken Wilson, the editor of *Mountain* magazine, published a photograph taken by the Alaska pioneer Bradford Washburn on its front cover – of the 'Unclimbed North Face of Mount Huntington'. I was mesmerised by it. Here was a face with Eiger-like qualities, easily as sinister, perhaps more beautiful and devoid of a human footprint.

Huntington rises 5,700 feet out of the west fork of the Ruth Glacier, the very locale we had chosen. Together with the photo was some advice from Washburn – that the face was too dangerous to be climbed. Well really, *we* would be the judges of that.

The mountain seemed to have chosen itself.

4
A NEW WORLD

Just the very act of driving in California entertains me. It is like seeing a parallel world that I have only witnessed on TV, never believing that it would actually look and sound exactly the same in real life. Jack cannot understand why I think Modesto is so amusing; he just sees it as a place that gets in the way on the journey from Santa Monica to the Valley. The long drive is boring for him but not for me. Just hanging my head out of the window like a Border collie is enough to keep me amused.

For Jack the drive to Yosemite is made lighter by my demeanour; every twist and new view heightens my expectation. I thought I would be well prepared for the first view of Yosemite Valley, but I was wrong. I make him stop the car every five minutes so I can get out and stare.

Jack is British American, born in the US to British parents and consequently he has a transatlantic drawl. I am a young Brit who has inherited the mimic vein from his actress mother and we play on this: he calls me 'man' like a Woodstock hippie and I call him 'mate' like a cockney Dick Van Dyke.

Jack is a 'Stonemaster', one of a group of elite Yosemite rock climbers who are pioneering big-wall and crag climbs in the valley. I am not in that league. I have never climbed on this type of granite before. Jack has thought about all of this and selected our first climb carefully. It will be the west face of Sentinel Rock, for a variety of reasons: firstly, it is big enough to satisfy me and we can spend a night on the climb as there is a big ledge. I have never done that before. In the Alps, yes, but not on a rock climb. Secondly it is hard enough to challenge me without being a serious contender for the main event. That is, unquestionably, to be Mount Huntington. It will be a test but it will be fun.

We have a schedule to keep to for our main game. Sentinel Rock will allow me

◀ Two local kids are fascinated 'cos [I] talk funny'. Jack and I stop for gas and lunch in Scappoose near the Oregon and Washington State border.

39

to scratch the itch that I have for Yosemite without being too time-consuming. We do not need to plan much for this climb – we can just go and do it. As for the big walls, they can wait until we come back later in the summer. We sleep next to the car that night after the guided tour is over – burgers, beer and an uncomfortable bed.

In the morning curiosity is mixed with just a little apprehension. I want to acquit myself well. I am aware that, after seeing a photo, Jack and I decided to go and make the first ascent of the north face of Mount Huntington. Just like that. With the exception of the Eiger with Wilco, I have never backed out of a climb, so I have no expectation other than success. But Jack and I have never done an alpine climb together. We are new friends and I am acutely aware of the importance of his confidence in me.

We trudge up to the base of the massive cliff laden with equipment, my gaze ever upward. Jack has chosen well, this is a magnificent granite tower. He explains that this climb had been one of the recent turning points in climbing ethics. In the past a lot of pitons had been used but now it was good style to climb it without a hammer. Since this was the only style of crag climbing I knew, he thought that this would be an appropriate first climb in Yosemite for me. Fifteen hundred feet of quality rock awaits us. No nails. No hammers. He has decided that I will go first.

The beginning is pleasant enough, up a corner and crack system, but when I have to belay, the anchors are not inspiring and I spend a lot of time setting up with an array of nuts. I can feel the vibrations coming up the rope from Jack: why am I taking so long? Then I need to hoist our haul bag, which is another first for me and I fumble that too. I have never rigged a haul before and getting the pulley and my jumars set up is painfully slow.

When Jack finally joins me I can see he is unhappy. I have created an untidy mess of a belay and not a very safe one at that. As he comes level with the belay he reaches to our right and clips into a bolt that has been fixed to the blank wall next to my stance.

I stare in disbelief. I had not seen it at all. In truth I had hardly seen bolts before so I had no expectation of them. The rock to my right was blank, so why would I look at it? There should be no anchors there! I had spent an age contriving a hanging belay on nuts and I could have just simply clipped the bolt instead. Jack is annoyed because he thinks I have avoided the bolt on ethical grounds at the expense of our speed and safety.

'Man, I know you Brits have all your high-flying ethics and all of that is fine but isn't this taking it a little too far? It's OK to use a bolt for a belay, surely?'

Jack in Yosemite getting set for some fun on the west face of Sentinel Rock. ▶

'Sorry, no, I just did not see it, really! It's practically the first bolt I have ever seen.'

We make peace and tidy the ropes and rack before Jack leads through. I will be much more attentive now I have embraced my British myopic error. Americans place bolts! We are finding out what is new to me, some of which is a revelation to my Stonemaster guide. I let it slip that I have never had to use jumars on a climb before. The penny really drops and mentally he makes an adjustment. I start to get helpful pointers.

I am climbing well, 5.10 is no problem at all and I have my head on engineering the protection. Our game becomes a competition to free climb as much of this route as we can without bogging down. I have no idea about the decimal grading system but Jack tells me that we are climbing some sections normally climbed with aid that are now 5.11. If we can't free something immediately we will aid the moves to keep momentum.

Aid climbing is a mechanical engineering skill and I have done little of it, although I am learning fast with Jack's help. He shows me how to set up properly and I am absorbing his wisdom and moving faster as a consequence. There is some fixed equipment on the route, it is easy to follow and this is a wonderful climb. But there is one piece of entertainment he has kept from me: a feature called the 'Expanding Flake'. I heard him say it once and in my mind I imagined a solid object that got bigger in some way, or a flake with a crack that just got wider. Either way, I imagined a *solid* thing.

Jack climbs for another sixty feet and sets up a belay near what will obviously be a traverse to the left under an overhanging flake, a huge overlapping block. It is not what I imagined at all. The wall below is blank, so the crack under the block will be the key. Since it is my turn to lead, I will have to fix my nuts under the flake and traverse standing in slings. I had not read the guidebook, so what I see is what I get. I think it looks OK, awkward, but just a traverse. Jack is watchful and alert. I start to lower my weight into the sling I have suspended from a nut I have cammed under the flake. It is difficult to make this look elegant and I am fumbling to place the next nut, and then the next. As I move my weight again I think I feel the nut move behind the flake. I look back at Jack just in time to see my last nut fall out of the crack. I am disturbed and confused; I had placed that hex very carefully and when I stood on it my weight should have bedded it in.

'What the hell?' I look at him quizzically.

'Expanding Flake, man, you made it move.'

'Shit, you mean an expanding ... *crack*?'

Sentinel Rock, Yosemite Valley. **Photo:** Mark Westman. ▶

'Kind of the same deal, man!' And he is grinning at me. 'I thought you understood.'

I keep very still while I consider my position. This massive block of granite is mobile, just jammed there somehow, waiting for foolhardy humans to apply a little leverage. By placing a wedge and applying my weight I have moved this massive piece of granite, so finely is it balanced. We have a short argument about the use of the English language, in particular the accurate use of nouns.

'You know, words used to identify a *thing* – concrete *or* abstract!'

I realise that Jack's belaying position is perfectly planned, and he has rigged it to resist the pull I will cause if I fall; it will be a pendulum swing. There is little to collide with on my imagined trajectory, so that at least is something positive. I am being observed closely, so I return to the task at hand. Now I know the flake is loose I place my nuts with great care and a total economy of movement. I move like a cat from one sling to the next, transferring my weight from one to the next like liquid, without any bounce at all. When I belay at the end of the pitch I am sweating. At least he says 'well done' in a roundabout way.

'Well, you ain't a Stonemaster yet, but you will get there.'

I read later that the flake pitch is actually the 'dreaded and feared flake pitch and is often a failure point for climbers trying the route'. It was the crux apparently.

It is a glorious thing to summit, a perfect first climb for me at the very altar of American rock climbing. The sun had shone on us all the way as I imagined it should. My hands are impressively scratched and my tan is looking good.

My joy is short-lived however: some bastard has smashed the rear window of Jack's car during the night and some of our equipment has been stolen, along with my passport and wallet, which contained my Visa card. I am seething. I can imagine what would happen to a thief caught stealing equipment in the UK; get caught doing that to a climber in Llanberis and a fate worse than death would ensue. Jack is more philosophical; it has happened to him before, more than once. It will not be possible to replace my passport and keep the schedule we had set so any thoughts of visiting Canada are gone. We will have to fly from a US airport and land in another, Anchorage in this case. We decide to drive as far as Seattle at least; it will give us some sense of the distance.

Revelling in the New World, more than enough was barely sufficient for me. ▶
Jack and I become easy company for each other on our road trip to Seattle. We drive through the streets of San Francisco, the streets I recall from the movie *Bullitt*. Albeit a little more slowly.

5
ALASKA

Anchorage is a surprise to me: wide, flat, spread out and with far fewer people than I was expecting. We have some shopping to do before we leave town, for fresh food, white gas for the stove, a snow saw, a snow shovel and beer. The hardware store is next to a small cinema, the Denali Theatre. It is showing *High Anxiety* and I point this out to Jack: 'It's a sign.'

While we collect our airfreight the manager at the cargo terminal chats with us about our plans and arranges for her brother Mike to drive us to Talkeetna in his pickup for $40 plus the cost of the gas. Driving out of town does not take long and soon we are speeding past lakes and small mountains with a little snow on them still. It is early June and summer is yet to fully arrive. We are rolling north on Highway 3, the main route between Anchorage and Fairbanks. If I was excited before, I am practically vibrating now. We will be in Talkeetna early this evening, but, being so far north, it will not actually get dark and so I will be able to explore. I notice that there are light aircraft everywhere, many of them float planes. Commuting in this part of the world obviously involves having your own aircraft. Jack points out one popular model, a Cessna 185. The company he has chosen to fly us into the Ruth Glacier uses the same type. It looks very small to me.

After a long uninhabited stretch Jack starts to recognise where he is.

'We are almost there, Si.'

There is a sign ahead pointing to our right down a minor country road: *Talkeetna*.

A mile from the village we crest the top of a small rise and suddenly the entire Denali range is visible. I ask Mike to stop so I can take it all in.

The village is more than I hoped for. From the bits and pieces of information I had gleaned from Jack I was expecting something small and quaint, but I was not expecting to feel like I was in a western movie. There is a home-made wooden sign under a tree at the beginning of the little road that is the main street. It reads *Welcome to beautiful downtown Talkeetna.*

There is the Fairview Inn, the Roadhouse, a store and a railroad station nearby. I suppose I am looking at strolling climbers, a few locals and many dogs. I am in heaven. I feel as if somebody is staring at me and I turn to see that Jack has been watching me intently. The smile on his face is like a question. In answer, I burst out laughing.

'What a great place!'

Our first stop will be Talkeetna Air Taxi and a meeting with Jim Sharp, our pilot. Jim lives in a log cabin built at the side of an airstrip. Both his plane and his pickup truck are parked outside. For Jack it is a reunion; he flew with Jim on his 1976 expedition.

There are several glacier aviators in Talkeetna. Kitty Banner is the only female pilot, and flies with Jim. Doug Geeting is another pilot – he flies a Cessna similar to Jim's, only unpainted to save weight. There is another famous aviator in town called Cliff Hudson, a real character by all accounts. Jim helps us unload Mike's pickup truck and at first I think this is just a friendly gesture but I soon realise he is adding up the weight of each box. The stickers from Western Air Cargo are still attached and they have the weight in pounds marked on each one. When the pile is complete he makes his pronouncement:

'You guys travel light. I can get you and all this in one load with the back seats removed.'

Jack and Jim chat about the weather, which is forecast to be fine for a couple of days. This is a good window for our flight. We need just a little time in Talkeetna to get ready. Our planning session is cut short by the intervention of the national bird of Alaska, the mosquito. They are big, painful and aggressive. We are forced to retreat to the safety of Jim's cabin where we pore over the map of the Ruth Glacier.

Later, we set up our little tent next to Jim's Cessna 185. It is a small plane but, I am assured, a great vehicle. It has skis mounted on the fixed-wheel suspension so it can either land on snow or the strip as required. Looking inside I can see that without back seats there is plenty of room for our kit, but that one of us will have to sit on the cargo.

'OK, mate, show me the nightlife,' I say to Jack. 'I want to see drunken cowboys sliding drinks along the bar.'

'The drunks won't be difficult to find,' Jack replies. 'Not sure about the cowboys.'

Jim Sharp's log cabin overlooking the airstrip, the home of Talkeetna Air Taxi in 1978.

We start at the Fairview Inn, just a short walk from Jim's cabin. A few beers and a hamburger deluxe later and I'm ready for the big time.

'Si, I believe you are properly prepared for a visit to the Tepee.'

We take a longer, mosquito-swatting walk to the edge of the village and the banks of the Susitna River and I discover the A-frame building known as the Tepee – because it resembles an American Indian 'wigwam', as we were taught to call them (no doubt inappropriately) by the early cowboy movies of the 1960s. Apparently this is Talkeetna's den of iniquity – the place to go when you have few plans for the next day. As the door is opened, Johnny Cash is our host.

Next morning, in our tiny tent, I am awakened by the whine of angry insects. The tent has a mosquito net and they cannot get in, but I need to pee, which means getting out to face the little bastards. This type of vile insect always occurs in alpine and sub-alpine environments in spring. When I used to go mountain walking with my dad, the midges in Scotland were murderous, but here in Alaska the insect problem takes on a new level. The 'skeets' are bigger and they know we are in the tent, poking their nasty stinging tails though the tiny holes in the net in an attempt to get at our blood. The buzzing eventually awakens my fellow camper.

'Morning, cowboy.'

'Ouch!'

'Jack, did we offend anybody last night?'

'Try that in Malibu and the cops would have turned up, but I doubt any folks really noticed in the Tepee.'

'Good. Pancakes please, and grits. I don't know what grits are but I have to find out.'

'Get all your clothes on and we will make a run for it.'

The main street in Talkeetna is busy this morning; there are obviously a couple of big expeditions in town getting ready to leave for the mountains. A group of about a dozen climbers is sorting boxes and bags of equipment. Jack explains that the boxes have 'Genet' marked on them because this lot are guided clients of Ray Genet and will be attempting the West Buttress of Denali.

He tells me that Genet is something of a famous mountaineer. Born in Talkeetna, Ray is a solid, swarthy man in his forties, with a shock of black hair tucked under a colourful bandana. His nickname is 'The Pirate' and the reason for the appellation is obvious. To complete the image he has a huge black beard. Summer guided ascents of Denali are his bread and butter, but he himself has actually climbed Denali in winter. Hell! I cannot imagine that.

I find Talkeetna intoxicating; we want to leave as soon as possible for the mountains and have agreed with Jim that we will fly tomorrow morning – so we have a lot to do today. We spend the day sorting out our equipment, repacking our supplies to make them aircraft-friendly and making sure our personal gear is in perfect shape. I spend hours adjusting my crampons and super gaiters so that they fit perfectly on my outer boots. We also register with the national park, as we must. There is a small fee to pay and we need to clearly state our intentions so the rangers will be able to keep tabs on us. It is a good system.

At the ranger station we meet park ranger Dave Buchanan. Dave is a friendly guy and very helpful but we get a big raised eyebrow when we tell him we are going to make the first ascent of the north face of Mount Huntington. He is an experienced local climber himself but he does not try to talk us out of our climb. Dave gives us helpful advice and explains how the park tracks the climbers on the mountain. We can pass information to the ranger station via the bush pilots we may encounter on the Ruth, or talk to them on our CB radio when they are flying close over the mountains.

When we are as ready as we can be, Jack and I pore over the Washburn aerial photo and our map of the Ruth Glacier area one last time before dinner. No high jinks tonight. I give Jim a few dollars so I can make a quick call home to let my family know we will be incommunicado for a while and that they are not to worry. To fool the mosquitoes we devise a technique whereby we leave the tent open and unattended, pretending that we are not interested in it. Then we run to it suddenly and dive in, closing the netting in one single movement.

The morning is fine, with a cloudless blue sky. We will definitely fly today: the weather is perfect. I am full of adrenaline, but I deliberately force myself to eat a huge breakfast. I may need it. The Cessna is fuelled and our gear loaded according to Jim's instructions, so that the balance of the plane is not compromised. I am a little apprehensive about the flight – I have seen a few planes take off and land at the strip and it amazes me how slowly they do so. I can see that Jack is keeping busy checking our equipment against the list we drew up over the past few weeks of preparation.

Finally it is time to get dressed for the mountains because when we touch down it will be on the west fork of the Ruth Glacier. Our climbing packs are loaded with ropes and basic climbing survival gear just in case we have an unpleasant surprise when we land. Jack is much more relaxed than I. You can actually see Mount McKinley in the distance from the rise in the road just outside Talkeetna, but not Mount Huntington. For this reason, the latter has no native name. McKinley was named after a president but, before it was rebranded by white men, it was simply Denali, which I prefer. Our mountain, Huntington, was named after a president of the American Geographical Society.

I climb into the back of the plane and make a nest for myself on top of our equipment. The views from the Cessna are panoramic and I have a good view of Jim's controls. I have my Olympus OM1 camera in my lap and spare rolls of film in my pocket – I expect to need them all on the flight. We are all aboard and the doors are closed. My goodness, it is noisy when Jim guns the engine to taxi on to the strip. He is talking on the radio but I cannot hear what he is saying. We turn at the end of the strip and pause only for a moment before he pushes the throttle and we rush forwards leaving a cloud of dust behind us. The Roberts-McCartney expedition has begun.

6
THE RUTH GLACIER

Jim's first turn gives me a start. The plane is unbelievably responsive to his instructions. I can see his hands and feet and any movement causes an instant change of direction. It reminds me of the sailing I did in my teens, when a pull on a sheet or a rotation of the tiller gave immediate results. With the little Cessna we are sailing in three dimensions.

We have cleared the Talkeetna airstrip and are heading west towards the snowy massif in the distance, gaining height all the while. We cross Highway 3 and we expect to enjoy forty-five minutes of spectacular aerial sightseeing on the way to our destination, the west fork of the Ruth Glacier.

The weather is perfect and we can see for miles. Soon we are over glaciers, dry of snow at first and strewn with moraines and rock debris that has been scoured from the mountains over millions of years. I have seen many glaciers in my life, but this is the first time I have flown low and slowly over such terrain. I am reminded of my geography teacher Hilda Sharp. She took a personal interest in me and I was a fortunate student. Looking down I can see the formative glacial forces at work as clearly as any 3D diagram in a textbook. Every fold and crevasse makes sense to me as clearly as a time-lapse movie might if you could film a glacier for a hundred years in one place.

I had wondered if, when our climb was over and we had rested in Talkeetna, we might either walk or fly in and then ski and walk out of the mountains, just for the experience. I had imagined that bears or river crossings might be problems but my view from the window shows me there are bigger issues: below the summer snowline the glaciers would be very time consuming to

◀ Pilot Jim Sharp gazes up at the north face of Mount Huntington.

cross and I abandon the idea now as I study the evolution of the terrain. For this summer at least, I have other priorities. When we are done on this Alaskan climb I want to go to Yosemite again. I have a list of climbs there that have almost chosen themselves: the north-west face of Half Dome to warm up, then the Nose of El Capitan.

There are some bumps as we hit air pockets. These are alarming at first but when they happen again, just part of the fun. With every turn, the landscape is becoming more spectacular. What on earth have we taken on with this little expedition? Many climbers must know about this vertical wonderland and I feel stupid that it is such a revelation to me. When I arrived in Chamonix for the first time I more or less knew where everything was in the massif. I could recognise the peaks and faces on first sight. My ignorance here, upon suddenly arriving in the Ruth gorge, might have been embarrassing in a way but is instead pure excitement as I realise the extent of the climbing to be had.

We round a corner in the terrain and are startled by the amazing sight of the great gorge of the Ruth Glacier. Even Jack turns to me and says 'Wow' this time. We are like two kids at Christmas. Coming to Alaska was a great idea. I am glad we chose this location, and we have not laid a hand on the mountain yet. There are so many new climbs to be done here, and that's just within the area I can see. We have travelled in time in a way, back to the golden years of alpinism. It feels, I imagine, like Chamonix would have felt in the fifties, when the obvious and great technical lines were being climbed for the first time. Chamonix is nearly all done now; all the classic faces and buttresses have been climbed, but in Alaska, even in just the Ruth area, Jack and I could keep busy putting up new routes for years.

We are over a steep-sided snowy glacier now. Jim reaches down, adjusting the trim for landing. He leans over to Jack and shouts to him while pointing downward. I look too and can make out the shape of Mount Huntington.

We are nearly there.

Massive walls tower above us on either side. Jim is busy now, studying the surface of the glacier below us intently. I can no longer take pictures, I am too absorbed in what is unfolding. The throttle is adjusted and the engine noise dips as we slow and descend towards a smooth glacier without visible crevasses. Because the glacier is rising towards us as we are descending, the distance is being closed more quickly than I expect and I notice that I am hanging on to a handle with white knuckles. I can see that there is a tent already pitched on the glacier ahead – we will have neighbours. It must be Charlie Porter and Peter Sennhauser's camp. Jim says that they are here for a first ascent on the Rooster

Comb's north buttress, the next peak to the east of Mount Huntington.

The plane is flaring gently. There is the slightest bump as the skis scratch the glacier and when they have settled Jim is immediately hard on the throttle, driving the plane through the snow for a long taxi before coming to a halt. He kills the engine and the echoes of the exhaust bounce off the valley walls for several seconds. The doors are opened and we all clamber out into ankle-deep snow in the middle of the glacier and more or less directly opposite the north face of Huntington.

Without any discussion all three of us stare up at our chosen adventure. My God, it is just over there! I have come halfway around the world to climb this mountain and we have simply landed at the bottom of it. It looks massive.

Jack and I don't speak and it is Jim who breaks the spell.

'Do you want me to take a picture of you together before I leave?' he asks.

We pose like tourists, staring at the face in a contrived pose, trying to look cool. Jim gives us some advice about the radio he has lent to us and clambers back into his seat. Jack and I watch silently as he guns the engine, spins the little plane on the spot and then roars down the glacier under full power. The Cessna takes off and slowly gains height by virtue of the descending terrain as it flies down the middle of the valley. We watch in silence as it gets smaller and smaller before disappearing behind the Rooster Comb. When the plane is no longer in sight, I find myself still staring at the point in space where I saw it last.

We are left alone. The only smell is of dissipating exhaust fumes from Jim's Cessna and soon there will be no trace of him, other than his ski tracks melting in the sun. I can still hear the noise of the engine when a sérac breaks off the Rooster Comb and crashes into the glacier with an impressive explosion. It is a perfect piece of theatre; the mountain is welcoming the new humans with a warning shot.

The only sounds now are of our own footsteps in soft snow, barely audible. But any notion that we are confined to a world of silence is soon dispelled by the creaking of another sérac and a crash of an avalanche somewhere else in the gorge. So this is how the mountains will speak to us: harshly. I can see that we are both in mild shock. Nine months of planning has ended and we are alone on a glacier.

Looming above us is the biggest climbing project either of us has ever undertaken. The north face is a massive jagged tooth, covered with razor-like runnels and flutes of ice. A steep rock band at its base defends the face from east to west. There will be no avoiding that. Above, a hanging glacier has formed a wall of extremely dangerous séracs, which are continuous except for one possible passage on the left. Of course we knew all this from the photo, but now, seeing the face first hand, it seems so much larger and more threatening.

We make a poorly organised camp and dig a hole in the snow to make an outdoor kitchen. We have dinner quietly, both deep in thought. Despite the shock of the rapid transition from plains to glacier, in my heart I am happy. I am high in the mountains where I belong, about to take another step in my climbing career. We celebrate our arrival with a tuna salad and a blueberry cobbler.

I have a full belly and it is warm in the tent, but I cannot sleep. It is either too quiet or I am too excited or we keep waking each other by accident in the tiny cramped confines of the tent.

JACK'S JOURNAL – JUNE 14

I've finally adjusted to the fantastic scenery around me. We landed here on the west fork of the Ruth on Saturday afternoon and we were completely blown away by the size of our project. That is to say that Huntington is much, much bigger than I had imagined. I am speechless about what appears to be a never-ending summit pyramid of rock, ice and snow, blending into the sky above so perfectly that the top cannot be seen.

Next to the north face of Mount Huntington is the Rooster Comb, almost as impressive – maybe more technical but far less serious. On Huntington there is not an obvious line that comes out to hit you and say 'climb me'. You have to study the face and pick the safest route.

The Rooster Comb has two obvious lines to be done.

The summit of the Rooster Comb is 3,600 feet of vertical rise above the glacier. Huntington is nearly twice that.

All around us are mini-buttresses from the south-east spur of Mount McKinley; all themselves smaller grade IV alpine routes without even taking into account that they are all only a part of 'Big Mac' himself.

We are camped next to Charlie Porter and Peter Sennhauser. They have left camp for a ski trip, I suppose. Charlie has made a scarecrow out of some aluminium poles and his climbing helmet. Still it will be a little more pleasant having two other people (that I know) around. It will help to break up the isolation on the glacier. In another way I think I am also disappointed that they are here because I was actually looking forward to some isolation. Not real sure about how I feel about being here.

Part of me wishes that our preparations had been more thorough and elaborate. But if they had been, some weight and bulk would have been added, it would have been less in the spirit of the trip.

Old friends meet and new friends made for me. Charlie Porter left, Peter Sennhauser centre and Jack Roberts.

I do regret not taking skis. I really regret that.

We settle down, get some grub and chat. We look at the face, listen to the noises and search a route.

We think we have spotted a line, one which goes from the centre, passing the séracs on the left, goes right and then back again left before climbing an obvious ramp feature directly to the summit.

With his usual impatience, Simon wants to go up tomorrow, or at least says as much. I want to watch the face and really study it before I decide.

The weather is perfect and this increases Simon's optimism, but I want to be sure.

Later on Charlie and Peter ski up to our camp, we see them coming far away; it is good to see old friends. Charlie and I talk for hours about past climbs, mutual acquaintances and new gear, catching up on all these years.

I had heard of Charlie Porter many times, naturally. Many of the serious climbers in the world read *Mountain* magazine and Porter would often get a mention. What I did not know was that Jack knew Charlie well. He also knew Peter Sennhauser, Charlie's climbing partner.

Charlie is the outgoing one of the pair, never lost for a topic or an anecdote. He is full of himself, but in a good way. I had no idea what to expect from him, but I find him highly entertaining. There is no arrogance about him either; I could imagine such a famous climber being full of self-aggrandisement but he has none of that, quite the opposite. It is Jack who whispers to me that Charlie climbed the Cassin Ridge two years ago, solo. That is really impressive; I know that the Cassin Ridge is currently the hardest route to the top of the highest mountain in America.

Peter is an affable personality but quieter and more considered. It seems we have become welcome neighbours and we also share similarly ambitious climbing plans. I listen carefully to Charlie when he describes his intended route on the Rooster Comb in case I can learn something; it looks hard and will require the utilisation of the big-wall techniques pioneered in Yosemite in an alpine-style climbing application. He has a home-made 'Porter-ledge' with him so that they can set up a hanging bivouac on a vertical section of rock if they have to. All this talk spurs me on.

I want to attack our climb straight away; I am not accustomed to hanging around looking at the mountain. Everything I have done up to this point has been climbed quickly. If the weather is good in the Alps when you arrive, you go for it. Waiting and thinking requires a patience I struggle to find within myself.

I push Jack to pack for the climb today because I just cannot wait. During our final preparations to leave there is a loud crack and part of the sérac band avalanches directly down the path we intend to take. We would not have survived it and we drop our packs to the ground on the spot, staring dumbly at the scene of devastation that unfolds: huge blocks of ice are tumbling and exploding exactly where we were intending to climb.

Charlie and Peter saw the entire episode and the looks on their faces required no words of translation. Jack and Simon are staying at home tonight – kids grounded for being reckless.

JACK'S JOURNAL

Later we get out a bottle of Scotch and we all get drunk telling tall stories.

We drank the Scotch because we aren't going on the face right away. Simon and I did prepare for it and were about to leave when a medium-sized avalanche went down the bottom part of the route we had picked which convinced us to stay in camp a little longer. Three hours sooner and we would have been under that avalanche. The end result was too unpleasant to contemplate.

Today the weather has deteriorated with poor visibility; the fog started rolling in at about 10.30 and had set in by 1 p.m. Wet snow starts to fall and keeps falling lightly through the day and evening.

I am excited and I want to climb too much to be able to read a lot, but I am anxious.

We decide to eat only half rations while it storms to conserve food and avoid getting fat.

The tent is too small.

We do not have enough Ensolite padding.

Tent life is terrible; the tent is much too tiny for a base camp and I am constantly aware that I may awaken Jack by simply shuffling on my Karrimat to get comfortable. Worse still, the snow is building up on the tent so quickly that we cannot sleep a night without it starting to collapse under the weight. This means we have broken rest because we have to take turns to get up and dig away the snow. Of course this awakens us both anyway so we both lose sleep.

The constant snowing makes cooking difficult and we decide to improve the 'ice kitchen' so that we can shelter the stoves. We dig down far enough so that we can make a roof to the 'kitchen' from a plastic sled borrowed from Charlie and Peter. Now we can cook in semi-comfort, even when it is snowing.

Yesterday was mostly spent in Porter's tent. All four of us are complaining, farting, talking and chewing almonds.

Visiting Charlie is quite pleasant for Simon and I because their tent is a JanSport three-man dome and it has much more headroom than our little bivouac tent.

The weather is still bad, really wet snow or 'splosh' as I call it because of the 'splosh' sound it makes hitting the tent.

Jack and I have our own ways of passing time. I have calmed down since the first aborted attempt and I have resigned myself to a Scottish-climbing-type mindset: there will be lots of bad weather and not much climbing, so I might as well save energy and get my head in good order. Fortunately sleeping is one of my favourite hobbies in the mountains and if I cannot do that we have plenty to read. We are swapping books with each other and, to our mutual surprise, quite liking titles we would have never normally considered. Jack has become immersed in Mervyn Peake's *The Gormenghast Trilogy* from my pile of soggy books and I am surprised by the fun I am having with his copy of *The Monkey Wrench Gang*.

If Jack gets bored with his book he falls back on his other favourite pastime: redesigning our climbing apparel. Neither of us is happy with our down parkas and we discuss their shortcomings. Now he is content because he has a project and he will write and sketch in his journal for hours. Jack likes to draw; he is a creative soul to be with.

Yesterday we made a snow cave, not a particularly large one but one that will do if our tent should cave in. It is really snowing heavily and steadily now.

Simon evidently loves digging; once the hole is big enough he sets about creating little improvements like creating a kitchen with a work surface and cut-outs in the walls to store our supplies. When the hard work is done I leave him to it.

Later I see he has skilfully used his ice axe to carve out a mock television set in one of the walls. To complete the humour I stared blankly at it for a while, as if it was fascinating.

Yesterday (June 15), the sun came out for a short period and I rejoiced at the sight of it, it felt so good, even for half an hour. But I got up at 4 a.m. to piss the tea out and it was snowing again.

It has probably snowed three feet now, every time I walk around the tracks are filled with inches of new snow and the light is so flat that I stumble about like a drunken fool. Each time I step off the packed trail I sink up to my knees in new snow.

We spend our time going from the cave to the 'igloo' which is how we refer to Charlie and Peter's tent. We tell jokes and stories. Charlie is telling us about trapping seals in the Arctic and living among the Inuit people in Greenland. Also an epic climb on Middle Triple Peak with Russ McLean. Story after story he has.

Every few hours a big avalanche cuts loose with a '**crack**' and roars down Huntington's face. Someone (maybe me) will look outside to see if it can be seen, but everything is so white that not much can be distinguished.

I have become used to the noises and they no longer awaken me as they did at first. But last night there was a much louder bang followed by a long rumble that did wake me fully. I thought about getting up, but the noise died away and in the end I stayed put in my pit.

It stopped snowing in the night and I now have a clear view out of the cave if I sit up and crane my neck from the sleeping nook I have created. Curiosity about the conditions on the face drives me out of my sleeping bag. Boots loosely on, I trudge up the steps and am horrified to find that avalanche debris has tumbled down the mountain opposite Huntington and only stopped a few feet from our camp. It has not come from Huntington, the usual offender, but from the north side of the valley and a mountain that we had regarded as innocuous. So innocuous I do not even know its name. I am the only riser.

'Hey, Jack, you had better come and look at this.'

His voice drifts up to me from the cave.

'What is it, man?'

Half a minute later he comes up the steps behind me and discovers that I am looking in the opposite direction to his expectation. His gaze follows mine after a 180-degree turn.

'Holy shit!'

'Quite.'

Charlie has become curious about our cursing and pops his head out of the dome tent. There is a short pause while he takes in the scene, and then an expletive. We are camped in the very middle of the glacier and yet the avalanche from the least precipitous and threatening side of the gorge has nearly overwhelmed us. Charlie and Jack wander about in the debris as if fascinated by it. Jack shouts to me, 'Should we move the camp?'

I pause for effect. 'No need, we are totally safe now.'

It raises a smile.

Things are not so harmonious between Peter and Charlie. They seem to have had a falling out about their proposed climb. Charlie has always been totally gung-ho about their prospects of success. Peter has been reticent, as if he is ana-lysing all the things that could go wrong and, to be fair, there are a lot. We discover today that Peter has decided not to climb the Rooster Comb with Charlie.

I stay out of all the discussions, but Peter's decision leaves Charlie frustrated: here he is, camped on the west fork, just an hour from the base of a beautiful and bold first ascent, but he has no partner. Charlie starts trying to talk us into going with him on his route. I have serious reservations – it is a fine line, but not what we came for. Charlie's only option is to recruit another climber from Talkeetna. Peter wants to leave but can't until the weather allows him to do so. There can be no flying at the moment. His only means of partial escape is to ski down to where the west fork of the glacier meets the great gorge, a place Jack calls the 'amphitheatre'. Overlooking this, perched on a rocky knoll, is the Don Sheldon Mountain House. If you are in the mood to leave the mountains it is a very comfortable place to wait for your plane and no doubt a more appealing prospect than brooding in the same tent as your ex-partner.

Jack has ants in his pants today; he has become worried about his physical condition because we have been loafing around for a few days. I am not worried about it at all. We were in great shape when we arrived and a week of dossing won't hurt in my opinion; at least we have been acclimatising. My climbing ca-reer thus far has been littered with long spells of 'dossing' when the weather was being unhelpful. As far as I am concerned we will find a way to stay here until we succeed in climbing our route on Huntington and that is that.

JACK'S JOURNAL

Starting with the original snow cave, we have enlarged it and dug out a much bigger snow condo with separate sleeping compartments, our only exercise for the day. Simon is as happy as a gopher and he has created a new place for every-thing we have and the improved kitchen is a work of fine architecture. Simon likes to cook and takes pride in it; I quite like cooking but I let him do it as it distracts him from his impatience.

I am trying not to eat too much food but just enough to keep healthy. If you get sick here it takes twice as long to get better. The dampness also seeps into everything.

I found out the real reason for Charlie and Peter's separation (if indeed what

Peter told me can be said to be true, what indeed is truth?). Peter thinks that Charlie is underestimating the seriousness of the line they have been planning.

Climbers are essentially alone. When you are on the sharp end of the rope you are up against yourself and your own fears. The truth is not hidden; it is out there for all to see. It is against this that we face ourselves or rather, the part of the truth of our selves.

Charlie feels that Peter felt that the attempt on the Rooster Comb was too serious, so they split. Peter agrees but in more words.

Building the big cave gave me an appetite and at least helps me sleep better. We have been eating up the granola and peanut butter steadily.

Tea is very popular but coffee is my favourite. Simon dislikes the honey we have and prefers the sugar we don't have.

I slept in the 'Ice Palace' last night. Probably the best night's sleep yet. Spent half a day in bed half sleeping and dreaming.

JUNE 17

When I did awake it turned out to be a particularly bad day for me; I didn't want to get out of my festering hole at all.

I am starting to pick out a few minor things and letting them irritate me, such as Simon using all of the cord locks for his own use. **My** cord locks!

No big deal but it seems to bother me and lets me dwell on something different for a change.

When that seems old I ask Simon if we should not take it easy on the milk, but that too is probably for the sake of novelty and nothing else.

The inactivity is bad. So I start to dig out the tent (again) and Simon joins in. We repitch it and redo it so it looks the best ever.

I walk alone for a while towards the Rooster Comb. I feel like the last planet spaceman all wrapped up in yellow Gore-Tex, seeing the storm through Vuarnet eyes, kicking up moon dust and just walking along until I seem to be sweating too much and I stop to pee.

I stare into the drifting sea of white nothingness and silently turn about. I wonder what everyone else in these mountains is doing. I begin to feel a slight bond with all of the other poor souls who are stuck in the same storm, probably doing the same things I am.

I try to make the perfect imprint of my boot sole as I plod back towards camp.

Put foot here; gently sink in to the knee. Bring the foot out without breaking the snow's crust and repeat and repeat.

Living underground is much better than the tent. It is cold but I sleep better because Jack and I are not crammed together and we no longer disturb each other needlessly. Cooking, reading, dressing and hanging out are all so much easier in the ice cave.

Jack has again taken to designing climbing and bivouac equipment to pass the hours. His sketches are very clear and give us something else to talk about.

Normally I cannot find the patience to spend time considering 'what if' scenarios about things I might or might not be able to have in future. With Jack, however, I have the strong sense that, even though we have not even begun our scheduled climb, I know that it will not be our only one. I find myself taking an interest in Jack's designs because I have begun to believe that on the next climb I will be using them.

Jack helped Charlie build a gym by digging another snow cave which is fitted with exercise bars made from the frame of Charlie's 'Porter-Ledge'.

Jack has gone for a walk and I let him be, obviously deep in his thoughts. Much as we get on well, living in a hole in the snow for so many frustrating days is becoming claustrophobic and we have both been a little irritable at times.

JACK'S JOURNAL

When I get to camp I go into Charlie's chamber and crank off sixteen pull-ups.

Coming out it seems I have seen this scene before, the one that looks like a deserted snowy death camp …

The snow dome here.

The outhouse there.

The ice cave over yonder.

The tent next to the hole.

Skis and poles looking like scarecrows in a burned-down cornfield, bent over and waiting for something to scare, anything to frighten away.

The snow drifts get bigger and tracks are soon filled in again and again.

The morning greets me with the quiet swish of wind and snow.

The temperature drops and as I cool off, shivers start to arouse me and drive me back down into the hole where I will spend 'time', my sentence for coming to Alaska.

Doing much as I do before I write some, rage a lot, read less.

I start to wonder what Siberia would be like. In the summer.

JUNE 18

6.05 p.m. Just finished the most satisfying meal to date: turkey, peas and rice. Washed down with coffee it really rang a bell.

Got up late today (1 p.m.), to be greeted by the familiar swoosh of powder snow flowing outside. Same as yesterday, white-out conditions with snow falling.

I had tea with Charlie and I guess he is going to ski to the mountain house with Peter to help him move over there. Peter is exasperated by the weather. For him it has been fifteen days without climbing. It is probably better that he moves to the mountain house and waits for Jim Sharp to come and fly him out, than be waiting here with us.

We have given Peter a list of food to buy for us and give to Sharp to bring to us next time he passes over sometime, enough for at least another week:

3 pounds of peanut butter

3 pounds of cheese

2 pounds of rice

2 pounds of margarine

2 pounds of granola

2 loaves of bread

6 4-oz cans of tuna

1 gallon of milk

Coffee

5 big packs of Tiger Milk bars

We may not need it but if we get any more big storms we will be glad of the extra rations.

JUNE 19

3 p.m. It snowed nine inches last night and increasingly the storm shows no sign of abating. Simon and I broke more trail last night towards the Rooster Comb. We were going to finish it today but there seems little point in doing so, bummed out again!

7.45 p.m. The snow has stopped and the sun has begun to burn away the remaining mist until the glacier is clear and the sky above is blue.

Everything is plastered with new snow and ice. I yell inside the cave to Simon and he quickly slaps on his boots and runs up the steps of the cave in leaps and bounds to meet me out on the glacier.

Sun, the first in almost nine days!

Even though there is a cold front coming in and the east wind is blowing, we stand outside taking pictures. We point at Huntington and pray for how nice it will be tomorrow.

Huntington is completely iced up; the lower rock band will actually be easier now with a new coating of ice.

Feet of snow.

Tons of snow.

Gobs of snow.

Back inside the 'Ice Palace', or 'Hotel California' as Simon now refers to it, we fix up a super meal, the first of the day. Turkey noodles supreme with carrots and scrambled eggs and bacon bits, washed down with delicious hot honey cream tea.

Full belly but I wish it was warmer inside the ice cave.

The improvement in the weather is a timely boost to our morale; I had begun to think it would never stop snowing. A little sun and a cold snap have given me determination to get on with our climb, but we will need to wait another day. If we were sensible we would wait many days, but we are not sensible.

Huntington is really plastered; will this be better or worse I wonder?

JUNE 20

I did not sleep much at all last night but today is beautiful, just a few floating clouds and blue sky and **sun**!

We got up and lapped it up like two thirsty dogs that have not drunk water for days. Actually I feel more like an alcoholic who, having not touched a drop of booze in weeks, gets to such a state that he falls off the wagon, gets drunk and feels that the whole world is a better place than before.

We strip down to the skin and dry off. Everything goes outside to be aired and freshened up.

I reckon that I must be pretty smelly by now so a little sunbathing might help. Perhaps the UV will kill the microbes. I take off my shirt and the sun feels good.

Jack strips all his clothes off and hangs them on a washing line made from climbing rope and sets up to sunbathe naked. This means I have to do so as well and we are soon laughing at the comedy images we are taking with our cameras. Our constitutional is interrupted by the unmistakable drone of an approaching aircraft.

JACK'S JOURNAL

Doug Geeting flies in and gets stuck!

He has with him two guys from Washington State, half of a team of four who want to attempt the French Ridge, the north-west ridge of Mount Huntington.

Everyone helps dig Doug out except us three and then when all the hard work is over, we all help to push him out of the hole in the snow that has buried a ski of the undercarriage.

Conversations are passed back and forth with the new arrivals and soon Simon, Charlie and I all leave the lads to their tasks.

According to Geeting, more often than not, when landing in virgin snow, getting stuck is an expected part of the process of delivering climbers to high-glacier locations. This spot, the west fork of the Ruth Glacier, is notorious for deep snow and provides a bit more of a challenge for him. Of course, with experienced climbers on board, with strong backs, it really was not a concern getting stuck. It was fun for him, sitting on the top of the wing like a human counterweight and waiting for the climbers to dig him out and pack a runway in the soft snow by simply stamping it down with their boots or skis.

I stop to chat with the new neighbours and I make friends with Rob Newsom. He has a strong southern drawl – it is as if I am speaking to a caricature of an American. Rob is also a natural comedian and the slow delivery of his observational humour has me smiling constantly. Jack finds him even more amusing than I do.

I had been initially resentful of the arrival of another team but Rob has changed my mind. He is an asset, so different from the rest of us in demeanour, and yet at the same time so closely connected through our chosen lives as climbers. At this moment we are specifically connected by the simultaneous invitation and threat posed by Mount Huntington.

Newsom has with him three other climbers, all Rainier mountain guides – Eric Simonson, Rom Lee and Craig Reininger – who, along with Rob, are calling themselves the 'Too Loose Climbing Expedition'.

Rob does not know Simonson or Reininger well, but he is a regular climbing partner of his friend Rom. Rob wanted to be a Rainier guide but they wouldn't let him because he has long hair which he refuses to cut!

Simonson wants to do 'Big H', as he calls it; he is au fait with the French Ridge (the Lionel Terray route). This is fascinating for Jack and me because our intention is to descend this north-west ridge as our escape and we know very little about it. I make a dinner date with the Too Loose boys so we can have a chat.

Jack and I leave them to their march up the valley and resume our sunbathing. The good weather and the Washington State team's arrival have us in high spirits. Roberts is in particularly good form today, scaring the tourists by running around naked apart from his climbing gear. After many days of sloth and boredom all the activity is stimulating and the arrival of more climbers helps to allay the nagging fear I have been developing that we might have been nuts to come here.

Well it seems that Charlie may split with Doug to get Gary Bogarde out here to climb.

Doug has just landed again and dropped two more guys. Again he leaves with Charlie still here on the Ruth. This is becoming quite absurd, very silly.

Hudson lands again and drops off another two climbers. These guys are going for the south-east face, which just happens to be on the other side of the mountain on a different glacier, but they seem like happy guys and don't seem to mind the fact that they [will have to] climb and haul the loads over. They inform us that there are four Colorado climbers going for the same route. There are also six or eight Japanese over there too. What a zoo!

Simon and I packed for our climb and left at 10.30 p.m.

Love to all.

7
CRAPS

The séracs at the toe of the hanging glacier are the most dangerous I have ever seen. They are weakest at the left-hand end, petering out below the diamond-shaped buttress that sits in the very middle of the north face. There lies the only possibility of success for us. To make this work we would have to climb the rock band so that we emerge close to the left-hand end of the sérac wall and then find a way around it, giving us an entry to the easier ground above on the hanging glacier. From there we plan to pass the diamond-shaped buttress on the right and then trend back leftwards over mixed rock and ice to access the ramp feature that runs almost all the way to the summit.

After leaving camp Jack and I take turns breaking ground in knee-deep snow. We talk very little, each of us deep in our own thoughts. There is no wind and the only sounds come from the crunch of our boots sinking into the crust and our heavy breathing. Then 'crack!' – a noise like a gunshot is followed by a crash. The report is repeated every second by an echo in the valley. A piece of the sérac wall has calved and fallen to our right. The ice explodes in a cloud of ice particles and billows towards us. My camera is around my neck – I have just stopped to take a shot of Jack kicking the way towards the face – so I am ready to take two quick photos, one of the explosion above me and a second of the avalanche cloud rushing towards our position.

We both stand still and stare at the cloud hurtling at us. Somehow I feel that we will be OK; we are far enough away that the heavy contents of this avalanche will not reach us. I even have the presence of mind to put my camera inside my overalls. The blast of wind hits me and, a second later, the cloud of

◄ Jack kicks deep steps towards the bergschrund at the base of the north face of Mount Huntington.

airborne particles envelops me. I am pelted with small pieces of ice, half expecting worse. I lose sight of Jack. A minute passes and the cloud slowly settles, revealing Jack dusted with ice from head to toe. Jack shudders, repelling the ice like a dog shaking off seawater. We stare at each other across the twenty paces that separate us without speaking. I wonder how he is feeling after the near miss. He is the first to break the silence:

'The mountain says hi, man.'

Good, he has made light of it. Some might have had second thoughts, but not us. We have come too far and waited too long. He turns and resumes kicking steps without further comment. I crunch along behind him.

We reach the bergschrund. It is easy to cross because it is filled with avalanche debris and we decide to keep moving without taking out the ropes. We climb the steepening snow slopes and head towards the couloir we have chosen. As we get close we begin to see a line that looks like it might be faster and we chop out a small ledge at the base of some heavily iced rocks, set an anchor and rope up. We left camp only two hours ago and we are already getting to grips with our challenge. There is no discussion about which of us will lead the first pitch. Jack is in front of me and it is less complicated if he goes first. I gather the ropes, our eyes meet and I nod. He places his picks and steps up; there is no talking, just the sound of his crampons scratching on icy rock.

The rope is run out quickly at first and I am encouraged. However, after eighty or ninety feet, Jack's progress slows to a crawl. The change in tempo is also accompanied by some bad language – Jack is cursing the mountain for some reason I cannot see. He is chopping out vast amounts of snow and, as he is directly above me, I am being pelted with most of the debris.

Twenty minutes pass for the gain of only ninety feet; we had hoped to dispense with entire pitches of 200 feet in less than that time. After a little more grumbling I hear him shout 'safe' and the ropes are taken in.

Alpine climbing is a battle against time and we had both agreed that whoever was following a pitch would climb as fast as possible, ignoring any sense of style. The rope above the second climber would always be tight and you would get up fast and in any way you could. My plan to race up to Jack's position soon changes as I see what the problem is: deep, wet snow, which has stuck to everything – even vertical surfaces. It cannot be climbed on in any normal way and Jack hates it.

JACK'S JOURNAL

It turned out to be wet snow plastered on steep rock; real shit mixed climbing. The couloir appeared to be thinly iced slabs in the back of a small narrow gulley, but pitches of hard mixed climbing on snow-plastered rock followed.

I met Simon in Chamonix the year before and I knew the guy could climb. We had both done the north face of Les Droites that summer with different partners. I had confidence in him but I always figured that I was the stronger rock climber. But in this vertical crap of steep rock, ice and wet plastered snow, he has this vertical grovelling technique that is uncanny. I guess he invented it in a soggy storm in Scotland or North Wales one winter. First of all he would burrow into the vertical snow and reprocess it by compacting it with his feet or hands or both. Any excess material he would chop out and thoughtfully jettison so it just missed me. He was building a ladder, a set of compacted steps, for himself made out of dangerous rubbish with little or no protection. It is fascinating to behold, but horrible to follow.

We did fifteen pitches in six hours, not bad in the conditions. Usually we swing leads but not always; Simon is happy to deal with the horrible mixed snow.

He leads two more 'grovelling' pitches and he lets me take a couple of extra leads on more normal iced rock pitches. We complement each other well.

Then the sun hits us and then suddenly the entire face becomes unclimbable and any sane semblance of decent climbing is lost. The mountain has immediately started shedding its coat of wet snow all around us and it has become very dangerous.

Simon located a ledge which we used to our advantage immediately to attend to our particular needs at the time, sleeping, cooking and taking cover from any falling debris from above.

It was a snow ledge, a build-up of snow and ice under a rock overhang, giving us protection from the séracs above and a good platform from which to survey the already impressive drop below. We chop out a ledge big enough for us both to lie down and cook; it is really very cosy. Simon reverts to gopher mode again and makes the floor perfectly flat for lying down behind a parapet wall of compacted snow which is nice and secure. How he loves to dig!

The ledge is a godsend; if we had been caught out in the open things could have been fatal for us. We will spend all day here and hope that it freezes tonight. I am disappointed that we did not pass the rock band in one push as we planned. On a cold day we would certainly have made it to the hanging glacier above with the pace we had. In my mind I feel that the loss of twelve hours on this ledge is not a disaster, but I certainly did not want to stop so soon. Our height gain has given us some much better views of the Denali massif and I pass some time staring at the new parts of this massive mountain that I can see. Jack and

I eat and lounge about and talk a little. It is time to get some rest and we both settle down in our sleeping bags.

JACK'S JOURNAL

This day I can't sleep. I'm worried or just plain freaked out by our route.

I am as disappointed by the condition of the snow and concerned as to how it will affect our upward progress, more than the sérac danger. The temperature is too high, too much running water on the rocks. We can't even see our own breath.

There are clouds moving in and out, but still just thin layers. I pass the rest by worrying about everything and yet being unable to speed up the progression of the route, or do anything at all until the temperature drops. So I worry and worry. Simon and I eventually discuss this 'Eiger wall' feeling he knows from before and I am comforted that he too is feeling the pressure and that helps some but I can only doze an hour here, an hour there.

The four other climbers attempting the south-east buttress are spotted and hailed. They are on the col between the Rooster Comb and Huntington, hauling loads over the pass. Planes land and people walk around below us. Planes get stuck and it all seems amusing until the time to pack and leave arrives.

It is snowing lightly and still much too warm but off we will go, ready to leave in one hour. We drop down and around a corner that takes us to a ramp into the couloir. I lead into the couloir and we uneasily make very fast progress (three pitches in twenty minutes) under the séracs. Too dangerous I feel, just a feeling that I have that everything is wrong.

The discussion is had, the decision is made, down we go, two raps and out of the couloir and rapidly back to our safe ledge under the overhang.

Eight minutes later the sérac cuts loose and it avalanches. A **big** avalanche lets go, which is followed quickly by two more equally big ones. We are hiding again on the snow ledge and back into our bags. The entire face suddenly comes alive. There are avalanches to our left and right and then shooting over the overhang above us.

We brew tea and watch the visibility disappear in proportion to the size of the snowflakes. Nasty!

Avalanches spew over us and although we are protected from them directly, the blasts send heavy spindrift into the small area we occupy.

About six hours pass while we brew drinks and eat Tiger Milk bars. Finally when the snow recedes we begin the retreat. Rappel follows rappel for ten rope lengths, and 1,600 feet lower, we emerge on to the glacier, four hours after beginning the descent. A very casual retreat!

Pilot Mike Fisher tends to Jim Sharp's Cessna, clearing the snow twice a day.

We had been forced to beat a retreat, in good style at least, but the score was Mountain 1, Climbers 0.

Climbing at this level with Jack has been encouraging; we had been put under a bit of pressure and have stayed cool-headed. We each have our own particular strengths and skills that mean one or the other of us is slightly stronger on a particular type of terrain. We worked like a machine on this first attempt; there was very little discussion required. Of all the great climbing partners with whom I've had adventures, Jack is looking to be the strongest of all. He seems to feel the same way, so morale is good despite being chased off by the mountain. We will just have to be smarter and faster next time.

We are not going away.

When we get past the bergschrund it only takes an hour of steady step-kicking to get us back in camp, where Charlie has had a surprise visitor: the pilot, Mike Fisher – 'Fish', who is now resident in our cave. Fish had flown in to fetch Charlie in marginal weather and in the short time he was on the glacier the clouds closed in and he was trapped.

Both are pleased to find us OK and safely back down. Charlie brews the drinks while we steam away the body moisture in our Gore-Tex suits. We describe what has happened in the last two days. Charlie listens intently but is quieter than is normal for him; I think his frustration at not climbing is really getting to him and it is not helping that Jack and I have had an exciting outing, even if it was not a successful one.

Later they return to Charlie's tent and we eat a big meal of rice and tuna. Sleep comes very easily.

JACK'S JOURNAL – **JUNE 24**

I awake to find big snowflakes blowing into the cave and covering all the food boxes. I get up at 5 p.m. after seventeen hours of sleep!

I went over to the Porter residence and listened to more of Charlie's stories of Alaska, Patagonia, Greenland plus many others until 10.30 p.m. I am pretty restless.

We have new supplies of food, care of Fisher:

6 pounds of cheese

3 loaves of rye bread

6 pounds of peanut butter

2 pounds of margarine

2 pounds of minute rice

2 bottles of Tang

Cost: 32 dollars.

It is nice to eat peanut butter and jam sandwiches and that is what I eat all day plus granola and trail mix.

Simon and I cleaned some of the ice and snow out of the cave, as well as improving the steps down into our Ice Palace, now officially the 'Hotel California' according to Simon.

The weather is warm and a lot of the snow has melted into slush in the entrance tunnel as a result of it.

The tent is dug out and repitched. We expect only to be found buried again tomorrow.

Fish has not only brought us supplies, there is also some mail from my mother. At first I wonder what it could be and worry that something is wrong at home. I had left the address for Talkeetna Air Taxi with my family, but I was not expecting to actually get any mail, especially not up here on the glacier. I need not have worried; inside the envelope I find a new Visa card with my name on it. It is the replacement for the one stolen in Yosemite. I laugh out loud – how funny that I would be issued a credit card up here of all places! My chuckles have piqued the curiosity of my fellow cave dweller.

'What's so funny, man?'

I pause for a moment then hold up the shiny card proudly.

'Jack, mate, just name the restaurant of your choice tonight and I will pay for everything.'

He is laughing with me now.

'Anything I want?'

'*Anything* you want.'

It is the high point of a boring day.

JACK'S JOURNAL – **JUNE 25**

I get up late as usual and did nothing. I went over to Porter's residence for tea and coffee.

On the retreat down the rock band we lost:

3 horizontals

1 ⅝-inch angle

3 stoppers (4.5, 5 and 6)

3 slings.

We have enough spare hardware so it won't be a problem when we go back on the face.

Simon and I enlarged the cave some more today and made his bedroom larger, large enough to allow two more people to sit down inside when we have guests. I couldn't work with him after a while, so I left and let him work by himself. I suppose the weather and the closeness is affecting my disposition.

We do have dinner guests tonight – the best way to combat the boredom and raise morale is to socialise so Charlie and Fish are invited. I fixed up a dinner of chicken salad, rice, peas and more chicken with cheese melted on top; very tasty.

Listened to Charlie's stories for a while and then when Simon and Fish went to brush the snow off the plane, Charlie and I went over some maps, discussing first ascent possibilities.

I draw up plans for a future expedition with Simon that includes multiple climbs in the Ruth as well as McKinley.

I think I consumed 1,500 calories today, just mooching around. It is snowing heavily at bedtime.

Poor Fish, he is stuck here with us and completely out of contact with his family in Talkeetna. We try to make him as comfortable as we can but it is uphill work because he does not like our food much. The only thing we have plenty of that he can eat is Tiger Milk bars, but he's not too sure about them either. We offer him items of warm clothing but he does not like down feathers. We have decided to have dinners together to try and keep his morale up, but he looks haunted.

The plane needs constant maintenance too and twice a day we help him clean the snow from it. Fish is working for Jim at Talkeetna Air Taxi and the Cessna is the same N1047F we flew in on.

JACK'S JOURNAL – JUNE 27 & 28
'Woke up, got out of bed, scratched my head, smelt like I was dead.'

The weather is supposed to improve by evening so Charlie tells us that Fish may fly him out, leaving his gear in his ice cave until he can decide what is to be done.

The great novelty of snow-cave dwelling appears to be wearing thin on Fish. More and more he is retreating to the plane to read or be alone, I think.

Charlie is crazier than ever, changing his mind every other hour about what he wants to do.

The beginning of our commodious snow cave; the excavations were a welcome distraction. ▶

Simon wants to climb and do everything but asks me what I want to do in such a way as to insinuate that our original plans don't hold. I just agree to shut him up and hope that his arrogance will melt away like the water-drenched snow outside our dwelling.

We ski up to the 'Too Loose' expedition camp and marvel at the constructive ingenuity as well as the architectural instability of the igloo they have designed and built.

JUNE 30

I enlarged my hole and dug for many hours, improving it considerably. The weather has turned again and it is snowing lightly although it is warm outside.

My bag was getting damp due to bad air circulation and cooking in the same location sending all the steam towards me but I have solved that problem now with my re-design.

I don't feel like writing more. I guess there is not a lot more to comment on. Bad weather, I am trying to understand why it is so bad. It seems like madness to me to be here for so long and only dig snow holes. Realising the absurdity of this makes me crack up and laugh for a long time.

I feel quite mad today, just plain **cuckoo**. Why did I leave Yosemite? Why did I leave the Malibu beaches? Fuck if I know, this is a madhouse!

JULY 1

Today marks the twenty-first day we have spent in this particular part of Alaska! It snowed six inches last night.

I finished Si's copy of *Gormenghast* by Mervyn Peake last night and started *Titus Alone*.

I have not enough motivation to get out of the sack so I will fester and write or read. The snow continues to fall and, solemnly, Si and I continue to read throughout the day and night. We are living the life of the undead like vampires who only come out of their coffins at night when the sun is down.

JULY 2

I got up late at 2.45 p.m. Blue sky is breaking up the grey heavens. Then we have a blue sky with friendly white clouds. We dry out the gear and tonight we are going to go for it.

Love to all.

10.10 p.m. We're going on to Huntington for the second time.

Mike Fisher tries to enjoy our climbing rations. ▶
He is sitting in the area of our snow cave reserved for guests.

July 2

Got up late and by 2:45 the blue clouds broke up the grey heavens into blue sky with white clouds. Gear is dried out and tonight when the tempreture is cold were going to go for it.

10:10 pm

We're going onto Huntington for the second time

8
ROULETTE

JULY 2, 1978

It would be sensible to let a few days of stable, clear weather pass and allow the mountain to shed some of its debris before starting our second attempt. We, however, are not sensible, and so we will not wait.

Having lived in a hole in the ground for two weeks, more or less, we are wound up like tightly tensioned springs. I am entirely devoid of patience, a quality I possess little of at the best of times. Jack has been more controlled, outwardly anyway, and tolerant of my mood swings which have tilted between hyperactivity and total slothfulness. He gives less away about his feelings than I, but I think the waiting has been silently driving him to distraction.

We both get up late, which is fine if you are trying to align your rhythms with climbing at night. I would like to take credit for deliberately planning this strategy but it would be a lie. It never really gets dark in Alaska in summer and up on the snow it is always bright enough to see what you are doing, so day and night have less meaning than usual.

The cave is now so commodious and deep that the rising sun does not disturb us in the same way it would in a tent. And so it does not immediately dawn on me – forgive the pun – that we have blue skies outside. I only discover it because I feel the need to pee.

As I climb out of my bedroom I notice that there is a different quality to the light filtering down into the Hotel California. I catch my first glimpse of blue sky as I put my boots on. I jog up the dozen steps and out into sunshine. It has stopped snowing and although there is still some cloud, it is breaking up and lifting. I let out a hoot as Americans often do. This rouses Jack from his torpor and he joins me squinting at the brightening scene.

We eat brunch in the sun but only after we spread all our damp equipment out to dry. We say little to each other, but by this time we have spent so much time together on 'the moon' that we are using telepathy. I imagine we are thinking the same thoughts as we chew silently and stare at the face. If we had any brains we would sit and watch the face for a day or so to see what the mountain looks likely to throw at us, but that is not going to happen. Without any debate we have both decided in our own way that we are going to go up tonight.

'What time are we leaving?' Jack asks.

'When I can't eat any more,' I reply.

Packing is hardly a chore as we have planned our food and equipment a dozen times, down to the last detail. It is a task made easier by the fact that we were not intending to take a lot of food or equipment anyway. Weight is a big problem and we will travel as light as we dare, paring down our rack to contain only eight ice screws (two of which are the drive-in type; six are the tubular screw-in type), one deadman snow anchor, twelve nuts and various pins, a selection of slings and karabiners, and two 60-metre ropes – one 11-millimetre and one 9-millimetre in diameter. We plan on four days' full rations, with dehydrated meals supplemented with Tiger Milk bars, some bacon bars and boiled sweets. We will take individual Gore-Tex bivouac bags only – no tent.

We have been eating all afternoon and into the evening and I feel overly full as we take turns to kick steps from the Hotel California to the bergschrund at the base of the face. The sky is clear and it is much colder than it was during our soggy first attempt. We have also adjusted our line of ascent a little. Rather than get involved in the indistinct vertical world of crud-coated rock in the couloir, we have picked out a line on the buttress next to it.

We have already established that the key to the entire route is the approach to the hanging glacier, guarded by the line of séracs. If we attack too far to the right we may succeed in passing the rock band, but will run into unclimbable séracs. We know the séracs get smaller to the left, and it looks like there is an easy couloir there to pass them by. We hope to reach the top of the rock just to the right of this couloir. We don't wish to climb directly below it because it looks like it drains snow and debris from a major part of the face. Perversely it feels better to be under a sérac for reasons I cannot properly articulate. If we arrive at the right place we should be able to climb diagonally left around the last part of the sérac wall and this will give us 'easy' access to the hanging glacier.

In my Eiger-dreaming mythology, the entry to the first ice field on Huntington is like the entry into the Eiger's second ice field; it is our Ice Hose, unlocking

Jack exits the rock band on the first day, séracs above.

the door to the heart of the face and to the problems above. Above this we will be screwed, a technical term meaning we cannot retreat. So we climb the 'schrund again and start up the first couloir, this time traversing rightwards out of it after a few hours on to our friendlier buttress, the second on the right.

Hard mixed climbing follows for ten pitches. They pass quickly as we swing leads, with less disgust from Jack than last time in the soggy snow – it is colder and the climbing better, although the rocks are still very heavily plastered with snow and ice. I think it is actually faster because of this.

The mountain is not grumbling; nothing is thrown at us for the moment. The climb is going better than last time and we are moving confidently. The sun begins to rise into a broken moody sky behind our hunched shoulders.

Several difficult pitches follow – icy slabs, icy corners and broken, steep ground, worthy of Scottish grade V all the way. I do get to lead one pitch of the horrible snow-plastered variety that we had encountered on our first attempt and I can hear Jack groaning about 'vertical granola grovelling' as he calls it. Fortunately there is only one pitch like this.

The angle of the rock band abates a little and we sense that we are close to the séracs, but where exactly? I find out one pitch later. The rocks roll away and, on a relenting ice slope, I arrive beneath a monster sérac. We are free of the face's rocky defences, but too far to the right of the Ice Hose – the sérac above us is huge. I belay on good ice screws and bring Jack up to join me. His tail is up and he arrives at a sprint. The sky has clouded over a little but we have obviously improved on our previous high point, so he is happy. So happy, in fact, that he seriously considers a full attack directly on the sérac wall above us. A bull at a gate.

He sets off with great gusto, but I am concerned: Jack is a big strong monkey but a direct attempt is surely too steep. My anxiety must have run up the rope. He stops and puts in a couple of the longest Lowe ice screws we have, and I go to join him. The ice is nice and white-blue, but silly steep for so early in the play.

'Matey, this is not the way, we have got to move to the left.'

'OK, let's give it a try, what's your plan?'

'Pendulum rappel: we need to get left into the Hose.'

It is a manoeuvre used to move to the left or right of your climbing line when you cannot climb higher on the ground on which you find yourself and it is too difficult to traverse. One climber lowers themselves using tension from the rope and then tries to claw and 'swing' in the direction they want to go, until they can belay in a better position.

Andreas Hinterstoisser used a similar technique in 1936 to gain access to the first ice field on his attempt on the north face of the Eiger. His successful tension traverse was also the cause of his demise; once the traverse was made it could never be reversed and in attempting to retreat, he and his friends all died. For a moment the sense of history plays on my mind. Jack had made traverses like this in Yosemite, on rock, but this was not the same at all.

At least Jack's attempt at a sérac *direttissima* has bought us some useful height for the rope manoeuvre. So I let him belay me down as I try to claw my way as far to the left as possible, like the bob on the end of a pendulum with a mind of its own. My heart is in my mouth. I distrust ice screws and have never seen anybody take a fall on one as a runner or even put much static weight on one as an anchor. But what choice do I have now? I try to pretend I am not me but a lightweight cartoon, less troubled by gravity than normal humans. I am my own little white spider. A four-legged creature, not eight, I claw and pull left and over a little ridge to where I can belay again, on ice screws. I am happy because I can see that we can traverse easily into the Ice Hose from here. I am unhappy because Jack has to rappel diagonally to me and he chooses to do it from a single screw because we cannot afford to leave two of them behind. I turn blue holding my breath until he joins me and clips into my belay.

We have overcome the technical manoeuvre and found our route, but have failed to notice that the weather is turning dreary. It begins to snow with determination.

Jack leads through and out into the Ice Hose and rapidly runs out a pitch with just one runner. I join him as fast as I can and lead through. We are in the middle of the funnel – which drains the parts of the face above it – as it starts to snow harder and spindrift is suddenly all around us. I cannot believe how fast the face changes its personality. I expected another hour or two of snowfall before conditions would turn against us like this. We are acutely aware of our exposed situation and as with our first attempt we must run and hide to avoid being swept away like vermin. But where?

The climbing is easy-angled because we are now on the left flank of the hanging glacier. If we climb straight up into the diamond-shaped rock buttress above, we hope we will be less exposed to the increasing snowslides threatening to sweep us from the mountain. We need to get away from the funnelling effect of the Ice Hose as quickly as we can and what ensues is a race for survival in the form of some rapid leads with minimal use of equipment. On a fine day we would have dispensed with belays on this ground and just moved together, but today we are in an unstable washing machine of swirling snow and we must protect each other with the rope.

As we approach the buttress we can see that the rock is very compact and heavily coated with ice. My heart sinks as I scan ahead, hoping for an overhang with a bit of ledge under it, or at least one where we could cut a ledge, but I cannot see anything encouraging. By now the sliding snow is flowing around the picks of my ice axe. As I look down to kick another footing I see that the moving snow is forming bow waves over the toes of my boots. I am very anxious, but at least I am moving. Poor Jack just has to wait like a rabbit caught in the headlights until it is his turn to follow.

The spindrift has already turned into heavy snowslides and debris is beginning to pour over the buttress above us. For the lack of any better plan we press on, one lead from Jack, one from me and then … we look to be screwed … But now, above me, I finally see the bergschrund at the top edge of the hanging glacier. I couldn't see it earlier because of the foreshortened view from below. It's a great big bergschrund. Of course, Stupid! You saw it on the aerial photos but you were too busy looking at the technical parts of the new route to study the face properly. Of course there is a great big 'schrund – this is a hanging glacier after all!

I climb up to the lip and look inside. I cannot believe our luck. It is cavernous and the roof overhangs the lower edge, so snow avalanches won't slide into it. There is a big horizontal ledge inside, strewn only with a few loose rocks that have been pulled from the rock ceiling above it. From the entrance the ledge runs back at least six metres.

'Jack, mate, we will be OK. Hotel California Two!'

He cannot hear me.

'Wha … ?' Jack starts to form a question but stops talking as I disappear head first into a hole he cannot see. Only one leg is left outside momentarily and then I vanish.

I wonder what is going through his mind. Whatever it is won't take long because I whack in one of the drive-in screws as fast as I can and pull up the slack. I belay Jack from the lip of the 'schrund so I can see what is happening to him.

The scene outside is truly awful now; he must be counting his lives. I can hardly see him because there is so much snow swirling around. I want to reassure him by telling him I've found a safe ice cave, but any attempt to shout to him is lost in the chaos. The message is too complex and the mountain is roaring now, shedding everywhere. The first really big avalanche begins to bellow. I need to give him simple climbing signals and I shout at the top of my lungs:

'On belay! Climb when ready!'

It is inadvertently comical: Jack finds British climbing calls amusing. ('Climb *only* when I'm ready? You sure about that, man?')

I hope that if he hears me making a joke he'll get some sense that the worst of today is nearly over. He understands and very quickly starts to follow. Jack can hardly see where he is going and just follows the rope like a robot that has only one simple program: pick left, pick right, kick twice, and repeat. He hardly looks up for fear of collecting a snowslide in the face. The conditions are so bleak that he cannot see me, or the 'schrund. I can see him, however, and I have never seen his face look so harrowed. I could shout all sorts of encouragement about the cave I've found but it would just slow him down, so I let Jack perform his own ice dance in silence at the end of a very tight leash.

And then he is close, close enough to see me and I am smiling at him, which just confuses him and his face becomes even more anguished. Maybe he thinks that I am being nice to him at this moment because we are about to meet our end. We are almost face-to-face at last after the longest ten minutes of our lives.

'In you come, matey, sling a leg over.'

He just does what I tell him and we are inside together, collapsed on the floor of our new bolthole. Jack is panting with effort, his anguished expression slowly turning to confusion and then … he stands up and looks around. Unless the entire hanging glacier decides to avalanche, we are safe in here. He does not speak so I do:

'Toto, I don't think we are in Kansas any more.'

I had spent a ridiculous tequila-fuelled evening with him and two of his friends watching *The Wizard of Oz* back in Santa Monica. I get the tiredest of smiles.

'If you *had* a brain, what would you do with it?'

'I told you, mate, another Hotel California.'

And now he laughs with me, but there is a tear not far below the surface for both of us.

We start the housekeeping immediately. By keeping busy we avoid the need to start discussing our broader situation. It is a five-star luxury bivouac. We have a place to hide and a big bay window. There is room enough for every need and after moving a few stones we can stretch out while we wait for the stove to melt the ice for the brew we are craving. We ignore what is going on outside because it is best to do so. The snowslides pass with an incessant rumble past the window.

It is a wonderful place and a terrible place. We are safe from bombing raids and are comfortable and dry; we can spread ourselves out and get organised. Cooking is easy and since this is our first stop, we have enough food to cook ourselves a decent dinner. But we know we will have to leave our shelter as soon as conditions improve and this prospect is daunting, as the noise of regular, massive avalanches interrupts our attempts at sleep.

The day has traumatised us but we are in good shape physically. We agree on one thing: we will not retreat.

'The way off is up,' Jack says.

It is probably not impossible to retreat, but the chances of surviving if we got caught in the open in conditions like today would be very slim. We will go up. We are totally committed and I prefer it this way because it makes things simple. We have made rapid progress and tell each other that the worst is over. We will find our way back to Kansas.

The mountain clearly does not like us and has been throwing punches since we first set foot on it. We retreated from our first attempt, but today we have dodged these punches, made rapid progress and found a safe place to hide. Mountain 1, Climbers 1.

Dozing, eating and chatting, we make a plan. We are carrying one of Washburn's aerial photographs of the face, similar to the one we saw printed on the cover of *Mountain* magazine, and we can see where we are, more or less. We are below the big rock diamond that sits in the middle of the face above the hanging glacier. Above that is what I have decided to call 'the Ramp' – another Eiger reference, this time to a massive ice feature that descends diagonally leftwards from the summit ice field. Our Ramp passes the left side of the Diamond and we briefly considered climbing it before abandoning the idea. It looked too dangerous as the base of the Ramp is full of séracs, and also would take us too far left of centre, where we didn't want to go for reasons of style. If we are going to make the first ascent of this face, we should take the best line we can, so that no one can come along later, 'improve' on it and declare a north face 'direct'. We would use the Ramp higher on the face but we would reach it by passing the Diamond buttress on the right-hand side. This would be no more difficult, but more elegant and a little safer, we hoped.

We have taken a detour to the left of our intended line and we must move back to the right, towards the centre of the face. Our plan is to traverse diagonally along the line of the bergschrund and then cross it, aiming for the 'Runnels', a sinuous system of steep but shallow ice gullies, and weaving our way past the scattered rock outcrops that lie to the right of the Diamond. When we have enough height to climb diagonally leftwards, we will pass the upper right flank of the Diamond to gain the Ramp and climb its ice to the top. We expect this section to be the crux of the climb as there is obviously going to be some hard mixed climbing, maybe not as hard as the rock band, but totally committing because we have so little equipment. The rock band still allowed the possibility of retreat, but we cannot get back there from this position. We will remain forever on the face if we cannot climb it. The Ramp is tall and narrow, stretching down perhaps 4,000 feet from the summit. We expect to enter it with approximately 2,000 feet to go.

We will wait until the mountain is quieter, which we hope will be soon because we are travelling very light, and if we get pinned down we have scant rations to sit out any storms.

So here we are, Jack and I, sitting in our hotel in the sky with very few options, but harmonious in our resolution and with no complaints. I feel lucky that he is here with me, strong, solid and reliable. I want to talk about it, to say, 'Well, Jack, normally climbers get to know each other through a few easier climbs.' This is our first 'Alp' together after all. But I think better of this; it might sound as if I have concerns, so I keep these thoughts to myself.

I sleep fitfully, disturbed by the sounds of avalanches thundering down the face.

JULY 3

It has stopped snowing although the clouds look like it could start again at any minute. We cannot wait too long; we don't have the luxury of time. I want to move and Jack agrees, but I can see that he is as uneasy as I am.

I lead off out of the ice cave and climb diagonally rightwards towards the heart of the face. I stay just below the bergschrund to make the traverse easy and I run out a full rope length as quickly as is sensible. We are well rested and fed, so physically we are both in good shape. Our minds are less so.

Jack is quickly past me and it is soon my turn to follow his footsteps. It feels good to be moving fast again, but the weather has already started to turn and flakes of snow have begun to fall. As we cross the bergschrund it is snowing a little harder. I know what Jack is thinking: I hope like hell that the snow stays light. We are disappointed two pitches later. The clouds close in and the face disappears as a repeat performance of the first snowstorm begins.

I can hardly see as I follow Jack's lead. We want to run and hide, but are slowed down by the steepening ice and the fact that we must pause to place ice screws, in case the sliding snow causes one of us to fall. I reach Jack and he passes me the rack without comment or delay, like a relay runner passing the baton. I shoulder the little sling of equipment and move on without a pause. From the photo we had studied we believe that we should run into some patchy rock outcrops soon. We may be in luck; when I am eighty feet above Jack's belay I see a small black rock looming above me.

'I am going for the rock above us.'

'OK, man, go, go!'

Snow is running down the face all around me now. I need to be methodical in my haste and I belt in one of the drive-in ice screws to protect against a fall; I must not lose my head. If I get knocked off in a snowslide I doubt Jack's anchors will hold and we will both be killed. Jack can only watch forlornly, wiping snow from his goggles.

I reach the little rocky island and the disappointment is crushing – it only sticks out above the ice by a foot and a half. This is not enough to protect us, but it is too late to look elsewhere. Snowslides are beginning to pour down the slope and our situation is becoming tenuous. We could be swept away any minute. I chop out a stance and place one long ice screw and two pins, one of which looks good, thank heavens. 'Safe!' I shout, and instantly the irony of that climbing call occurs to me. At least with a solid anchor we can fight back, but we are anything but 'safe'.

'Come on, Jack!'

I take stock while he cleans his anchor. We are still not high enough to avoid the debris that I expect to come flying out of the Runnels any time now. I can almost get my shoulder under the rock, but the drifting snow pulls at my head and pack. The rock is parting the wave of sliding snow for me but not so for poor Jack. For him it is a deluge. He must climb on a moving conveyor belt of snow. I keep him on a very tight rope, to help his morale as much as to prevent a fall. When he reaches the ice screw I have used for a runner, I tell him to leave it; it will take too long to remove. He unclips the karabiner, leaves it on the rope above his harness and keeps moving upwards.

He is about fifty feet below me when there is a ghastly noise from above. It sounds like concrete being poured from a great height. I have heard this sound before.

'Jack, watch out!'

I hunch on my stance and brace myself, ready to take as much of his weight with my body as possible before the anchors are loaded. I have just enough time to see him look up. He acts instinctively and with two mighty wallops he buries the picks of his axes in the ice above him and lowers his head.

Thump!

This snowslide is much bigger. It bursts over the rock and over my head and I lose sight of Jack. The rope goes heavy almost at once. I take Jack's entire weight and then some more. Through the tension in the rope I can feel the snow pummelling him. For perhaps ten or fifteen seconds I cannot see, and then the angry white snake of snow is gone, off into the void below. And there is Jack, knocked off his feet but hanging by the wrist loops that we always attach to our ice tools. The front points of his crampons are no longer in, and his head is on the ice. He is not moving and dreadful thoughts race through my mind.

'Hey, Jack! Jack, you OK? Talk to me!'

It is only a few seconds or so before he moves but it seems like an age.

'Come up, come on!'

He moves his head and looks up blankly as he slowly heaves himself back on to his front points and I am released from his weight. There is a pause while he gathers himself, and then, without saying a word, he starts to climb, like a machine. His face is blank; he is climbing on instinct. The impact of the snow had briefly knocked him senseless, but his eyes are wide open and, after a few moves, he unleashes a tirade of the worst language I have ever heard. He is obviously shaken but getting mad helps him. On his way to me I see that he is using his picks like weapons, stabbing at the mountain as if exacting revenge.

Despite the near-death experience he is cogent when he joins me. He takes a good look at the anchors I have arranged. This is a huge boost to my morale; he is checking my work and so has his head on. Despite the chaos of our situation, he is thinking instinctively, like the instinctive climber he is.

We need a hole to hide in immediately and we shall have to create it. Like soldiers caught in an ambush we need to dig in. The most expedient way to do this is for me to belay him while he chops away under the rock. This way he can move around freely while I protect him with the rope. We are in great luck. The rock itself is undercut and the ice underneath must have formed from wind-blown snow rather than water ice and is formed from big, fragile crystals that shatter easily. The surface has a dense skin, but once the first foot has been cut away, it is quick to excavate.

Soon Jack is out of the firing line and the adrenaline is abating. I am proud of us: we had just dealt with a potentially lethal situation without complaint or discussion. We are well enough hidden that the mountain's endless supply of ammunition can harm us no more. But we are pinned down again and we need to be more comfortable than this; we need to be able to get warm and prepare food and liquids. We may not get swept away, but we may yet fade away. We cannot sit cringing under this rock for long.

We dig through the rotten ice for about four feet before hitting solid ground. We take our packs off and, now belayed on slings, coil the ropes and stow them out of harm's way. Digging holes has been our life on the Ruth for weeks, so why stop now? I turn to the wall of ice formed to my right by the ledge we have cut. I leave the hard skin-ice on the surface and burrow away at the rotten stuff behind it. It is easily removed and I shovel the debris behind me for Jack to jettison. This is a gloriously calming task. Before long I have progressed so far as to have dug a full body-length into my ice mine, and there is nothing stopping me as yet.

'Where do you want the kitchen this time, mate?'

I get the first smile out of him today.

We keep digging until we have penetrated fifteen feet parallel to the face of the mountain, creating a long thin cave in which we can lie down end-to-end and cook in the middle. It is a burrow a scared rabbit would be proud of. Jack is uncertain of the cave's structural integrity, so we place another ice screw and keep our boots on loosely and our equipment tied down.

Because we are head-to-head in a tunnel three feet wide and three feet high, it takes us a long time to get sorted out. Everything must be done sequentially. I insert myself feet first, followed by my kit, followed by the stove, followed by Jack and his kit. I just hope I don't need to take a dump before we can get moving again. We brew and eat a little and the trauma of the day subsides, although, outside, the mountain remains angry. It roars at us like a bear that has lost sight of its prey, longing to find and kill it.

Poor Jack. For all he knew, he had looked up and seen his end coming in the avalanche. He looks OK, but we are both in sombre mood despite the fact that we are warm and dry in the cave. The problem is the same as last night: soon we will have to leave it.

The score is slipping. Today there was a knock-down. Mountain 2, Climbers 1.

9
THE RAMP

The two rabbits have a restless night in their burrow. If we felt committed at the last bivouac, we are certainly lost for options now. Jack is obviously as concerned as I am but we try to keep the conversation light-hearted. We have no choices any more; the mountain is dictating all the shots, so there is no point opening a can of worms by discussing the seriousness of our predicament.

Jack likes to read me the fortunes that are printed on our Salada tea bags. One seems close to the mark: 'The biggest tumble one can take is falling over one's own bluff.' No problem then!

We brought with us four days' food and we have eaten half of it – but it is likely that we are far from halfway back to camp. I can easily imagine spending another two days just to reach the summit. We are certainly going to go very hungry at some point. It is simply a question of when.

The progress yesterday from the Berg Bivouac to our Rabbit Burrow was pathetic; we need a big increase in pace and distance tonight. We need to try and finish the climb in a day or we'll be sorry. We are also expecting that the difficulty of the climbing will be sustained between our current hiding place and the Ramp, which will be our road to the summit.

I am awakened, this time by silence. It has stopped snowing and all is quiet on the northern face. It is time for the rabbits to run away. It takes an age to pack, because we can only prepare one at a time. We brew and eat a little, then Jack gets his kit organised and packed. All I can do is wait, trapped in the back of the burrow. No matter, it must be done step by step.

Eventually we are packed and standing together on the very spot on which we were cowering twelve hours ago under our life-saving rock, surveying the coming attractions above. Jack is busting to get a flying start. I am happy to hold

◄ Jack leading in the Ramp, sometimes simple, sometimes desperate.
We will have to climb that sérac.

the ropes for him and soon he is far away. I have the sense that he feels today is make or break, and I can tell by his every move that he wants to be gone before we get any hungrier. The first few pitches of ice are quickly dispensed with.

It is cloudy, but it is not actually snowing. The face is quiet and we are left alone to get on with our job, our spirits higher than yesterday. We reach the icy rocks and this makes us happy because, although the climbing will get harder, the terrain matches our crumpled aerial photograph as we hoped it would.

Getting to the Ramp takes all day. There is steep ice and mixed climbing that just cannot be rushed as we take a diagonal line leftwards past the Diamond buttress. We climb methodically with economy of effort. It feels that we are climbing at 'normal' and not 'trauma' speed now.

We cross the last of the icy slabs and several moderately angled ice pitches connect us with the Ramp. Jack is the first to get there. He has belayed and is safe, but before he gathers in the ropes to bring me to him he pauses to stare at the Ramp, which I cannot see well from my perch.

'How is it, mate?'

'Umm, steep, err, steeper than … '

I join him fifteen minutes later and we stare together at our planned 'highway' to the summit. It *is* steeper than we had thought. Bits of it are vertical or worse. We thought we would be out of the woods by now and on the summit quickly, but this will obviously not be the case. From where we have joined the Ramp there will be several hundred feet of steep but manageable ice, some snow pitches and walls of rounded séracs stacked one after the other. Some can be skirted, perhaps, but not all of them. There will be a battle every other pitch it seems, easy snow followed by steep ice. We will have to bivouac again before we summit. Any thoughts that we could just climb through to the summit today are gone.

The first of the severe difficulties are many pitches above us so we decide to dispense with the moderate ground and look for a safe place to rest just below the next hard ice-climbing section. For the first time on this mountain we will have the luxury of deciding where we will make our bed. It is a bedroom we had hoped to avoid, but at least we are not fleeing and hiding.

We climb on through the remains of the day, slowly. We have become tired due to the shortage of food. Run-out follows run-out, but the seventy-degree ice is good quality. We look for a place to spend the night, but find that we can only chop out a little ledge under an overhanging sérac. We will sleep in the open tonight. Using a sérac for protection seems ridiculous and yet sensible all at once.

The day's climbing has been much better and we have improved our odds. Jack had designed and sewn bivvy bags for us and they work very well. Despite the uncomfortable perch, we sleep like dead men. The score is Mountain 2, Climbers 2.

In the morning we have enough fuel to make tea and, while we aren't dehydrated, I notice we have both taken to eating bits of snow and ice. I also notice that I am cold a lot of the time, even though I have taken to wearing my down parka over my other clothes. Obviously we have gained some height, but I think we feel the cold because we are hungry. I can sense that I am losing weight rapidly. My Whillans climbing harness does not fit normally any more and I have to tighten the waist strap to the maximum. At least our packs are also losing weight.

The day starts with solid, strenuous grade-VI ice climbing. Jack puts in a fine lead and I am puffing and panting when I follow, pulling myself over a steep ice bulge. We are amongst a dense field of ice bulges that have formed at the top of the Ramp. It does not look this way on our aerial photo, but then, years have passed since Bradford Washburn took the picture. The terrain is made up of sixty- to seventy-degree ice and some snow, interlaced with blunt sérac bulges that are much steeper. The game will be to thread the path of least resistance through the obstacles, but we cannot avoid all of the very steep sections.

We evolve a strategy to cope with this. We cannot just run out the rope and swing leads; we must plan to deal with each of the obstacles so that whichever of us is more rested attacks each hard section. We have to climb to suit the terrain.

On hard ice we climb in shorter pitches, which helps us manage the lack of equipment. We have only seven ice screws left and cannot climb far on such difficult ground without taking ridiculous risks. Every belay and runner must be placed with great thought, economy and care.

Jack has belayed almost immediately after his first bulge and above him is an easier section, topped by another little ice cliff. I climb on sixty feet and belay below the next bulge, taking off my pack before bringing Jack up. I have had an easy ride on the last half pitch and I have a little time to rest and study the next problem, which I will lead.

We are climbing safely but slowly. Nine pitches reward us with just 500 or 600 feet of height gain. I am cold and tired and it is becoming obvious that we need to rest. Jack feels the same. He gets the last bulge of the day and it leads him to a big snowy ledge under the steepest sérac bulge we have seen so far, a gently overhanging wall of ice that blocks our exit from the Ramp.

We kid ourselves that all we need is a 'short' rest and chop out a comfortable ledge upon which to lie and try to get warm. The skies have cleared to high thin cloud and watery sunshine. We can see all the way down to the glacier, where we spot four colourful ants. Apparently they can see us too. There is absolutely no wind and we can hear whoops and screams faintly echoing around the valley. Who else would they be screaming at? It must be the Too Loose team. There are four of them and they are coming from the direction of Rob Newsom's camp. I am sure it is them; I tell Jack I can make out Rob's southern drawl in the way he shouts 'WoooooHooooo!' We reply and they answer again. It is wonderful. We have been alone in the clouds for four days and to make even such distant contact with other climbers boosts our morale. Somebody knows where we are!

The effect is immediate: we do everything a little faster, get organised a little quicker and chat incessantly about getting to the summit in the next short push. It must be so close now as we are looking down on peaks which Jack knows, and knows the heights of – they are all lower than our current position.

We eat the last meal we have but we are not despondent. We will sleep a little and then find a way over this last cliff and reach the summit. Maybe there will be a message there from the Too Loose team when we arrive. Maybe we can follow their footsteps down the French Ridge.

EXTRACTS FROM ROB NEWSOM'S 1978 JOURNAL – JUNE 30 [on the French Ridge, several days before sighting McCartney and Roberts high on the face].

I lead out in a warm bright fog, poor visibility. One hundred and fifty feet I stepped into a 'schrund. I jump back and adjust my line and then carry on for thirty feet past the 'schrund when 'crack' and I saw God and his North Face beneath my feet. At least fifteen feet of corniced ridge has disappeared and I dove head first into the insecurity of the 'schrund. I was ready to go home, be home, stay home. I've never been so scared climbing in my life. I was sure that I was going to die.

Shaken I brought the other boys up and showed them my footsteps going off into the sky …

JULY 1. I am lying in the tent with Rom crying my heart out. We are going to bail off this mountain. It is hard to write anything; I just cry. After this long we are on the line, going for it or coming back alive …

We are going to try to get back down. We are four days out and three to four days from the summit …

The climbing is the most severe, and the conditions the worst I've ever seen. If we go on we will run out of food and fuel and probably luck before we can get down, because the down climbing will be harder and slower than the ascent. This leaves no room for mistakes, being pinned down in a storm, unforeseen technical difficulties and any other of the bad things that can happen on a mountain like this …

Deep down, I know I could reach the summit but the odds are against our getting down with all four of us alive. This ridge is unrelenting, it is harder and more dangerous than I ever imagined.

JULY 5. Yesterday, while packing our rather overloaded packs, Jim Sharp flew over looking for Jack and Simon. We radioed him and he said he would have Cliff come and pick us up. It started to rain so we used Porter's old snow cave for dinner and the McKinley tent for sleeping.

Sleeping by Huntington's north face is like sleeping by an angry ocean with huge breakers crashing all night, the continuous avalanching never ceasing.

In memory of our climb:

Mount Huntington, Mount Huntington, my old friend
I wonder if I'll ever come to climb you again
You're steep, you're beautiful, you're dangerous, you're mean
You're the baddest mountain I've ever seen
The avalanches never seem to cease on your face
You make an old southern boy feel out of place
But despite my fears, my obvious dismay
We are one and the same, I'll be back some day.

JULY 7. Yesterday I spotted Jack and Simon near the summit of the north face and it appears that they have made the first ascent, a very bold undertaking.

The face is very quiet today, and we strain constantly to hear the sound of Cliff's Cessna coming to take us home.

10
THE SURPRISE

We are both too cold to sleep so, after a few hours of shivering and shuffling from one frozen buttock to the other, we give up. The stove is humming, melting snow to make tea. I find the process soothing – I am doing something positive.

We confide in each other that we have had enough of this face. It is time to fight our way out of the mountain's grip and finish our first major climb together, the first ascent of the most beautiful but terrifying face I have ever seen.

Breakfast does not take long, because it is a mug of tea. Getting ready does not take long either, because all we have to do is tighten our bootlaces and put our crampons back on.

Jack has decided that it is his turn to lead and is leaving his pack with me because the next pitch is too steep to climb carrying any extra weight. He is starting up the steepest piece of ice we have yet encountered and he is doing so at nearly 11,500 feet. If it had been me, I would have tried to wriggle around this ice bulge any way I could.

'Mate, can we have a look on the right maybe?' I suggest.

He has already placed an ice screw as a runner so that, if he falls, the pull on me as the belayer will be upward. He has planned his lead and he has made up his mind. He is going to attack the ice bulge straight up, no matter what I say. I want to argue but it is too late. He has begun and it is against the holiest of climbing codes to give the leader unhelpful distractions. I am forced to watch events unfold, paying out the rope like a string of worry beads. I am belayed to just one long tubular screw and I wish I had three of them. At least I placed it hours ago so it should be well frozen in place.

As strong as Jack is, I can see after a few moves this is not going to be our way out. I can hear the exertion, the increasing unnecessary movement of a rapidly tiring climber. I brace myself as best I can for the fall that will surely follow. Do we really have to play such extreme games now, after all we have been through on this climb?

When he does lose traction we are fortunate that he is only twenty feet above me. There is the normal shout and the metal clinking noise that always comes with a fall. Then there is the passing of a lifetime in a second. Jack arrives flat on his back in the deep, soft snow six feet away from my belay. Cruuuuump! I quickly lengthen my belay anchors so I can crawl over to him. He is badly winded but uninjured. When his breathing returns we have our first argument.

'You bloody Americans have a far-too-lax attitude to falling, why the bloody hell don't you listen to me?'

I was annoyed because his fall had been frightening and we'd had plenty of that already. I tend to get cranky when I am frightened. I can't tell if he is repentant or not, but I receive no argument when I suggest he might like to take a rest. We are changing over the ends of the rope on the belay when he says, a little hurt, 'You shouted at me, man!'

It feels like a scene from *The Odd Couple* and I am Jack Lemmon.

I start my passage around the obstacle with a traverse to the right and, out of sight of his stance, I find that there is a steep little gulley that sneaks around the end of the sérac. It is not easy, but I can just climb it with my pack on. I have five ice screws and I use three of them for protection on the steepest part. I am too tired to take risks any more than I have to. I have two screws left, so there are no more options; I must belay even though I have run out only thirty-five metres. The angle has eased so it is convenient to belay where I am. I chop out a step in the ice big enough for both my feet, place my two screws and attach myself before taking in the remainder of the rope.

Jack can feel the rope being taken in although he cannot see me or hear me well. I hold the line tight enough so I can feel the fish. When it goes slack, I know he is on the way. Looking around I can see that the bulge atop the ramp really has relented – we are finally above it. There are séracs above me but they are no longer channelled into a funnel, they are scattered and set across a wide ice field. We will be able to weave and avoid nearly all of them. We are out of the Ramp, above the bulge. I dare to believe that the summit ridge must be only several rope lengths away.

I am full of chat as he comes up to join me.

'Jack, we are almost there!'

I get a tired smile from him, but not much conversation.

'Let's get out of here,' he replies as he kicks his way towards a gap above us.

After that I get an easy pitch, but Jack gets the last little bulge because traversing around it is actually worse than climbing directly over it. The summit ridge is visible on the next pitch and we agree to belay each other carefully all the way rather than move together. The snow has formed scary fluted cornices and we are tired and cold; this is no time to fall victim to clumsiness. Saving a few minutes by moving together is not worth the risk of being dead forever.

I feel like I am in a dream when I reach the crest. I have arrived on the north-east ridge and it looks like I am, at most, one rope length from the summit. We really have done it! Even the short argument I have with a little cornice I have to chop away can't keep the smile from my face.

Jack does not speak at first when his head appears above the cornice. He looks around, taking in the situation before clambering on to the ridge. The ridge itself is narrow and plastered with heavy snow, sculpted by the wind into 'meringue pie' cornices.

'OK, we should belay all the way, man,' he says.

'No argument, take your time.'

He leads past me and sets the last belay, which is just where the angle of the ridge steepens slightly. I pass him a few minutes later and trudge up the short ridge to the summit. The sky is misty, with just a little wind. We are on the bottom edge of the cloud layer and we can see all the way down to the glaciers at the base of the mountain. For the first time we can see both the Tokositna and the Ruth glaciers. The summit is virgin. There's not a single footstep or even a hint of a buried footstep to be seen. This means, surprisingly, that nobody else has been here before us this year. Jack was sure that one of the two teams attempting to reach this spot from the south-east or north-west ridges would have been here before us. If it was the Too Loose boys we had seen on the Ruth yesterday, then they had failed to make the third ascent of the French Ridge, the very route we had chosen to descend. I am sure we are both thinking the same thing: why had they failed to climb the French Ridge?

It is 2 p.m. on July 6 1978. Jack takes a picture of me and we set off to the west. We are both shivering but the feeling of elation at beginning our descent has us in good spirits. I wonder if we can get down in a day or two. I am very hungry.

How can it be that the only footprints are our own?

Leaving the summit requires us to be careful of the cornices that have formed on the rim of the north face and we skirt them well to the south to reach a big snow-shoulder that levels out so that it is almost flat for a hundred metres. What a pleasure it is to be able to move about so easily after our six-day battle with the north face. Oh please let it be like this more often than not!

We are able to look down from less-steep angles and make a plan to follow the French Ridge on the west side as the overhang of the cornices is consistently on the northern side of the ridgeline apex. The shoulder rolls away and steepens, more and more, until I have to stop and retreat. Disappointingly, we soon need to belay again.

We have only one deadman snow anchor and Jack duly places it so he can protect me. I know how to use a deadman but I had hoped never to have to depend on one. The theory that, under load, the blade will cut deeper into the snow always seemed flawed to me; what if the alloy plate or the wire leash hit something solid? It would just pull out. I am pleased to note that Jack has dug a big hole to sit in, making himself more secure. Jack will pay out the rope while I go and have a look.

My first stab is hopeless – the slope steepens dramatically. We are on a huge snow mushroom which is higher than our ropes are long. It is unclimbable because it is made of snow and is overhanging at its base.

'Mate, this is going nowhere, I am coming up.'

I trudge back up the hundred feet.

'Si, is there any way around the side of it?'

'No, it is undercut … wait, hang on, watch me. I want to go closer to the edge of the cornice, maybe we can climb around it by going back on to the edge of the north face.'

My idea is that if we climb down on to the north face until we're just below the cornices and snow mushrooms, we might be able to pass the worst of the obstacles by traversing pitches. Then we could regain the ridge and descend more conventionally. Perhaps. The only way to test this theory is to have a look. To do this I need to find a gap in the cornices, or at least a little cornice that I can cut through. I am searching on the end of 100 feet of rope.

Crack! The snow and ice give way and I fall through the collapsing cornice. Jack is attentive but the stretch in our climbing rope means that I fall further than just the slack rope between us, about twenty-five feet further in fact, on to the north face of Huntington. My right foot makes the first contact and the crampon bites like a pivot, flicking me upside down. There is a searing pain in my right ankle as I crash into the ice below. I am looking straight down at the Ruth Glacier as the chunk of collapsed cornice accelerates sickeningly down the hideous fluted ice runnels below me, exploding as it hits the shallower-angled ice of the hanging glacier 3,000 feet below. A 9-millimetre rope and Jack's attention is all that saves me from the same flight of death.

Jack is screaming.

'Si, you OK? Si …'

He can hear me screaming too, in pain.

'Sorry, Jack, sorry … I've hurt my ankle. I don't think it is broken.'

I kick with my good left foot and I can take my weight from him. Pain washes through my ankle like molten lava. Most likely I have a bad sprain; I did this once in a cross-country race at school, jumping over a ditch. When I landed I turned the same ankle and had to pull out of the race. There would be no pulling out of this race.

'Give me a minute, man.'

I chop a step and get two solid placements with my Curver and my Charlet Moser axes. My racing pulse subsides and the pain eases a little. I find I can put a little weight on my right foot on the chopped step and I force myself to stand on it.

'I'll be OK, man, let me take a look around.'

From where I am standing I have a less-obstructed view of the French Ridge. There are enormous cornices and snow mushrooms all along it, as far as I can see. It is truly awful to behold. We are the two stupidest climbers in the world. How on earth could we ever have thought we could climb down this ridge? We should have asked Jim Sharp to make a couple of circuits of the mountain when we flew in so we could check it out. It seems idiotic now that we didn't do that.

I take my time. The burning liquid feeling in my ankle is abating.

I want to be able to give an accurate and convincing verdict to Jack, so I look very closely. It is hopeless on the north face. Looking to the west I can see that the terrain is a geological nightmare of deep fluted ice ridges and runnels, all topped with cornices. We cannot climb any of it.

I make twenty painful little moves upwards and grovel back on to the ridge. I cannot disguise the limp as I climb back to Jack and his face is full of concern. I slump in a snow seat so I can rest beside him and we discuss the pointlessness of persisting with the French Ridge. From where we are, the only terrain we can possibly descend leads off the west face. A large snow slope looks easy to start with, although it steepens into mixed ground. It may be an escape if we can conserve enough equipment. We are all out of choices. We will head down the west face and pray for better luck. To cheer me up, Jack tells me that the west face has been siege climbed at least once recently, so the way down will have some kit and fixed lines on it to give us some clues. It is called the 'Harvard route', apparently.

I find that if I tighten my bootlaces and the ankle strap of my right crampon they support my hopefully only sprained ankle. It still hurts but I can climb on it.

As we get ready to leave, Jack says, 'Man, before we go I just want to say one thing.'

I am transfixed. Surely he is not going to get all philosophical on me now. We had been doing so well at pretending not to be frightened.

'You bloody Limeys have a far-too-relaxed attitude to falling, don't do it again!' Smiles all round for the Odd Couple. For the time being anyway.

On July 9 1978, Angus Thuermer Jr, Kent Meneghin, Joseph Kaelin and Glenn Randall had made the first ascent of the south-east spur of Mount Huntington, believing that their climb would be the fourth new route up the mountain.

ANGUS THUERMER JUNIOR, HUNTINGTON JOURNAL – JULY 9 1978. The sunrise was magnificent with a sea of low clouds over the Ruth. We set off, bunched beneath the séracs on the hanging glacier at first, then good cramponning with Kent kicking. I took over near the top and was the first to turn the corner to see the south face, what a place! A sweeping carpet of snow that arcs up to the ridge séracs and cornices, wow! We took many pictures.

Kent took the lead and took us over to the south ridge. The snow on it is sugary and unstable, very disappointing. I take over near the top [and] get into difficult ice below the summit ridge …

We are surprised to see footprints coming up out of the middle of the north face and we follow them to the summit. It seems our climb will be the fifth first ascent, not the fourth.

1 Set free of their farms after the war, Lantau water buffalo happily roam the island. I love these gentle monsters and it is a joy to meet them on a hike. Here at the end of a coastal hike, they seem to love the beach at Pui O as much as we do. **2** Happy as always in the mountains, Dave 'Wilco' Wilkinson on our first ascent on the Fiescherwand. **3** Wilco below the Hinterstoisser Traverse on the Eiger nordwand in summer.

4 Wilco on the central pillar of Brouillard with a storm brewing: the technical difficulties are over, the weather difficulties are about to begin.

5 The storm on Mont Blanc is just over and Wilco and I are the only ones stirring, almost reluctant to descend into the clouds.
6 The sorcerer and the apprentice on the Argentière Glacier on the evening before our ascent of the north face of Les Droites.

7 Jack Roberts in Anchorage on his way to collect our airfreight, June 9, 1978. **8** Beautiful downtown Talkeetna, June 10, 1978. The Roadhouse is on the right; the white building on the left at the end of the street is the famous Fairview Inn: 'saloon – rooms'.

9 The entire extent of the Roberts-McCartney expedition is gathered under the wing of an old abandoned Douglas C-47. I am forced to wear the hood of my parka as a defence against skeets. **Photo:** Jack Roberts. **10** The adventure begins. An hour from now Jack and I will be on the west fork of the Ruth Glacier. I look more relaxed than I am actually feeling. **Photo:** Jack Roberts.

11 The west fork of the Ruth Glacier. The Rooster Comb is closest the camera and Mount Huntington is behind, the north face overlooking the glacier. **Photo**: Bob Kandiko.

12 A sérac collapses on the north face of Mount Huntington, a regular occurrence. According to Rob Newsom's journal, 'Sleeping by Huntington's north face is like sleeping in the ocean with huge breakers crashing all night – the continuous avalanching never ceasing.' **Photo**: Mark Westman.

13 Our neighbour Charlie Porter in camp on the west fork of the Ruth Glacier, June 1978. **14** Smelly me and my damp clothes, all out to dry in the glorious sun. The north buttress of the Rooster Comb in the background. **Photo:** Jack Roberts. **15** Jack attends to drying his equipment.

16 Jack making a monster chilli in the luxury of the Don Sheldon Mountain House. **17** The Ice Palace (later the Hotel California), as seen from the guest entertainment area.

18 The north face of Mount Huntington from the slopes of Peak 11,301. **Photo:** Mark Westman. **19** Jack waiting for nightfall under the rock overhang that saved our lives on the first attempt on the north face.

20 Jack makes the last rappel in our retreat from the rock band on our first attempt on the north face. **21** We live to fight another day. Jack arrives inside the bergschrund at the top of the hanging glacier, the shelter that saved our lives on the first day of our ascent of the north face.

22 Heading for the Ramp on day three of our ascent. **Photo:** Jack Roberts. **23** As I place a screw I turn to Jack and say, 'so you are convinced the outlook is bleak?' I have my pack off so things are clearly getting serious. **24** Jack climbing in the Ramp on day four.

25 'Good morning, man.' Jack in our first bivouac in the Ramp on day five. **26** Jack leading in the bulge on day five. Sometimes we could skirt the séracs and sometimes we could not.

Nose roof pitch

Rope found stretched down this snowfield, snagged against base of Nose roof.

27 The line of our descent on the Harvard route on the west face of Mount Huntington. **Photo and annotations**: Mark Westman. **28** Twenty years after we lost our rope on the descent of the Harvard route it is discovered by Mark Westman – it is the purple rope on the left. Joe Puryear is the climber. **Photo**: Mark Westman.
29 Exhausted, Jack and I cross the north-west ridge that separates the Tokositna Glacier from the west fork of the Ruth and our salvation on the final day – day ten – of our traverse of the mountain.

30 The British contingent assembled above Kleine Scheidegg in February 1979. L–R: Tony Saunders (back to the camera), Howard Lancashire, William 'Bill' Barker, Dave 'Smiler' Cuthbertson (of course) and Stevie Haston. **31** Smiler crossing the Hinterstoisser Traverse.

32 'A lad of life, an imp of fame.' It was impossible to be bored in Chris Hoyland's company; he sought and extracted the maximum life could offer every day.
33 I am heading for the Exit Cracks at the top of the White Spider on the last day of our climb. Photo: Chris Hoyland. **34** The passing of time makes no odds, the atmosphere and the fact you are climbing over ghosts on the Eiger cannot be ignored. As Joe Simpson eloquently described the feeling, 'it gets in your head!'

35 North-west Europe is lost in cloud and the sun shines only for Chris and me as we near the end of a perfect adventure on the Eiger.

Yesterday was high clouds drawing
Post meridian depression..
Today dawned hazy with mid
morning clearing. I lingered on my
breakfast for hours — enough for a few
hours. Had coffee, tea, eggs +
not enough of anything else
Wonderful to exist here alone.
Nothing good — all [illegible]
The most stories here been
screwed for two days. Today we
combined the good taste of [illegible]
+ now have a [illegible] again.
Yesterday I spotted Jack + Simon
near the summit of the N.
face and it appears that they've
made the first ascent — a
very bold undertaking. The
[illegible] very quiet today. So
to the [illegible]. We strain
constantly for the sound
of Hudson's cracks, coming to
bring us home to civilization
+ all the things we need...

Every time we stop in the McKinley,
Simon stocks a "pile-up". HA! HA!
After dinner
Sitting out on the glacier
by the tent, using a [illegible]
old my pack for a back rest
Drinking a pot of hot [illegible]
mint tea. It is just right.

Mount Huntington, Mount Huntington
my old friend
I wonder if I'll ever come to
climb you again?
You're steep, you're beautiful,
you're dangerous, you're mean.
You're the baddest mountain
I've ever seen.
The avalanche never seem
to cease upon your face...
[illegible]
But despite my feelings, + my
obvious disloyalty,
Wherever I go, in the game [illegible]

An extract from Rob Newsom's 1978 journal. 'Yesterday I spotted Jack and Simon near the summit of the north face and it appears they have made the first ascent, a very bold undertaking.' The underlined text was by Rob himself.

11
SHEER LUCK

We cannot see what we are getting into because the convex slope below us is too steep. What we do see is that we can certainly descend the next 1,000 feet of snow and ice, after which it will become mixed ground, and much steeper. I have some recollections of pictures of the west face, but I had paid scant attention to them. As soon as I heard that this face of the mountain had been climbed already, I lost interest in it. How I wish I had studied it now! Too late. We have no choice and so we climb down the easy slopes that fall away from the shoulder and descend into a funnelling amphitheatre. We follow the right-hand edge, looking down.

Jack is looking after me. I climb down with my limp while he is the attentive sentinel above. At the end of the rope I belay and he climbs carefully down to join me. The movement helps my ankle. It hurts but the lubrication caused by front pointing backwards is helping keep the joint supple.

We descend six pitches before I find myself on icy ground, with rocks becoming more common. It is getting too steep for this game; Jack is taking big risks by down-climbing now and a fall will kill us both. It is five times harder to climb down than to climb up, and the angle is changing so that the ground below cannot be down-climbed in any sensible way. We need to rappel, but have so little equipment to use as anchors. I scan the slopes below for an answer. My prayer is granted: I can see some old fixed equipment on a rock outcrop below and to my right.

'Jack, there are fixed anchors down here.'

'See what you can find, man.'

I set off again on a tensioned rope, to the little bright flash of colour that has drawn my attention. It is a pair of pitons tied off with old frayed tape. Somebody with lots of kit has set up a rappel anchor here. I give both pins a good hit with my North Wall hammer. Jack can hear the ping of metal on metal and I see him start at the familiar noise. I replace the old tape with new.

'On belay, come on down, carefully please,' I instruct and, as good as gold, Jack gingerly picks his way down backwards to join me. It will be rappels from here for about 3,000 feet.

I am dispatched first. The joy of sliding down a rope so easily raises our spirits. My mission is to find another anchor.

God bless them, the last climbers to pass this way have placed many anchors and left them all behind. One hundred and fifty feet further on I spot more old climbing tape away to my left. I need to traverse to reach it. The route our unknown friends have taken trends into a little ice field and a system of diagonal ice-filled cracks. I rappel on crossed karabiners as an improvised brake, and now fold the low end of my ropes around my leg and diagonally across my opposite shoulder, so as to add enough friction to lock the rope. This way, I can take both hands off the rope and use the picks of my axes to claw my way over to the next historical anchor. Whoever laid our unintended escape route had time and application on their side. Love your work, mate, whoever you were. Another two pitons tied together with tubular tape are just what the doctor ordered.

Jack and I discuss tactics for our salvation. He does not know much about the west face, but he reckons that we are now definitely on the Harvard route. This is a mid-sixties adventure climbed in siege style that has been repeated once, in similar style, by a Japanese team about three years ago. It seems we are the grateful beneficiaries of the fixed equipment from that ascent. We don't have enough of our own equipment to get down, so we must follow the trail laid by the Japanese team. We will remove the existing pitons that are surplus to requirements and reuse them lower down. It is sheer luck.

The route seems to be following the diagonal strata that runs through the mountain, following an icy seam in the rock. It is almost a traverse in places and we have to down-climb. However, the trail of old equipment is unmistakeable and easy to follow; there are even white fixed lines in places, partially buried in the snow and ice.

Another rappel brings me to the top of a large block. There are several obvious anchors in the block itself, but the trail of old equipment stops here. I scout a little further down the seam but there is no sign of previous climbing. I clamber back to the block and belay.

Jack joins me a few minutes later and we discuss the direction we should take and both conclude it must be straight down. The block is overhanging and we cannot see properly what lies below. I volunteer to go to the lip and take a look. I back down over the block until I can peer over its edge, below which is a vertical wall. At the base of this wall is a gently sloping snowfield. The ropes we have thrown are lying in coils and loops in the snow below the wall, so it is less than the ropes' length to that point. This leads to another cliff, beyond which there is moderate mixed ground to the right. I can even see some more fixed rope. I relay all these facts to Jack.

'OK, man, away you go then.'

Our anchors are second-hand so I gradually let my hip slide over the edge of the roof and lower myself into space without bouncing on the rope. Hardly touching the wall, I slide down on to the little snow slope. I estimate that I have some of the rope left and I want to use it. I gather up the ropes below me and pitch them into an open gulley – the obvious way down – and descend into it until I run out of rope. There is white fixed rope, which appears to be in quite good condition, and so I anchor myself to it. The retreat is going so much better than I had expected.

'Come on, Jack!' I shout, and share my optimism: 'This is looking good!'

Soon he appears on the skyline, pausing on the edge of the roof, as I did. He carefully lays the ropes so that they will pull down without getting twisted around one another. We always do this; the last one down would run a finger of his bottom hand between the two ropes to keep them separated and in the same orientation that they were laid at the anchor. The purple and gold rope is on the left and the blue and gold rope with the knot is on the right. The blue rope is the one we will pull. Methodically and cautiously Jack slides down to join me.

The rope is very difficult to pull down and at first we can hardly move it. This is deeply worrying – if we jam the rope and lose it we are in fatal trouble. The wall above us is too much for us to reclimb: it is obviously a pitch climbed using aid and we don't have the equipment for that. We try to loosen the rope by flicking a big loop in the purple end while pulling on the blue. This has happened to me many times and I have always managed to get the ropes to move.

Jack climbs up and to my left so he can get a better angle on his flick and it works, just. I load the blue end with tension and as the loop of purple rope runs up the line like a pulse, a little bit of the blue rope comes down. With each pulse I get a little more.

The psychological tension is awful. We seem to be winning but Jack will have to let go of the end of the purple rope soon, which means no more flicks. He looks at me with the last metre of purple rope in his hand, as if asking a question. I shrug, what else can we do? He gives the tail of the rope one more flick as I pull down on the blue rope. For a few metres it comes down more easily and then … it jams completely. I heave with my entire weight, but it will not budge. I try the flick technique to no avail. Jack is wide-eyed. Of all the places and times to lose a rope, *please* not now!

We work on the rope for an hour, flicking loops to the left and then the right, but even with our combined weight we cannot pull any more of it down. The consequences of our predicament are devastating. This could be the knockout blow and we watch one another like hawks for a sign of weakness, or inspiration.

The two ropes are tied together in the middle and inexplicably jammed above us. We only have hold of the end of one. With our backs to the wall, we devise a plan. It is not a plan we like. We will climb back up as far as we can so that we can cut off as much of the blue rope as possible, abandoning the rest of it along with the purple rope, which is lost above us. We should be able to get about sixty feet. We will then down-climb the gulley as best we can, following the fixed line wherever possible. I will excavate as much of the fixed line as I can from the ice so that we can make up a retrievable double rope again. It won't be nice rope – it will be full of knots – but beggars can't be choosers.

We make some tea before we go. It will be a long and dangerous retreat and we will not stop to bivouac tonight. As we drink, I stare at the glacier below and try to calculate how high we are above it. I am also struck by the most obvious fact that the Tokositna Glacier is where we will wind up, not the west fork of the Ruth where our base camp is. Between the two glaciers lies the French Ridge, or at least the continuous geological spine of it. I turn to Jack and he is staring at the same thing. He cuts me off:

'Yep, when we get down on the Tok we will have to climb over that ridge too.'

The progress is initially painfully slow. We down-climb when it is possible and make very short rappels when it is not. All the while we collect bits of white line and knot them together. After many hours we have enough line to give a rope that is similar in length to our remaining blue one. Unfortunately the white side has two knots in it, which makes rappelling very tedious and a little dangerous.

Day turns to night again as foot by bloody foot we make our way down. We are both exhausted but we are moving so slowly that one of us gets a good rest while the other is climbing or making rope manoeuvres. And so it goes all through the shadows of the night. I am cold and shiver when I'm not moving.

When at last the morning sun comes, it brings us hope that we will escape from the shadows later in the day and be warm again.

We are fortunate that the climbers who fixed lines clearly wanted for nothing in their supply of hardware and there are surplus pitons driven into the cracks at many of the anchors. We rearrange the pitons to ensure their security and remove the excess hardware so we can recycle it below.

After perhaps twenty-four hours of this, we have some luck: Jack finds a stretch of line that is as long as the blue rope and we now have a knotless sixty-foot rappel rope.

In the middle of the second night, we come to a dramatically steeper rock section, below which is a snowfield. We long to be there and an hour later we are both standing on it, having successfully retrieved our ropes.

'We are going to get out of this, Si.'

Jack finds my attempts at American accents amusing, so I try one in the style of Rob Newsom:

'Dang straight, boy!'

We have to keep it light.

It is time for a brew and the last of the boiled sweets, two each for dinner. We allow ourselves a short nap, but it is too cold to enjoy it. After another brew we are on our way. We had got the food situation hopelessly wrong but at least we have a little white gas left for the stove.

The snow slope is dealt with slowly. Jack looks OK, but I am getting a bit wobbly. It is actually easier on slightly steeper ground where I have the security of 'crawling' on my front points and can use my ice tools. Climbing over snow while standing up feels much less secure.

The snowfield descends to a horrible-looking arête with nasty-looking teeth and gendarmes, all of which are covered with corniced snow sculptures. I hope like hell we can avoid this and Jack says as much too. Below, the snow-field becomes part of the ridge and there is a short but steep rock outcrop we have to rappel in two steps to the snowy ridge below.

We are in luck. From this point there is a couloir that leads directly to the Tokositna. We like the look of this. Our Japanese friends must have also liked it as there is an anchor at the rock step and a piece of frayed white line sloping away from it, frozen into the ice of the couloir. It is like a signpost that reads 'Salvation – This Way'.

The rest of the night and some of the early morning is spent climbing down where we can and rappelling where we have to. It occurs to me that I am witnessing the second sunrise since we started downwards. We have been in purgatory for more than forty-eight hours, yet neither of us has uttered a word of complaint.

Jack continues to look after me selflessly. I manage to keep up my end of the teamwork and not always have him down-climb last, but it is obvious that he is in better shape and consequently it is less dangerous for both of us if he is above me.

The weather finally gives up trying to torment us and the skies clear – just as we begin to believe that good weather no longer exists. The sun beams out of a dark-blue sky and my spirits rise. I take this as a good sign that we will survive and rejoice that I will be warm again soon. We cross the little bergschrund and step off the mountain and on to the Tokositna Glacier.

Any attempts to keep it light, British-decorum-style, are futile; Jack is going to hug me no matter what. Neither of us actually cries but we hold hands for a very long minute while neither of us can talk. Jack's big rock-worn hand.

Eventually I manage a few words: 'Thanks, mate. What an epic! Thanks for looking after me the last couple of days.'

'Forget it, man, you were so solid. I have never been that far out on a limb with anybody.'

We are sure we will be free; just one ice-ridge to climb over and surely we can deal with that. We have abandoned the rock anchors as we know we no longer need them, and have two ice screws left and the deadman snow anchor – enough kit to do the job. We know there is an icefall on the other side of the French Ridge and we will certainly have to take care, but so long as the weather is fine we should be able to find our way well enough. One last big push and we could be back in the Ice Palace. And then eat a proper meal for the first time in what will be five days … or will it be six by then?

We will go no further this morning; we must sleep.

My ankle hurts. Now I sense we are going to get away with this adventure, it's as if I'm subconsciously allowing some pain to enter my body. I am getting the wobbles and I need to rest. We have been descending for fifty hours and the sun will soon make the snow horrible to climb on. We will rest in the sunshine and set off for home tonight, when it is cold. We spread all our kit out to dry and make a brew. Now we have time to talk about all the little things that had to be blocked out over the past eight days.

'How do you feel, mate?' I ask.

Jack's concern is for me: 'Let's have a look at the ankle.'

I flop down on my Karrimat in the sun and am warmed by the physics of the universe rather than my own shivering.

We take our boots off for the first time since the Ramp. I want to look at my swollen ankle to make sure that I am not compounding the problem by leaving it laced up in the boot. As I remove the inner boot, extra blood flows through my foot. It feels like hot liquid, painful but good. More good than bad anyway. My ankle is badly swollen, but it won't stop me now.

Jack is tending to his own feet with great attention. He has special feet and I have always marvelled at them: huge bone spurs stick out near his big toes, and that is just the beginning. The Hulk has prettier feet than Jack Roberts. But something is wrong: he is *too* intent on his toes.

'You OK, Jack?'

His expression tells me he is not OK and I join him on his Ensolite pad to see the issue close up. He rubs the ends of his big toes, which are white and wooden-looking at the tips.

'What is it?'

'My big toes are numb, can't feel the ends properly.'

I am alarmed: 'When did this start? Last night?'

'No, on the summit.'

'Shit! Why didn't you say?'

'What was the point?'

He has been holding out on me for days, climbing all the way down the west face knowing he had a problem but not saying a word while I yelped like a puppy every time I got a stab of pain in my ankle. I had already decided that whatever damage I had done would heal – it was just another little ordeal I would have to climb around. But Jack has the beginnings of frostbite or, hopefully, just frost nip.

Examination reveals that he has sensation up to the last knuckle, so perhaps it is not so serious. Because Jack has terrible-looking feet at the best of times, trying to ascertain if there is more damage than normal by comparing the condition of my feet with his is inconclusive. Any examination might lead a scientific person to believe we are two separate species.

While the stove is running I get Jack to place his feet close to it to warm them. Aware that sensation in his toes is a problem, we both keep our hands close to the stove to ensure he is not overheating his damaged feet. Then we pack them, along with the rest of him, inside his sleeping bag. We can do no more up here.

After a short time, I pass out, rather than fall asleep.

The sun is doing its half-hearted Alaskan version of setting when Jack wakes me up. It seems I have passed the entire day comatose on my back.

'You OK, Si?'

I cannot see well. My eyes are blurred, as if dazzled by a bright light. Every part of me hurts.

'Sure, mate, never better. I just ran out of batteries. Did you sleep?'

'Yeah, but not like you, man, you slept the whole day. I even checked your pulse, I was worried about you.'

Jack has been looking out for me. We take stock of our situation: we have just enough white gas for one more brew, but we must save it. We have had zero food for four days, apart from a few boiled sweets, but we are at least hydrated. The rope situation is no longer a major issue as we will be on snow terrain during the last stage of our traverse of the mountain.

Jack has been considering our exit strategy from the Tokositna while I have been unconscious. He has picked out the same point on the north-west ridge that I saw when I looked down from the west face. We should climb to and over the 'Petit French Col', as he has chosen to call it, a low point in the north-west ridge directly opposite where we have been resting. It will be easy snow-climbing – thank goodness – but we must reach the ridge at just the right point to gain the easiest entry to the icefall over the other side and the Ruth Glacier below. From there we can reach Base Camp and our salvation. In good visibility we should be able to find our way down the complex slopes on the other side but we will be navigating down an icefall we have never studied so if the weather turns against us we could be in trouble. We must go now, and go quickly, while the going is good.

The exhausting effort of getting dressed and packed is offset by the growing excitement of our imminent escape. Despite the pain in my ankle I even manage to summon the vinegar to share the trail-breaking with Jack. He says he can do it but I tell him no – I want to share everything, 'otherwise I shall have to buy *all* the beer!'

Trudging across the Tok is hard work. We have few energy reserves left because our bodies have been eating themselves to stay alive. I try to keep the tone positive with my own running pep talk.

'Mate, what we are about to do today is an alpine traverse that would probably rate as a good day out on Mont Blanc.'

And then, 'We are starting this last round on day nine of a climb that was started with four days' food. We have made the first ascent of the north face and we have made the third climb of the west face – upside down. Not bad!'

Jack looks at me with the extra wisdom of those few years' difference in our ages.

'Save it for the bar, man.'

I continue quietly with my wading in the deep, crusty snow. I do think of the bar actually – what a celebration there will be when we get there.

We cross the little bergschrund at the base of the north-west ridge and kick our way up the steepening snow slope.

We move together solo climbing until we are close to the ridgeline but once there, we become more attentive and rope up. Jack says he would prefer it if I don't fall through any more cornices. No need to worry – the route-finding has been almost perfect. When we crest the ridge we are treated to a revelation: we only need to move a rope's length to the west to be at the ideal entry to the slopes that will take us home. We need to avoid some mixed ground directly beneath us, and traverse beneath the cornices to reach a bluff. This will allow us to reach the hanging glacier that is spread out below. We will be able to descend that, no doubt wading down most of it in deep snow.

But this sight is eclipsed by the view of the Ruth Glacier below, the glacier that had been our home for nearly four weeks. There is only one tiny blemish on its surface – all the crowds have gone and all is still. We are the only climbers in this vast wilderness. This moment belongs to Jack and me. The mountain is all ours.

The sun is rising and now casts a shadow upon a small lump in the snow below the north face. It is a pile of excavated snow debris. It is the Hotel California.

'Toto, there's no place like home, no place like home!'

Never have I felt such affection for such a windswept place. Crossing the English Channel, homeward-bound after a long sojourn, seeing my family after half a year abroad in the mountains – all wonderful homecomings, but none that could match the joy of this view. We can see our salvation: there, in that hole in the snow, is food and a radio. The weather is set fine and all we have to do is carefully climb down to that very spot and Jim Sharp will come and fetch us. Even Jack, who has been playing 'let's not count our chickens until they are hatched', allows himself a wry smile.

The sunny view lets us find energy we did not know we had. The few downward pitches of ice climbing below the ridge are slow, due to the short rope, but after an hour we are on the snowy bluff and descending big open slopes, weaving to avoid crevasses. It is exhausting and we are weak but we're making our fastest progress in many days.

The last few hundred feet are annoying as the slope steepens just above the glacier and we are forced to front-point, facing backwards, down through the jumble of a little icefall.

The bergschrund is almost indistinguishable as it is covered in snowslide debris, but, as sure as gravity itself, the terrain levels out and the mountain's claws finally release us on to the benign river of ice and snow that is the west fork of the Ruth Glacier. Within an hour or so we will be at our ice cave. We are talking all the way now.

'Si, I'll get the stove on and get a chicken dinner going. Can you get the radio warmed up?'

'Sure.'

And then I ask, 'Do you think we can get out tonight? Is that what you want to do?'

'Man, it seems like a shame to just split straight away but if the weather turns I don't want to be stuck here like we were before.'

He is right: on a sunny day back in camp we would be focused on eating and resting and staring up at the face we have just climbed. I would have been happy to spend another day just looking at it, but if the weather were to close in we could be stuck again for a long time and we are in very poor condition physically, Jack's feet especially. It could quickly become awful. We will leave tonight if Jim can get his Cessna in.

'Jim Sharp, calling Jim Sharp, come in please, this is McCartney and Roberts.'

I make several calls over twenty minutes without reply.

I repeat the call ten minutes later and almost immediately after I release the transmit button the radio crackles into life.

'This is Geeting, glad to hear from you after so long. You guys OK?'

'Hi Doug, can you ask Sharp to come and get us ASAP, we are back at the landing site, we are OK but we need to get out.'

'Standby. Sharp has been looking for you guys for a few days.'

There is a long pause; Jack and I are staring at each other and the radio alternately.

'West fork climbers, this is Geeting.'

'Doug, go ahead.'

'Talked to Sharp, he is in the air and headed for Talkeetna to refuel, he'll come in to get you on the next run, please be ready.'

We spend an hour staring up at the mountain, pointing and remembering where we climbed, or where we had fled and hidden. We celebrate our achievement by recording it as accurately as we can.

Jack sketches the face and the line we agree upon. He has an innate and simple way of drawing that captures the features and character of the mountain.

The Hotel California is emptied of its boxes of food. Everything is dug out

Jack's hand-drawn topo of our route from his journal, courtesy of Pam Roberts. ▶

and stacked so that we can load the Cessna quickly when it lands. I notice for the first time that we smell very bad.

The radio suddenly comes to life and startles us.

'Jack, Simon, this is Jim Sharp inbound.'

There is a rush to grab the radio; Jack wins.

'Hey Jim, this is Jack, over.'

'Jack, ETA five minutes, please be ready to load up and make yourselves visible.'

'*Roger that!*'

12
COMING DOWN

We hear Jim's Cessna before we see it; that droning sound makes our hearts beat faster and we are suddenly as happy as clams. There are so many resounding echoes in the west fork that we cannot tell exactly when our little bird will appear, but it is definitely getting louder.

'There! Hah! There he is – there!'

We can see him coming at us – but too high to land. Jim flies over our camp and completes a loop; he is studying his landing site. He heads back down the valley and then turns toward us again. This time the approach is lower, the engine note deeper and he parallels the upwardly sloping terrain of the glacier, perhaps thirty feet above it, heading directly for our camp. I can only stare.

The engine note is throttled and the little plane drops. In slow motion, the little bird touches gently down and a trail of debris is launched into the slipstream as the tail-skid ploughs into the snow. The ballet is not yet over; Jim guns the engine and powers up the slope, setting down a long set of tracks. Just short of the camp he applies what seems to be full throttle, spinning the plane 180 degrees. When he comes to a halt the Cessna is parked perfectly in the tracks he has created, facing downhill.

Jim is languid and cool as he steps from the plane. It must be satisfying to be a Denali glacier pilot if every client is as pleased to see him as we are now.

Apparently the weather is stable so there is no need to rush, but still Jim makes it plain to us that he wants to pick up and leave smartly.

'I was looking for you guys. Rob Newsom saw you near the summit but you took a long time to come down.'

The plane is packed quickly – there is not much left of our stores. I am struck by the contrast between our arrival and the time we spent here and this hasty departure: we will be gone in fifteen minutes. Another forty-five minutes and we will be sitting outside Jim's place in Talkeetna.

I guess we must smell really bad because, without either of us asking, Jim offers us a shower at his place after we land.

Our climbing packs are the last things to be loaded. We climb in and close the doors. Jack passes his camera to Jim to take a picture for posterity. I am overcome with a mixture of emotions. Relief is one, gratitude for the dependability and grit of my climbing partner is another, and I am pleased to learn Jim has been looking out for us.

The engine spools up, but this time I am relaxed during the headlong acceleration down the glacier. I am an old hand now. No, it is not that. We have survived and I have no room left in my mind to worry about a glacier take-off. I hold out my hand to Jack as we fly down the west fork and he grasps it with that powerful grip. The poignancy of the moment lasts for a long time and I have a lump in my throat, but when he smiles at me with that big goofy grin of his we both burst out laughing.

We cannot talk over the engine so for forty-five minutes I am alone with my thoughts. My brain is buzzing. Freed of the prime directive of survival, I have time to think of many things: my girlfriend Judi, contacting my family, writing the story of the climb … but there is something underlying all my disorganised and half-considered thoughts. We are almost in Talkeetna when I finally identify the emotion: it is pride.

The plane is parked in front of Jim's cabin and the engine killed. Jim is the first to speak:

'The shower is in the back on the left, guys. I can get you some towels if you need them.'

Clearly forty-five minutes with us in the small confines of the Cessna has been more than enough for him.

Washing is novel; a layer of scum is rubbed away when I scrub myself, similar to sunburn peeling skin, only more disgusting. There is a mirror in the bathroom and I am shocked at my appearance. I have never been so skinny. I look like I have lost many kilos. It is time to do something about that.

When we are both changed we have the presence of mind to put up the tent near the row of parked ski planes. I can't be bothered unpacking anything more. We are too hungry to spend longer and we set off to walk to downtown Talkeetna. We limp there actually. Jack says his toes have sensation again but that the sensation is mostly pain. My ankle hurts too and we stagger and sway like two scrawny derelicts into the Fairview Inn.

We plan to start with a burger and jug of beer. Then I decide that, actually, I can eat two burgers and I order two hamburger deluxes, imagining I will be rewarded with one plate with two burgers on it. I am a little embarrassed, and so is Jack, when two dinner plates arrive for me alone.

Although my hunger is gone and I can have a beer, I am not in the celebratory mood I thought I would be. I thought that by now we would be running wild with celebration. Jack is quiet too. The journey from the mountain to civilisation has been too abrupt and I am dazed by it. Last night we dragged our tired and damaged bodies out of the trap the mountain had set for us, escaping with our lives. A forty-five-minute flight had delivered us suddenly to a green world where nothing is dangerous.

The intensity of the last ten days has evaporated and now there is a void. At first I think my mood is a symptom of my exhaustion, but it is more than that. I had thought that our ascent would feel complete, as if I had laid a demon to rest, but it doesn't. Rather than smug satisfaction, I am agitated, as if I had slain one dragon only to find I have awakened another.

I am tired and the first jug of beer has clearly gone straight to our heads. Somehow I feel lost. Each day of the last two weeks has been so intense. Every move was planned. Now I have no idea what we will do tomorrow. I have spoken only to Jack and even then, not much. Most of our communication was done telepathically, aided by a look or a nod. We have actually been tied to one another for ten days, during which time we defended each other constantly. Now we can stagger about with the rest of humanity without the need of a plan. It feels insufficient.

Jack is obviously deep in thought too and we hardly speak on the walk back to our tent. Annoyingly, we remember at the last moment that we forgot to lay out our lightweight sleeping bags and pads and we have to dig them out of our stores. We are savaged by the skeets that have been waiting in ambush but, despite the loss of blood, sleep comes easily.

We sleep, sort of, for fourteen hours and afterwards I feel better both physically and mentally. I am adjusting to a more normal life in which I can do what I want, eat when I feel like it, or do nothing if I so choose, without having to fight for survival. Jack is also in better shape today and is back to his normal, outgoing self. Sarcasm and out-of-context conversation have returned to him, so all is well. We can both walk, almost without limping. I am very happy about this because Jack's toes worried me, what with his feet looking like a problem even on a good day.

'Matey, about your toes … ' I begin.

'Not too bad today, man.'

'Jack, it's a well-known fact that alcohol thins the blood and promotes circulation in the extremities.'

'Si, I think I see where you are going with this.'

'I feel like celebrating today, I was down last night, let's have a nice lunch and write to *Mountain* magazine.'

'Anywhere I want?'

'Anywhere you want.'

On the way to lunch we call in on Dave Buchanan at the ranger station. We had checked in with him when we entered the park. He had been dubious about our plans when we first met, but now he is full of questions about the climb and particularly the descent. Dave digs out some pictures of the west face and with his help we piece together where we went. We did go straight down the Harvard route apparently. It turns out we owe a big thank you to some Japanese climbers who left all the white fixed line.

Jack does most of the talking and I watch Dave's animated face, his big bushy beard waving to us whenever he speaks. This guy has climbed many mountains and we have earned his respect – we no longer get the raised eyebrow, instead we're rewarded with the smile of a brother sharing something special. A bond has formed even though we hardly know each other. Dave is impressed with the way in which we made our climb, in simple alpine style, totally self-reliant. I can imagine no other way of climbing so don't really understand his fascination, but I am proud of our effort all the same.

When we have finished downloading our tales, Dave gives us the news he has so far from the Ruth. None of the five other parties attempting routes on Huntington have made it to the summit yet, but the group of four including Angus Thuermer is thought to have made the first ascent of the south-east spur. Rob Newsom's team from Washington State was repulsed by snow mushrooms on the French Ridge. That made sense – so were we! The team of Thuermer, Glenn Randall, Kent Meneghin and Joe Kaelin planned to ski-walk and raft home, so we would have to wait for their story.

Jack is full of chat over lunch at the Fairview Inn. We are both getting over our adjustments to a more normal everyday life. This doesn't happen in the Alps, I believe, because as a climbing pair you are never isolated like you can be in Alaska. At the end of an adventure in the Alps you just walk back to the village you started from, rather than fly back after a month on 'the moon'.

What we have achieved is beginning to sink in. Dave's reaction counts for some of that, but as Jack and I relive the epic step by step we share things that we thought but did not say at the time for fear of upsetting one another. He wants to talk now, I can see, so I open:

'Jack, I have to ask, when that snow avalanche hit you, what … how did you … what went through your head?'

He thinks for a moment and replies, 'Snow mostly.'

We smile at the corny gag at first, but it's followed by a long pause. His smile fades, another thought has taken its place.

'Man, the only, *only* good thing about that climb, was that you were tied on to the other end of the rope.'

No one has ever said anything like this to me before and I cannot immediately reply. The climb had taken my abilities to unimagined new heights. The feeling I have is that, together, Jack and I can climb anything we want. I feel we are powerful as a team; we have subtly different technical strengths as climbers but on the one rope together, anything is possible.

The next road trip beckons and we will head south in a day or so. This time we will hitch a ride in a Cessna back to Anchorage. The fire we had in our bellies before our climb on Huntington has started to burn once more.

It seems a shame to leave Talkeetna so soon. Apart from the skeets it is a wonderful place. I am bitten by love for the village and mosquitoes at the same time. But it is easier to say goodbye to a lover if you promise to come back, and so it is with Talkeetna. Jack and I are running away to play on the sunny granite of Yosemite, but we have every intention of returning. We have unfinished business with 'Big Mac', as Jack calls Denali.

We make a tour of the village and say so long to everyone we know: Jim, Kitty, Doug, and the friendly folks at the Fairview and the Roadhouse. Before we fly out we make one last visit to the ranger station, where there is a huge blown-up photograph of one of Washburn's aerial photos of Denali. It shows the Cassin Ridge and the two walls either side of it. The south-west face draws my eye.

'Has that been climbed?' I ask.

I get the Roberts wry grin.

'Not yet.'

13

'AN OBSESSION FOR THE MENTALLY DERANGED'

Colonel Strutt, president of the British Alpine Club, describing in his 1937 valedictory address attempts hitherto to climb the Eiger Nordwand.

The rest of the summer in America did not play out as I had hoped. Jack and I left Alaska with our tails up, heading for Yosemite and feeling unstoppable. The journey down Highway 1 from Seattle was a delight to me, a journey along the rugged young geology of the San Andreas Fault, the junction of the Pacific and North American plates, each creeping determinedly in opposite directions.

We stopped the car barely an hour or two from Santa Monica to do some bouldering on little cliffs near the road. We were as skinny and light as we had ever been and full of ourselves. Climbing warm rock in the sunshine felt wonderful and within an hour we were attempting moves that were at our limit of ability. Jack committed himself to a leering crack in a tall boulder and got stuck, high enough that when the inevitable fall happened I was almost powerless to cushion his landing. He smashed into me, and the ground, injuring his back. All I managed to do was to prevent his head from striking the hard rocky surface. Jack could hardly breathe because of the pain.

The reception at Jack's family's house was not as bad as I feared. Jack's mother was full of concern, but luckily his condition had improved a little by the time we got there. Or he was faking. Or both.

The revelation that Jack had injured himself was met by his sister Chris with a sister's love and concern but also with the scorn of expectation. The inference was that Jack was always going to have accidents like this because he repeatedly indulged in foolish and dangerous behaviour. Chris was training for a career in law enforcement, and consequently she was an organiser who took charge of the situation. It was as if Jack was the perpetrator and the victim of the crime, and I was surely the accomplice.

Jack had compressed one of the discs between his thoracic vertebrae. He would recover but there would be no climbing for him for a few months. Our dreams of the big-wall classic climbs in Yosemite were postponed for the year.

Before heading home to the UK, I did climb one wall in Yosemite: the west face of the Leaning Tower with a friend of Jack's. The Leaning Tower is the biggest continuous overhanging cliff in the Sierras and the climb was immense fun. Halfway up we bivouacked on the commodious Ahwahnee Ledge and drank beer as the sun went down.

The next day, as the shadows were just beginning to lengthen in the valley below, I battled around a roof near the top of the route. We knew now that we would be off the climb that afternoon but we would not try to get all the way down to the valley that night. We were in good shape, we had food and water and we were having fun. Even the problems with an awkward haul bag could not dent my mood.

The last pitch gave way and we were united on horizontal terrain at last. Without haste we packed up and began to pick our way towards the few rappels that were the beginning of our descent. We were tired and it was obvious that it would soon be dark, so we slept by the creek. The sound of the water was like a lullaby. Before sleep came, my mind strayed back to home, to Judi and my family, and I wanted to be with them.

I dreamed of being in the mountains. A familiar shadowed peak presented itself: in my dream I was standing again in Kleine Scheidegg, staring up at the north face of the Eiger and it was frowning back at me. There was snow everywhere – it was winter. Of course, I must climb it in winter for to make a summer ascent would no longer do; my climb must have some of the hardship of the first ascent and to have that the deed must be done in the dead of winter. I slept easily that night, totally content with what I had done already that summer, and now equally content with what I would do on my next trip to the mountains.

Back in the UK, the one person I wanted to see most was Judi. We had met at school at the age of fourteen and consequently had been close for a long time. While I had been away she had decided that her philosophy degree at Lampeter university was not what she hoped it would be and had decided to waste no further time on it. Judi was back in Woking with her family: her mum, dad and brother Jim.

There was another reason Judi had come home from Wales: her mum had terminal cancer. Our joy at being reunited was tempered every day with the knowledge that her mother was so poorly. Judi was a devoted daughter, helping her dad, Bill, care for her mum.

My immediate alpine climbing plans also caused Judi concern. She'd had reasonable expectations that as I had only just returned from an epic summer expedition, she would be safe from the afflictions of another expedition, at least until the following spring.

I had tried to sell the idea that a winter ascent of the Eiger was a short-term undertaking; it would not be an alpine season, just one climb. I had been in America for months but we were only talking about a couple of weeks, 'tops', for the Eiger. Of course I was kidding myself, but not her.

One of our favourite treats was to go up to London and see a play. Before the show we liked to eat at the Swiss Centre near Leicester Square, where the food was decent, ample and reasonably priced. The interior of the Swiss Centre was decorated with huge, floor-to-ceiling posters of classic views of Switzerland. All of the scenes one might expect were there: the chocolate-box pictures of the fountain at Lake Geneva; that view of the Matterhorn, looking up the Hornli Ridge with the west face in sunlight, set against a clear blue winter sky. There were cows with bells around their necks taking in the views from high alpine meadows. But there was also an elephant in the room. I inadvertently sat down at a table overlooked by a mountain view from the Bernese Oberland: that of the three famous icy sisters, the Mönch, the Jungfrau and the Eiger. And within the image a two-metre-tall north face of the Eiger occupied pride of place, glowering down on our dinner table as if we were eating on the outdoor viewing deck of the Restaurant Eigernordwand itself.

I tried to avoid staring at it but there was no fooling Judi. She knew exactly what it was. My eyes would stray to the big photo and trace the line of the 1938 route.

'When are you leaving?' she asked.

In truth I did not know exactly. All I could tell her was that the trip would be after Christmas. I had arranged a partner, but we had yet to come up with a precise plan.

Dave Cuthbertson was the first person I thought of for the Eiger. Only his family called him Dave; to the climbing community he was famous as 'Smiler'. His nickname is his demeanour, his endless enthusiasm, good humour and West Midlands drawl all coming out through that endless grin. I met Dave 'Wilco' Wilkinson through Smiler; he told me that Smiler held the world record for the fastest descent of Ben Nevis, having fallen 800 feet down a snow and ice gully and lived to tell the tale. Typically, Smiler was up for the Eiger at once.

He was always naturally enthusiastic, but this time he bowled me over with his excitement. He launched into the planning, full steam ahead, and I was soon bombarded by phone calls. All I had to do was knuckle down and raise some cash, working at Alpine Sports during the day and taking whatever work I could get at the big London exhibitions at night. Somewhere in-between I would need to train and sleep.

The London branch of Alpine Sports had become the axis about which the local London climbing scene rotated. In this group were Stevie Haston and Victor Saunders. I had climbed with both of them and when Stevie and Victor heard about the Eiger plans they immediately decided to join us.

Judi and I drove up to Snowdonia for a long weekend and crashed at Smiler's house. We would do some scheming, some ice climbing and some sociable drinking. It made it easier that Judi and Smiler got on so well. Come to think of it, I don't know anybody who has a bad word to say about him.

He tells me there is another pair that wants to come with us: Bill Barker and Howard Lancashire. They are very keen and Bill owns the most useful item of equipment for any alpinist in the UK: a Ford Transit van. We could all pile in the back with our kit and make the journey from the UK to the Alps cheaply and in relative comfort.

And so the caravan commenced. Starting in North Wales, Bill Barker collected his cargo, picking up Smiler and Howard and then headed south to London to collect Stevie and Victor. I was the last to pile aboard the trusty Transit van outside my family home in Woking.

There is a party atmosphere in the van and we stop only to change drivers or for calls of nature. In-between we doze and stretch out, but as we approach the mountains everybody is alert and staring out of the windows into an icy dawn.

Along the road between Interlaken and Grindelwald we see spectacular frozen waterfalls that would themselves be worthwhile as climbing projects. Our destination is the Lauterbrunnen valley, where we will make our base. Victor has arranged a room in a farmhouse – the Nature Friend House in the hamlet of Stechelberg. Sharing the cost six ways makes it affordable and it is only a short drive to the mountain railway station and the train that will take us up to Kleine Scheidegg at the foot of the north face.

None of us can wait to confront the mountain; we all want to see how the Eiger looks with its winter coat on. If the conditions look good we will pack for the climb the next day.

Stevie and Victor have a similar agenda but will climb independently of the rest of the group. The historical significance of a group of four climbers on the Eiger's north face is not lost on me as the train grinds its way from Lauterbrunnen to Scheidegg.

Our first attempt was a total shambles. The snow was deep and crusted and we floundered in it with our heavy packs. Moving as a group proved to be painfully slow and we got in each other's way. We were so slow that we ran out of daylight before we even got to the Hinterstoisser Traverse.

We chopped out a ledge under the Rote Fluh and settled in for an uncomfortable night during which the spindrift hunted us relentlessly. By morning we were wet through and all in a very bad mood. This was no way to start a climb on the Eiger and we unanimously decided to retreat, regroup and plan for a second, and hopefully much better, attempt.

Back in the Nature Friend House we have a council of war. One of the issues is that the dynamic of climbing in a single pair is very different to moving in a group of four climbers. With just two climbers, decisions are easily made and roles are shared, pitch by pitch. When there are four of you, a leader is required and we had no leader because none of us wants to tell the others what to do out of respect. This would be a very left-wing team then, an eight-legged committee.

We rationalise our equipment and reduce weight by avoiding duplication. We rest for a day and spend the time eating. The next morning is clear and fine so we go up to bivvy in a little concrete railway building above Kleine Scheidegg we had found, planning to make an early start.

We make much better speed over the lower face and make our early morning objective, the Hinterstoisser Traverse, with time to spare. I find myself in the lead again. I have been here before, with Wilco in 1977, and I am the only one in the group who has seen this famous traverse up close.

The Hinterstoisser Traverse is a psychological step. Everything before this pitch is almost inconsequential, feeling like an approach to a climb. Crossing that traverse makes me feel that I have started the climb proper. The Rote Fluh overhangs above us and the rocks below are undercut. It is like a door displaying the warning, 'Enter at your own risk.'

I am glad we are here in winter. I plan to only ever climb this face once and I have been waiting for my turn for years. The sense of grand adventure of the first ascent in 1938 can never be recreated, but at least we are engineering some hardship that would have been avoided by a summer ascent.

Bill and Howard are backed up behind Smiler now as he belays me. It must have been just so when Hinterstoisser first crossed this blank and steep slab with his three companions looking on, willing him to succeed on this desperately difficult pitch.

The Swallow's Nest, at the end of the traverse, is just big enough for all of us but is not the luxury ledge that it is in summer for a single pair. Despite the lack of comfort I do not want for entertainment. Bill, with his very dry sense of humour, and Smiler, the raconteur, entertain us as we chat and eat until we start to get cold and it's time to close the sleeping bags over our heads.

I had found myself in the lead yesterday and that made sense since I had been to the Swallow's Nest before. The following morning I just carry on, there is no discussion. I was closest to the first ice field on our bivouac ledge and so I lead off after breakfast, with Smiler ever-attentive, paying out the rope and the encouragement in equal measure.

I pause on the ice for a moment to remember standing on this very spot with Wilco and being chased away by a volley of stones in 1977. Looking about me I measure what has changed on the face now it has its winter coat on. All is quiet this morning. I am the only cause of any sounds. The crunch of my crampons and whack of my ice picks is followed by the tinkling sound the chips of disturbed ice make as they skitter away into the void below. The ice shatters like glass, brittle and as hard as hell.

The Ice Hose is in good condition, with a thick coat of ice, but it is steeper than I thought it would be. No problem for me today with my modern equipment, but I spare a thought for those that have passed this way prior to the development of ice-climbing gear as it is now. My crampons are razor-sharp spikes of steel that are almost part of my body, so seamlessly are they connected to me. I have never cut an ice step in my life, other than to rest at the end of a pitch of delicate and efficient front pointing. Kurz, Hinterstoisser, Angerer and Rainer passed this way back in 1936. My God! I hope it was rocky for them that summer because their ice-climbing gear was like farm equipment in comparison to mine.

As I come out of the top of the Ice Hose I am treated to my first panoramic view of the second ice field and I can see the Flat Iron and Death Bivouac far away and diagonally to my left. When Smiler joins me we have a chat about the line we will take.

We have a choice: I can climb diagonally on a beeline to the top left corner of the ice field, or I can take a steeper line to meet the rocks above and traverse

The north face of the Eiger in summer. Photo: Dave Wilkinson. ▶

horizontally on the junction between rock and ice. We decide to go to the top of the ice field and traverse as this line will be quicker.

At the moment we are not as fast as a single pair swinging leads. I lead a pitch and Smiler follows. Smiler then belays me leading the next pitch while also belaying either Howard or Bill up to him through a second belay plate. Impressive dexterity on Smiler's part, but this is still one pitch in three slower than just a single pair.

I connect with some old fixed line at the top of the ice field. Much of it is buried but it does speed everybody a little. Sometimes there is a gap between the ice and the rock above, making an easy place to hook the pick of my axe.

Looking back from my next belay I get a surprise when I see that in addition to Smiler, Bill and Howard, there is another pair of climbers on the second ice field below us. From the helmet colours and clothing it can only be Stevie and Victor and they are catching up fast. I am not at all sure whether this is good or bad but this mass British ascent must be causing amusement for the tourists in Kleine Scheidegg. The vibe is very different to my climb on Huntington with Jack. The silent fears and telepathy I found with Jack have been replaced with a noisy gaggle of pals. It might have been a bit like this on the 1936 attempt to make the first ascent, until it all went terribly wrong.

It has been a long hard day and I am grateful that it is easy to chop out a ledge at the Death Bivouac. It is just spacious enough for us all to sit, but bitterly cold and even with all my clothing on I can hardly sleep. I am also worried because Bill has broken his ice axe. The pick has failed at the first tooth and the point snapped off, rendering it almost useless as an ice-climbing tool. Perhaps the extreme cold and the hardness of the ice are the cause? The cold will not go away and most of us are using the same tools: Curver axes and Charlet Moser ice hammers. I will be tentative with my axe placements tomorrow, which is not good. The mountain has, by this inconvenience, sown a seed of doubt in my mind.

Smiler has brought a metal file and sharpens the broken stub. It cannot be used as a reliable tool on steep ice but at least it functions as well as the previous generation of ice axes: you can chop with it, if not hook.

Smiler and I huddle up in individual bivvy bags, as do Bill and Howard. Stevie and Victor have disappeared into their two-man bag for the night. I wonder if they are any warmer than we are. It occurs to me now that we are committed. If for any reason we can't go upwards, getting down will be even more problematic.

In fitful sleep I am troubled by the ghosts of Karl Mehringer and Max Sedlmayr, the poor devils that gave the name Death Bivouac to the ledge we are gathered upon. In my mind, I am sleeping on their bones. In reality their bodies were eventually found and one freed from the ice. The other had fallen, but here and now they seem to want to talk to me and I want to talk to them.

'What happened to you guys, Max, Karl? Did your final sleep come easily or painfully?'

Before they can answer, I am awakened by Smiler shuffling to get his circulation going. There is a chain reaction among my cold-but-living friends shivering themselves awake. We are all connected by one goal: a big brew of hot, sweet tea and let's be gone.

I cross the third ice field and enter the Ramp and belay. In the following group there is another ice axe failure: Smiler breaks the tip off his Curver axe pulling it out of the ice and he has a tough time following with one blunted and useless tool. This mishap makes a mess of the entire day. We are now so slow that another night will be spent at Death Bivouac because we cannot all move to a better place for the fourth night.

My Plan B for the day is to run out as many pitches as I can in the Ramp and fix the ropes. We will then return to Death Bivouac for the night and try to get a flying start tomorrow. I have never made such little progress on an alpine climb and I wonder if this is what winter ascents are supposed to be like.

The crowd at Death Bivouac is still cheery thanks to Bill. I have been listening to his repartee for an hour or so as I carefully made my way back down the fixed ropes. The advantage of being last home is that the cooking has been done and as soon as I get into my sleeping bag Smiler passes me a bowl of hot soup and, ten minutes later, a pint of hot, sugar-filled tea. The warmth this fuel brings me is welcome and I doze off immediately.

My comfort is short-lived; I am awakened just an hour later by the cold. I wonder if it is just me but Smiler confirms that he too thinks the temperature has dropped much lower than before:

'Fookin freezing, me!'

Even before the morning I cannot wait to leave. The Eiger has closed its grip on us in a frozen fist.

The climbing line of the 1938 route is a master stroke of boldness. All around are vast overhanging walls and we follow a sinuous path which is the only possible line between them. The Ramp steepens and I hope the steepest bit is not as hard as it looks. What were Heckmair, Vörg, Harrer and Kasparek thinking when they reached this point during their epic first ascent in 1938?

I am forced to take my mittens off to overcome some rocky mixed climbing and in so doing I freeze the skin of my fingers on both hands to the rock. It happens in a moment. The realisation of what has occurred shocks me. I had only taken my gloves off for a short while but having started those upward moves I could not stop. Eventually I have to peel my fingers from the rock and as soon as I can I put my gloves back on. Too late – the damage is done. The pain is not great but I can feel that I have partially frozen my fingers. I have often wondered how climbers manage to get frostbite; now I understand. I fix a belay and bring Smiler up to join me. When he is close enough I explain what has happened to my hands. He wants to look.

'Si, let me see.'

I allow one mitten and inner glove to be momentarily removed.

Smiler's face is full of concern and he stares at my wooden fingers. It looks like I have just grasped something very hot and scalded the pads of my fingers. Only it is just the opposite.

Victor is the next to join us. Smiler tells him what has happened and I get a rare sympathetic moment from Victor:

'Simon, you have done enough. Let somebody else take over.'

It was like a line out of one of those 1950s British war movies. I make no argument. I have been at the sharp end of the rope every pitch to this point and I am tired. Now I am also injured, I will be slow. We wave Victor through. Smiler and I stay put and allow everybody to overtake us.

There is a long delay before I move again, so I have time to stare about and take in the amazing situation. I look back along the narrow path we have followed between the huge overhanging walls, the ground below falling away into yawning voids. Debris, cut from above, falls constantly. Big bits of ice bounce off the rock near my little ledge and spin out into thin air, vanishing into the abyss. I imagine that they will only bounce for the second time at the foot of the face, 4,000 feet below.

The fact that I am no longer leading is a release; I can allow my concentration to wander and it does. I find that I have been dozing when Smiler stirs me. I continue climbing, but I am now in a daze. I have stupidly managed to avoid realising the most obvious and significant fact: we will bivouac in the Ramp tonight and it will be truly uncomfortable. They have been chopping bivouac ledges, hence all the debris. Another ice pick has been broken too, a twenty-five-per-cent failure rate … so far.

Unconsciousness will only come with the passing of enough worry and shivering. The mountain stabs at any sleeping souls with cold fingers of spindrift. Its name is so well deserved: 'the Ogre'. It hates me and I hate it back.

I am the last to rise; there is no point in getting out of my bag early. I might as well doze and dream while my mates deal with the immediate hostilities above us. When they have done their work I shall follow, but I have an hour or two to wait.

The tips of all my fingers have swelled up with lymph-filled blisters twice the size of my fingertips. I now have hands like a gecko lizard. I am comforted by the fact that all of my fingers hurt – the blisters are numb but everything else is painful. I know they will get better in time, but only if I don't do too much more damage.

I can see that Howard is at the sharp end this morning, toiling up a vertical corner with a bulge of ice at the top. Pack off, legs spread in a wide bridge, he is in full battle-mode, with scant protection. Then there is one last moment of total commitment, one more leg-shaking stretch and he brings the pick of his axe to bear on the ice slope above with a satisfying 'snick'. He wriggles over the bulge with a last scratch of his crampons on the ice-glazed rock and disappears from view. It looks like the last pitch of the Ramp has been climbed.

Victor is waiting with me.

'Did you see Howard's lead?'

'Fine effort.' I manage a smile. Victor is checking me out, I can tell. Am I OK or doing what exposure victims do when they first start to drift away into apathy?

Howard has been the snake charmer this morning. His bold lead has galvanised us, the spectators, and fit or not we must slither after him. My turn comes, last again. Smiler is above me, 'helpfully' telling me how hard it is.

When I follow, I let him pull on my rope as hard as he wants. For me any semblance of climbing style is cast away, I just want to be up and gone, preferably without taking my gloves off. I arrive on the ice slope on my knees and toil upwards just in time to see Stevie attacking the next obstacle: the Brittle Crack.

There are the remnants of old fixed rope in several places. Who leaves all this rope? What a mess. Today I pull on it without regret and dare to believe that if we all work hard we might escape to the summit, if not today then tomorrow.

The sun is long awake but it is still bitterly cold. The temperature is actually painful. Stevie must be discovering some hurt in his fingers too: he has his mittens off. I start to pay more attention – he is on a nasty little steep section, rock that would be so easy in summer but is not today in the cold. He heaves up and reaches for a hold above his head. He grasps it and … the rock breaks off in his hand. There is a yelp and he falls fifteen feet. Hell!

Luckily Victor stops the rope very quickly and the last running belay holds. All of the adrenaline glands of the group are connected to Stevie, as if by telepathy. My heart is in my mouth, a little fall like that would be bad enough on Ben Nevis, but up here the consequences of an incapacitating injury to one of us could undo us all. The Eiger has killed many teams in this way – 'sniper'-style – injuring one of a group and then claiming the rest as victims in the circumstances that followed.

Of the six of us Stevie seems the least troubled, apart from a spectacular outpouring of profanities. He gathers himself into an angry ball of muscle and ignores Victor's offer of a rest. I have seen him in this bull-terrier mode before. Falling does not seem to scare him, it just makes him mad. It is not his fault of course, the Brittle Crack is aptly named. The shattered rock is unreliable and any one of us could have pulled that bit of rock away. But Stevie won't be thinking like that. He will be embarrassed that he fell while leading a critical pitch on the most famous north wall in the Alps.

He climbs up to his high point and finishes the pitch. There is a collective sigh of relief. Smiler as always is the first to utter a word of congratulation:

'Greaaaaaat Steeevoy maaate!'

Victor and Stevie lead across the Traverse of the Gods and into the White Spider, by which time Victor has broken the tip from his Simond hammer. We now have only seven undamaged axes between six climbers. I can hear them shouting about it even though I cannot see them.

I am the last to heave myself carefully up the Brittle Crack and I join Smiler at the start of the traverse. What a place! I had seen pictures but they have not prepared me for reality: a narrow and sloping band of ice-covered rock that well deserves its dramatic name. The airiness and exposure is breathtaking. It is the only thread of terrain that is less than vertical here; the only climbable path to the final key to the Eiger's north face – the White Spider. It is like climbing sideways across the roof of a steeply tiled house covered in ice and snow. And the tiles are loose. It is not so much difficult as alarming, the consequences of a fall for the leader or the second are equally awful – the ground below is undercut and you may survive the fall only to perish hanging in the void, unable to climb back up. If that were not enough to focus your anxiety, the protection is terrible. A few old battered pitons litter the pitch, none of which inspire any confidence.

I am delighted when Smiler is all the way across and doubly delighted when I am too, but on the last few moves I break the pick of my Charlet Moser ice hammer. Just as with all the others, I wrench up on the shaft to remove it from the ice and, with a quiet 'clink', the last and most important part of the pick breaks off. Smiler and I are only feet apart and he sees and hears it too. For the first time we stare at each other and neither of us can find anything helpful to say. These broken tools may be our undoing. He is not smiling now.

I turn the corner into the White Spider. I am finally here. After all the books I have read and the pictures I have studied, I stand humbled at the sight of this infamous place. Today the ice is grey and shiny, polished like steel by the swish of spindrift. The ice-filled cracks that form the legs of the spider are plain to see. Only one of them holds the key to the summit and, as always on the Eiger, the most obvious choice is correct: it is the crack system directly above me, just a few pitches away.

Stevie and Victor are a rope length above me chopping a ledge on which to spend the night. Opposite me, Howard and Bill are doing the same. Smiler and I climb over to help them and, between us, we chop out a big ledge.

We dive into our bivouac equipment to avoid the biting cold and begin to mumble over our plans. We have only five useable ice tools left between six climbers and we need two each. I do not mention them, but everybody else talks of my blistered fingers and frostbite. Victor reports that Stevie is hypo-thermic and deteriorating no matter what he does to help him. The weather is clear but now so bitterly cold that, despite our superb clothing, we are all becoming weaker and weaker. We have also run out of food after more than a week of climbing on the Ogre.

We turn in for the night without forming a plan. One option is to wait for rescue. I hate the idea of it but the consequences of a storm hitting now would be fatal for some, if not all, of us. We can hardly climb properly as it is. Whoever is leading will need two good axes and that leaves only three other good tools to be shared by five climbers, one of whom (Stevie) is in a serious condition.

If any of us had any doubts about accepting a rescue, the events of the night put the issue to rest. The Ogre has no mercy and we are constantly pelted with spindrift and snowslides that force their way behind our backs, inching us slowly towards the edge of our ledge. The mountain is trying to prise the human parasites from its flanks using knives of snow, just as my father taught me to prise shellfish from the shoreline rocks with a penknife when I was a boy.

We wriggle in our bivvy sacks to try to displace the snow, but every hour we must unzip and dig away at it and in the process we inevitably let yet more cold and damp into our clothing. In the few snatched moments of sleep I imagine I am with the ghosts of Karl and Max again:

'Was it like this for you?'

'Ja, it was like this. We are sleeping with you now.'

'No, not yet, my friends, I have loved ones.'

'As do we.'

'I will awaken!'

'We will see, boy, we will see … '

Dawn brings little relief. There is no more warmth or any less spindrift, but the daylight lifts my spirits a little. The weather is still stable and we are in clear view of the many telescopes at Kleine Scheidegg. Hundreds of tourists will have been watching our every move every day now for a week. We will no doubt have been the subject of ghoulish debate over dinner every night. Amongst the watchers will be mountain guides and the Swiss mountain rescue. Our pathetically slow speed will have sent a clear message that we are struggling. The fact that we do not get out of bed this morning will send a signal that something is actually very wrong.

Smiler rouses me from an uncomfortable sleep in the mid-morning:

'Si, I can see a helicopter.'

I open my eyes and scan the abyss below me, searching for what he has seen. I have to follow his gaze before I can locate the tiny red aircraft just above the railway station at Kleine Scheidegg. I can just hear the whack of the advancing blades as it slowly ascends through the still, cold morning air. The helicopter is a flying Swiss army knife, a red body with a white cross. It is heading slowly but surely for our position.

Bill and Howard are out of their bivouac bags and standing on the ledge packing equipment – they had been anticipating this event. I scurry to get ready too. It is cold out of my sleeping bag but I am fully dressed already, so all I have to do is tighten my bootlaces and put on my crampons.

The helicopter is level with us now and the noise is deafening. It is hovering just 150 feet in front of us.

Stevie arrives on our ledge, lowered by Victor from above. He is indeed in a bad way, enfeebled by the cold, but able to talk. Hypothermia has a grip on him.

A person has climbed out of the cabin and on to the skids. It is a lightly equipped climber attached to the winch that extends from one side of the aircraft. He leans back to let the cable take the strain, steps off the skid and slowly descends on the wire. With incredible precision he is transported to our ice ledge until he is so close that Bill can stretch an extended hand to his and pull him in. His crampons bite and he immediately turns to signal to the winch man for slack in the cable before disengaging it and allowing the metal wire to snake away over the abyss in the down draft of the rotor.

The aircraft retreats perhaps 300 feet from the face and maintains an altitude level with our position. It seems rehearsed – clearly it is dangerous to hover too close to the Eiger.

As Stevie is in poor shape he will be the first to be lifted off. Our friend checks out Stevie's harness to satisfy himself that it is suitable and waves to the pilot with well-practised hand signals. The message is obvious: 'Come and get this one.'

Smiler talks to Stevie all the while. 'Stevie mate, you'll be OK. We'll all be in the pub in an hour.'

Our friend catches the hook with an outstretched hand and the winch man runs out a little slack so that any small movements by the helicopter will not put any tension on the cable. Stevie is clipped into a snap link and his hands obediently grip a circular handle. Our friend makes a signal with his hand to the pilot and, simultaneously, the slack in the cable is taken in while he unclips Stevie from the belay anchor on our ledge. The aircraft alone has him now.

My expectation is that Stevie will be gently winched upwards until he can board the aircraft, but I am wrong. As soon as Stevie's feet leave the ledge the aircraft simply banks away from the face and flies out above the valley with its human cargo dangling like bait. When the aircraft is clear of any risk from avalanche or downdraft from the face, it begins a stationary hover, level with our position but far enough away that Stevie will be looking straight down at a drop of at least 7,000 feet of clear air below him. All of us stare, first at Stevie's flight and then at each other.

'Fookin 'ell – that must have been exciting!'

Smiler and I lock eyes and we both smile for the first time in days.

Stevie is hoisted into the cabin and the helicopter swings back for the next victim, which, it appears, will be me, reluctantly. I would have liked a little more time to compose myself and so, as Victor has just descended to our ledge, I suggest that he might like to join Stevie first. He is having none of it and I am outvoted four to one. I shall be next to 'fly'.

The cable is again expertly flown into the grasp of our friend who attaches it to me and deftly releases me from my own anchor. Just a moment passes before the tension in the cable is taken in and my harness tightens around my groin and waist. My feet leave the ledge and the wave is given to the aircraft which means 'the parcel is yours'. The rotor is inclined and the helicopter banks away, launching me into space.

Like a pendulum I swing away from the White Spider. I glimpse Smiler waving at me as I rotate on the end of the cable, gripping the handle with all my strength. Seven or eight thousand feet below me, the ski slopes of Kleine Scheidegg are spinning. I am winched into the helicopter while we fly away.

We descend very quickly and I have little time to prepare before the skis touch down on the snow. The engine is kept running and the door thrown open.

Two men approach the helicopter in a crouching walk below the spinning rotor and beckon us out of the aircraft while signalling to keep our heads low. I may be cold but I am not stupid. Never mind, they mean well.

Barely have we walked away before the engine spools up into a frenzied scream and the helicopter lifts off and heads back to the White Spider to collect the next pair of benighted Brits. An official of some kind tries to get us to follow him but Stevie and I ignore him for a minute as we watch the tiny red bird become a speck against the face.

'Excuse please, please follow me.'

I cannot react at first because we are surrounded by hundreds of people, who take my full attention. All have given up skiing or eating or drinking to come and gawk at us. Some point and exchange whispered conversation; some just stare. I accidentally make eye contact with a family and they all wave at me like idiots. Somebody shouts a question in what sounds like German, and Stevie, weak as he is, snarls in anger at the intrusion. The question is not repeated.

'Please, follow me.'

'Sorry, where are we going?'

'Just to this building, it is warm. Don't worry, your friends will follow us.'

Numbly, Stevie and I trudge after the friendly rescue team member and the crowd parts to let us pass.

It is a little concrete building with shuttered windows and a wooden door. Inside they have prepared for us, not knowing what ailments we might be suffering. There is a stretcher on the floor and a table where an injured person might be examined. There is a hot stove and the sudden warmth of the room makes me dizzy.

A kindly but officious face arrives in front of me.

'Hello, I am a doctor, are you injured? Why don't you sit down?'

I do so and am interrogated in what is obviously a well-structured triage plan. These guys have trained for this. They will soon have six potential patients and they want to know what to expect and who to give priority to.

I explain that Stevie has hypothermia, but they have already figured that out for themselves, slowly giving him hot liquids while checking his temperature and the appearance of his hands. They are very attentive and well organised. One of the team is writing on a form.

'Name, age, nation of birth?'

The kindly face speaks to me again:

'Are you injured?'

I think for a few long moments. I have no money to be treated in Switzerland;

that will have to wait until we get home. I almost want to lie and tell him that I am fine but if I do that then he may think we all just gave up and that will not do either. I nod and open the palms of my still-gloved hands.

'My fingers ... '

This is what he wanted to hear; the diagnosis has direction now. My gloves are gently removed, exposing severely swollen and blistered fingers. Beyond the last knuckle of each finger each digit has swollen almost to the size of a golf ball. The doctor stares intently at each finger in turn, pressing and squeezing.

'Do you feel zis?'

'It hurts.'

'You are lucky, my friend, you will recover in time.'

The roar of the helicopter landing outside heralds the arrival of the next pair of sorry Brits. I feel I have to make an apology:

'More than half of our axes broke in the cold, you know?'

I am staring into his eyes to see if he believes me. I receive a polite smile.

'Zis must have been very inconvenient.'

14
UNFINISHED BUSINESS

We leave the Bernese Oberland the next day. Stevie is physically better but his mood is darker. Smiler is philosophical: 'We all got down in one piece after all.' Victor analyses where we went wrong, but nobody listens.

Our anger at failure was obvious. We had plenty of excuses if we wanted to look for them but none of us really cared to do so. We had been beaten. Worse still, we had been *helped*. And I hate that.

To make matters worse our Eiger episode was front-page news in the UK. I discovered this when I called Judi from a payphone in Interlaken. She told me that we had made the cover of the *Daily Mail* and that the phone at my father's home had been ringing all day with reporters chasing the story. It seems that our names and addresses, given to the Swiss, were not so confidential after all.

If the outward journey across Europe had been a party, the drive home was the opposite. It felt long and tiresome as we pressed on through the night. Bill dropped Stevie and Victor in London in the late afternoon and then headed west to Kingston, to my father's home, where I would leave the diminishing group before they headed north to Wales.

I navigated through west London and when we pulled up at my father's house I invited all the lads in for a drink. My dad, or Mac as I always called him, would be pleased to meet them all and, when I had called from Dover, Marianne, my stepmother, told me that she would have some food ready.

When Mac opens the door I get the usual 'Hi son' and the big hug, but immediately I can tell something is up. Mac is a meticulous man but he is overdressed for an evening at home. As I cross the threshold I realise that there is a film crew in the lounge and they are recording my homecoming. It seems we have not escaped the ghouls at all and they have anticipated our every move.

◀ Like so many young climbers before me, it is my turn to pose; a picture of confidence while the Ogre looks on.

Mac introduces me to the BBC News television producer who very politely asks if I will consent to be interviewed for the national news.

I really wanted to say no but I sense that Mac would be upset if I did. The family are all here: Mac, Marianne, my teenage sister Annette and my young brother Nic. Having a TV crew in the house is evidently exciting and I have little doubt that Mac has been proudly talking about my exploits while they have been waiting to spring this ambush. Mac means well; he would not understand if we told the TV folk to go away.

Smiler, Bill and Howard have bundled in behind me and are bewildered until Marianne breaks the spell and welcomes them into the lounge. Food and drinks have all been laid on and I can tell that the crew have been enjoying the hospitality for a while.

I sit on the end of the sofa and Smiler sits beside me, then Howard and finally Bill. It occurs to me that this was how we were sitting together on our ice-ledge bivouac in the White Spider. I am not the only one to think of it and it is Bill who speaks first:

'This ledge is a sight more bloody comfortable than the last one we sat on together!'

The TV producer tells me what will happen: I should look at him, not the camera and just answer his questions. Mac is watching me intently and I am acutely self-conscious. Nic and Annette are grinning at me from the kitchen doorway making faces.

There is a look between the producer and the cameraman, who nods in return. The sound engineer produces a big fluffy microphone and points it at me. Everyone is quiet. My interrogator looks down at his notes briefly and then asks his first question:

'So, Simon, you are the leader of this expedition?'

The question is a shock. He does not understand so I have to set him straight.

'No, there is no leader here. We are just four friends that like to climb together.'

He was not expecting that and is flummoxed for a moment. He makes a gesture to the cameraman and recording stops, after which we have a discussion about alpine climbing and he has to rethink all his questions.

We are then all invited to talk individually in turn and it is Smiler who is the star of the show. The rest of us are too reserved, while he is animated with his big smile and friendly West Midlands drawl. A string of questions are fielded: how did it feel to get stuck on the face? How cold was it? Did we think we might die? What went wrong? This really gets Smiler going:

'Wull, we couldn't gaw up and we couldn't gaw down!'

This was the stuff the TV producer was looking for – strong, simple statements.

I go down to the van to see them off. I stare down the road watching the Transit slowly disappear into the traffic. What a sad end to a trip that had been so full of grand ambition: stuck in a weeknight traffic jam in the outer suburbs of London.

Mac and I drink a couple of bottles of wine while I give him a day-by-day account of what happened on the climb. Everybody wants to look at my blistered hands; Nic prods one of my grotesque fingers to see if it hurts. Only when I have eaten and drunk all I can am I allowed to go to bed.

I would have been happy to stay in bed all morning but I am not allowed to do so because the *Daily Mail* is craving an interview with me – I am wanted on the phone. At first I am not interested but Marianne points out that if I don't talk to them they will write whatever they want anyway, so I might as well have my say. I take the call and agree to go into Fleet Street in London, home of the British print press, and meet a reporter.

On the train to Waterloo I find myself almost looking forward to the interview. It was this sort of caper that made Chris Bonington famous. I recall that in 1962 he was involved in the Eiger rescue of Brian Nally, and then returned *the same summer* to make the first British ascent of the north face with Ian Clough. The same summer. He got straight back on it! I have been in a dream since coming down from the face, but these thoughts of Bonington awaken me. I know exactly what I want to do: find a way to get back to Switzerland this winter and finally climb the north face of the Eiger. My fingers are already on the mend. The major obstacle will be finding the money and a partner who is available.

The interview is much less formal than I expected and the editor of the *Daily Mail* himself does most of the talking. The reporter asks if I have any photographs and I tell him I do, but that none of them are developed. He offers to process the film for me and the thought of being able to get my pictures developed today, for free, is a huge boost.

After lunch and several beers in an old pub in Fleet Street I am taken back to the office to look at what my camera has captured. There is quite a crowd gathered around the dark room: this is obviously interesting for the reporters and I cannot help being proud that they are so curious, despite the fact that they seem more interested in pictures of our faces than in the spectacular climbing shots that I find so exciting.

I am taken into the editor's office.

'Now, Simon, we like your pictures. Would you consent to allowing us to use some of them on an exclusive basis? We will of course pay you the current rate for any we publish.'

Pay me? My mind is racing. I had never made a penny from climbing and the cost had always been covered by months of work and saving. Now a newspaper is offering me money. I have the presence of mind not to agree immediately, but when he offers me £100 *each* for three of his favourite shots my face must have given the game away. I sign an agreement and I am assured that the cheque will be ready the next day.

'May I use one of your phones?' I ask.

I make a call to the head of security to see if he has any work for me at the London boat show, which I know is coming up. The boat show is a paradise for thieves and a large security team is required to prevent mass theft. I would make good money working nights because the build-up, show and breakdown collectively last at least six weeks. Working at night I could still get a little sleep and I could train and prepare for the Eiger every other day. My fingers should be healed by then too. I could be back on the Eiger in March.

I am in the city so decide to walk to the Alpine Sports store in High Holborn where no doubt I'll find some old climbing friends. I am greeted with a mix of sarcasm and good humour. *Nearly* climbing the Eiger in winter will not be quite enough to avoid some jibes at my expense and I know that. None of it will carry any spite and I know that equally well.

I am deep in conversation with Dick Turnbull, the manager, when we are interrupted by the very spirit of Yorkshire: Chris Hoyland. Bounding down the steps into the climbing basement, he arrives like a comedian bursting on to a stage of his own creation. An extrovert, Chris loves a crowd as much as he loves women and beer. Like most people in the London climbing scene, I knew Chris but not well and we had never climbed together. He is a natural athlete; he had tried out for the Yorkshire Colts and had become one of the regulars amongst the hardcore of the London climbers. Of all of us, he took climbing the least seriously.

My hands are the subject of some fascination. The blisters have started to peel away, taking with them all the calloused skin. The entire epidermis is missing, revealing the beginning of the dermis below, red and raw. All of my fingertips are like this, although for some reason my thumbs are OK. I am obliged to explain how the injury happened one more time for him.

I have never had a serious conversation with Chris but he is full of questions about the Eiger. He asks me about the Hinterstoisser Traverse and my answer just leads to another question about the Swallow's Nest and then the Ice Hose.

He makes me take him up the climb in words, until he has an epiphany and asks Dick to produce a copy of the climber's guide to the Bernese Oberland. We are in London's premier climbing shop after all – we might as well make use of the library.

The book is produced and now I can entertain Chris with the picture and route description for support. During the conversation I mention that I am going to work at the boat show and Chris immediately asks if I can help get him a job there too as he is at a loose end.

A few days later we are both working a night shift in security.

Built in 1937, Earls Court is a huge cavernous building and the boat show was the biggest exhibition of the year, filling every corner of every hall. This would be the second show I had worked on and I knew the place like the back of my hand. I had explored the caves in the basement and wondered at the pre-war technology that created the Olympic swimming pool, now a dry dock that could be flooded in the middle of the main hall. For the show, it has been theatrically themed as a harbour, and a building with a viewing deck has been constructed overlooking the moorings as if it were the harbour master's office. Below is an apron stage, themed after the fashion of a naval dockside in Portsmouth.

The Royal Navy are much in evidence this year; they have created the centre attraction of the entire show. Towering over the harbour is the mast of a tall ship, with all of its stays and rigging, so tall that the highest part of the mast – a single spike of timber with a platform for only one man – nearly touches the cavernous roof. The highlight of each day is when dozens of Royal Navy Cadet sailors climb this mast to the beat of a military band, clambering out on to the spars high above the audience, who sit with their faces craned upward to take in this perilous demonstration of discipline at height.

The finale of the display is performed by a sole sailor, the 'button boy'. When the rigging is fully populated and the crew stand aloft, stiffly saluting, the last of them, a young, fit-looking West Indian lad, climbs the slimmest and highest part of the mast and stands proudly atop the button. The music stops and a drum roll begins. We do not have to wait long. There is a heavy braided rope attached to the ceiling above and slightly behind the button boy and it has been tensioned to the edge of the dock below, pulled tight at about forty-five degrees to the mast, a metaphor for the forestay of a large sailing ship.

The sailor reaches up and grasps the rope with both hands and then pulls up and steps off the mast, rotating his lower body upwards and wrapping both legs around the rope. There is a gasp from the crowd; he is more than high enough that a fall would result in certain death. The drum roll stops and a whistle is blown.

Hand over hand the button boy descends the rope until he can drop down on to the dock where he stands at attention and salutes the crowd, to thunderous applause.

Chris turns to me; I know exactly what he is thinking. When everybody has gone home and it is dark we will have to climb up the mast and try that stunt for ourselves.

We have access to the entire building, but Chris and I are assigned to the main marina part of the exhibition. I know full well that the other members of the team are unlikely to be patrolling late at night, so we will not be observed. At about midnight, when all is quiet, Chris and I climb the mast together. For two able climbers it is a simple job, but I find myself taking a good look at the rigging as I pull on it. When we reach the highest spar we traverse out horizontally, just to see how it feels – it feels very exposed. Climbing on a steep cliff is one thing, but the rigging is quite another because it is a man-made contrivance. I am quite impressed with the young sailor's display now.

'Well then, youth, just one more to do,' says Chris, and he climbs up to the button and salutes nobody, just for fun. He reaches up, grasps the rope and swings his legs up and around it. The rope sags dramatically and he is involuntarily swung down several metres until the slack is taken up. It gives us both a scare and there's some colourful language from Chris. They must slacken the tension in the rope at the end of the day for some reason. He cannot get back to the button so he sets off down the rope hand over hand until he is low enough to let go and drop on to the dock. He is laughing – it's my turn and, as he has done it, I have no choice but to follow.

Standing on the button is airy. There is nothing between me and the ground except for a web of ropes and wires. Chris is cackling up at me:

'Go on or you're a big girl's blouse!'

I grasp the rope hard enough that it makes my not-yet-fully-healed fingers hurt. As soon as I have done so there is no going back as the sag in the rope pulls me away from the mast. I pull up and lock my legs around the rope and start down immediately because just hanging there is sapping.

As soon as I start moving all fear is gone. It is spectacular but easy, like solo-climbing a steep rock route you know well. Chris is still laughing when I touch down.

In some way this silly stunt was a milestone in our relationship. We had never been on a real climb together but we had shown each other some boldness. Over the coming days we talked about climbing a lot and I explained that I wanted to go back to the Eiger before the winter was over.

He told me that he wanted to come too.

The normal apprenticeship for climbing the Eiger in summer was to spend a few winters in Scotland and then many seasons climbing in the Alps. I know that Chris has done almost none of that and has very little ice-climbing experience, perhaps one Alp or two. To attempt your first serious alpine climb on the Eiger in winter would be regarded as lunacy by the climbing establishment.

Chris has no such doubts and his self-confidence is so compelling that I agree. We talk about the climb in detail. I know the way up the face intimately, as far as the White Spider anyway, and I have led almost every pitch. When I ask myself which pitches I am most worried about I realise that Chris will be a good choice for them. I am dreading the need to take my gloves off because of the risk of more serious damage to my fingers.

Chris can do the nasty pitch in the Ramp, the Brittle Crack, and the hard bit at the beginning of the exit cracks and anything else that requires mitts off. I am happy to lead all of the rest. From what I have heard he is a great intuitive climber and his talent on rock will be well suited to the bits I would prefer not to place my hands on.

And there it is: our ludicrously simple plan.

15
THE NATURAL

Stevie and Victor are also heading out for a rematch with the mountain and are a day or so ahead of us. Not that we think of it as a race or a competition; I am glad to know that they will be around. The Eiger north face has been climbed in winter before, in 1975 by Joe Tasker and Dick Renshaw, who made the first British winter ascent. There is no national pride at stake now, just my own.

Chris and I arrive at Interlaken in the morning. We take the Wengernalp mountain railway from Lauterbrunnen to Kleine Scheidegg, taking all of our equipment with us. With every grinding turn of the railway the higher peaks begin to reveal themselves. Chris has his nose pressed to the window, oblivious to the fact that I am watching him intently, searching for any hint of his mood.

At Kleine Scheidegg we jog up to the hotel with our heavy packs. There is only one thing to do. We must have a beer on the terrace and look through the telescopes at the Eiger, just like the tourists do. Only *our* examination of the face will be in great detail – every part of the route must be scrutinised. We assume control of two telescopes that are mounted a few metres apart so we can talk and we both press a few Swiss francs into the greedy machines – nothing is free in Switzerland.

There is an impatient crowd behind us but nobody dares to interrupt our running commentary. Pitch by pitch I direct the aim of his telescope up the face, describing the route. From time to time he will stop me and ask a question.

'So the Flat Iron is that triangular lump just below a ledge?'

'Yes, correct, and the third ice field is on the left, a short traverse into the bottom of the Ramp.'

Nothing about Chris's demeanour reveals he has any concern, just intense interest.

After we have rehearsed the climb through the Zeiss lenses twice he announces that he is content to sit in the sun and drink beer while staring up at the face. This pastime works for me; I can stare at the face for hours. Chris, however, has found another distraction. Some of the waitresses are young and attractive American girls and despite the yawning gulf between his Yorkshire version of the English language and the soft Californian drawl of the target of his attention, he manages to communicate his intentions very well.

That evening I make a solitary bivouac in the electrical building I found earlier in the winter. Hoyland has found somewhere warmer to spend the night.

The next morning we study the face over a late breakfast. The conditions look stable. When the sun comes out there is no sign of dangerous shedding; the snow that is on the mountain looks happy to remain where it is. The weather forecast is good so we plan to go up the following day.

We make pigs of ourselves on cheese fondue at a little chalet café. The poor girl running the place is rushed off her feet fetching ever more bread and cheese. We decide that we will get an early night, both of us packed and ready in the bivouac, which we will make by the railway. We plan to set out at five in the morning, climbing under our head torches.

I cannot wait to go. I wake at midnight, at 1 and at 2 a.m. I have always been like this; I have no need of an alarm clock if I have an appointment with a mountain. Chris on the other hand is dead to the world and I wonder at him. This, the most notorious climb in the Alps, in winter, will be his first proper ice climb and yet he can sleep while I cannot.

In the end I can stand it no more and the noise of my tea-making finally wakes him. I pass him a mug of hot, sweet tea.

We pass the early hours in silence as we flog up the initial snow slopes, climbing unroped in personal clouds of our own expired breath. We have not gone far when we discover the tracks of a climbing team that has passed this way recently, only a day before us at most. How can we have missed them? The footprints are so recent that the spindrift has only partially filled them and the broken crust of the snow is still sharp from their boot prints. I am sure it must be Stevie and Victor.

We make rapid progress, scratching with our crampons as we pass over the rocky steps that interrupt the snow and ice, passing the Shattered Pillar, following all the while the footsteps of our unseen friends.

We rope up below the Difficult Crack and Chris leads the first pitch, one that I do not want. I have done it three times before and want to avoid taking off my gloves today.

Up he goes, quickly and with a running commentary to keep me entertained. Solid and fast, I am impressed with the lack of fuss. The Difficult Crack in summer is worthy of tying on a rope and, in truth, is really just the 'Awkward Crack'. But this winter morning in the pale frozen dawn, there is verglas on the rocks and any less-than-vertical surface is loaded with snow.

I arrange the climbing above the Difficult Crack so that I lead all of it, including the Hinterstoisser Traverse. It is quicker this way: I know the route intimately. I spot a few 'holes' in Chris's ice- and mixed-climbing technique and offer tips which are immediately adopted. Just a rope length further he looks like a natural.

Crossing the Hinterstoisser is inspiring as always. It is not long in distance but spans five decades of torrid climbing lore and the heritage is not lost on Chris. He is on an Alpine-climbing history tour. At the steepest point he stops and leans out so he can take a good look into the void below – the void that claimed the life of Toni Kurz and his friends.

We arrive at the Swallow's Nest before noon. We are feeling good and there is more than enough daylight to continue, but I call time. This is actually the beginning of my ascent plan – Camp One. From this point it is easy to descend; we can still run away if the weather proves unhelpful, but after another day of climbing our options will become limited. We will spend the night on the best bivouac ledge in the Alps and attack the ice fields in the morning.

The Swallow's Nest has recently been slept in and made ready for us. We are two Alpine cuckoos. It must have been choked with ice and wind-blown snow, but when we arrive we find that our two unseen road sweepers have chopped out a bedroom for us. Chris approves of this. The fact that Victor and Stevie might have done the manual labour providing us with a comfy ledge amuses him greatly.

We while away the remains of the afternoon looking and listening to the skiers having fun below us, such is the contact we have with them in the still mountain air. I do not doubt that there are a hundred pairs of eyes trained on us; we are the added entertainment, the Kleine Scheidegg sideshow. I couldn't care less. I am warm and comfortable as I go through my lists and plans and when I turn to talk to Chris I am too late: he is fast asleep.

The dawn is very cold. In the tiny pool of light from my head torch I set out up the first ice field for the third time. An endless stream of Yorkshire humour helps pass the task of climbing the Ice Hose and the second ice field. As I have been here before, there are no surprises, just the feeling of a closing grip that the Eiger seems to exert as you progress upward. If Chris feels any pressure, he does not mention it.

Obviously my plan is to go a great deal faster than on my last attempt, but this hinges around what I consider to be the best bivouacs. I want this ascent to be as organised and as comfortable as possible. We will use prior knowledge and cunning to blunt the monster's defences. Night one will be spent at the Swallow's Nest, night two at Death Bivouac. We will be able to sleep well and cook easily on these two comfortable and safe ledges. On day three we will go for it. I am not at all sure that we can get to the summit in a day, but we will try hard.

The rest of the day passes easily. We pick and kick our way across the second ice field uneventfully. In winter the face is frozen solid and the summer-afternoon volleys of deadly stone fall are absent. I decide to lead all day because I think this will be the fastest way.

This part of the climb, 1,800 feet of traversing with only slight ascent, would be a drudge, were it not for the situation. While I belay Chris I have time to daydream, and my dreams are all glimpses of history. This is the point from which Kurz, Hinterstoisser, Rainer and Angerer retreated. Willy Angerer, it is supposed, had already sustained a head injury from a falling rock. This is of course conjecture, because none of them survived to tell the tale. Climbing back across the second ice field in winter is not something I would look forward to. To do so in summer would be more dangerous still because of the stone fall.

All the while I have that feeling of growing commitment but the weather is fine and the climb is going to plan. With every rope length, Chris gets quicker. We will reach Death Bivouac well ahead of schedule.

Stevie and Victor have done a fine job of excavating the bivouac. As I heave myself up to the ledge I am greeted by the sight of a beautifully cut sleeping area for two. There is even a little alcove cut into the ice where the stove can be placed out of the wind. Perfect. Thanks, lads!

Once Chris and I feel comfortable and warm in our bivouac bags we pass the dusk drinking tea and chatting. Thoughts of Karl and Max do not taunt me this time. So far the climb has gone exactly to plan. Chris knows that tomorrow will be a test. We have climbed a long way but the hard yards are in front of us. We have eaten and rested well at the end of each day. Our personal equipment is dry and we are just warm enough that sleep comes easily.

It is the wind that wakes me. The weather has changed; the unwelcome breeze is full of spindrift and this is worrying. We are relatively sheltered where we are, but conditions will be far worse out on the face. We have a discussion. Actually, it is more like me explaining to Chris that I have decided that we will press on with all possible speed despite the drifting snow. Nothing of what I say to him is questioned and we set off in a grim mood across the third ice field

Chris follows me across the expanse of the second ice field.

with little slides of snow all around us. None of them are heavy enough to wipe us from the ice but they are unsettling and unpredictable.

Surprisingly, when we are a pitch into the Ramp the clouds seem to part and blue skies return. Maybe we will be in luck after all. Chris takes the lead on the pitch where I had frozen my fingertips earlier in the winter and does a great job, fast and confident.

My happiness over Chris's fine lead vanishes under a torrent of spindrift that descends upon me as I lead a pitch just 300 feet higher. We are deep within the crevice of the Ramp, so we have a limited view of the sky, which has turned grey again. Snow begins to fall and it seems that much of it is being funnelled on to our heads. At first it is merely annoying, inconvenient, but it soon becomes stronger – and dangerous. The buffeting is heavy enough to sweep us from our tenuous purchase on the mountain. The tenuous pick of an axe or the grip of a cold hand will be little defence.

I had been optimistic of a quick result today but it seems the monster has other ideas. I bring Chris up to the same ledge that I had sat upon while Howard Lancashire had led over the difficult bulge. Chris has to duck several times as snowslides descend upon him. Memories of Jack on the north face of Mount Huntington come back to haunt me.

In these conditions the bulge pitch is horrible. Pulses of snow regularly burst out of the little ice field above the lip, concentrated by the narrowing gap into deadly torrents that would sweep a climber away like an insect. We have no choice but to wait until the storm and debris abates. This is not a good situation. We can bivouac here, but it will be cold and uncomfortable. It will be a struggle to keep the drifting snow out of our sleeping bags and cooking will be impossible.

Piece by piece the ledge is improved. In the process I unearth some red fabric frozen into the ice. Hell, it is an abandoned sleeping bag! Some other poor devil has been forced to bivouac in this terrible spot, which is bad enough, but there must have been so much more to his situation than that: no functioning climber would leave his survival equipment behind unless he had been rescued, or had perished.

If we are both thinking the same thoughts we do not voice them. We have both read the books – sixty ghosts are owned by this mountain. Was the owner of the red sleeping bag the sixty-first victim?

We manage to squeeze into a little niche that is just far enough out of the fall line of the little snow avalanches that we are not struck by them directly. However, as they pass, the clouds of spindrift try to get into our equipment and we have to keep our Gore-Tex bivvy bags zipped up tight. I would love to make a hot drink but it is out of the question. We pass the night shifting the weight from one arse cheek to the other. Each time we shuffle we invariably wake the other; not that we are ever properly asleep.

I can tell that dawn has come from the dull green glow I can see through the fabric of my bivvy bag. I open the zipper just enough to see what the mountain has in mind for us today. The sky is broken with five-eighths' cloud cover, it is still windy, and the clouds are steadily moving beyond the vertical horizons of our little nest. Still the scene is an improvement; maybe the little storm was just a passing front. Because of where the Eiger sits, on the edge of the Alps, it is completely exposed to the north-west and is the first major terrain to be hit by incoming weather.

We will wait a few hours to see if the drifting snow eases. The crux of the climb is just above us and if we can get past that we should be in better shape for going up, not down. We cannot even think of that.

The morning does improve. The wind drops and the spindrift becomes manageable.

'Hey, Chris, let's go, it looks good enough.'

We pack very quickly because only our sleeping bags and bivvy bags need to be stuffed into our packs. We do not spend time trying to get the stove out to melt ice for tea; we want to be gone, thirsty or not. We can brew up later. The weather is improving but we have lost half the day already.

Chris leads an awkward short pitch and belays in the same spot that Bill Barker had used below the bulge that is the key to the Ramp. The cramped night has left me stiff and awkward but the upward movement soon loosens my joints. I climb up to Chris, my head lowered so that the wisps of drifting snow stay out of the hood of my parka.

I leave my pack with Chris at the belay, clipping a karabiner to one of the straps before taking it off and securing it to the anchors he has set up; I will take no risk of dropping anything on a climb. The lack of weight on my back will help me enormously on this difficult pitch and I will have more room to move.

I study the task that waits for me in the next forty metres. I can see how the Ramp has formed geologically and once again think back to geography teacher Hilda Sharp. She went out of her way to make physical geography interesting for me and gave a memorable lesson one afternoon about the formation of the Alps, fault tectonics and the Knapp folding of sedimentary rocks. For me it was a eureka moment. I already spent all of my holidays and as many of my weekends as I could in the mountains or down in wet limestone caves, immersed in geology.

Back in the present there can be no more prevarication. I will use the yellow rope for protection and leave the blue rope free so that I can haul my pack when I belay beyond the bulge.

The climbing is not difficult at first and I gain height quickly, clipping into a couple of aged pitons on the way. The next section is the key to the entire climb. The overhanging yellow rock on my right continues like a frozen wave, but the shattered black rock that I am forced to climb on steepens and closes from a steep gully into a vertical blockage. Pinched into a narrow 'V', a swell of ice has formed a bulge which is slightly overhanging for a metre or two.

I know full well that when I start my attack on this problem I will not be able to stop or reverse. I toy with the first move, stretching up a little to take a look at what is above, practising the footwork that will follow in my mind. I step back to the last good resting position and glance down. Chris is staring at me, a picture of total attention. There is no need to talk, everything about our situation is obvious. If we cannot pass this difficulty we are screwed. My protection is poor and if I fall I may rip the poor pitons from the rock and take a big plunge. I will hit the rock and ice below many times and be badly injured. If Chris cannot hold me because his anchors fail, we will both be killed.

By using small adjustments I regain my high point, trying to sneak up on the problem.

There can be no more procrastinating. I am on the brink. One more little move and I will be unable to reverse. It is time to see what I am made of. I have rehearsed the next three steps in my head and one by one I observe myself making each move in turn. I bridge out to the left and jam a cramponed boot into the fold on my right. My left foot steps up so that I can jab my front points into a tiny crease, the steel and limestone making a screeching noise as metal settles on rock. I stretch up and out, forced off balance by the bulge of ice, and hook the pick of my axe into the unseen ice slope above. The first blow makes a good noise. Snick! The placement sounds OK. I am totally committed now, off balance and only connected to the monster by a few millimetres of steel. It is time for the finale. I must trust the pick placement of the axe I cannot see and pull hard.

I do. Uncoiling like a spring I relinquish the frozen handhold I have been gripping with my right hand and fetch my ice hammer, which has been hanging on its tether, waiting to be called. I reach as high as I dare and swing awkwardly at the unseen ice above, not too close to my axe – the impact may shatter the ice and collapse the only purchase I have.

Snick.

I am spreadeagled on the bulge and my left leg, which has been taking most of my weight below the overhang, must now join the rest of my body above it. I can contrive no elegant way of doing this. I heave on my axes and scrabble with my left crampon, clawing at the slick rock for momentary traction, inch by inch until my body is hunched over my axes and I can finally lift my foot high enough to plant the front points into the toe of the little ice field. I take my weight on my feet again and pull my right axe from the ice and pick a new placement a metre higher. It is done.

Chris speaks for the first time in twenty minutes:

'Well done, youth!'

I want to belay soon and I can see that Stevie and Victor must have felt the same way as a step has been hacked in the ice just fifteen feet above me. A dozen swings of my axes and kicks with my front points later I step on to a comfortable foothold and can relax my calf muscles while I place two ice screws.

And ... breathe.

I have been planning the rest of the climb in my head. I had decided that I would ask Chris to lead the Brittle Crack and the first pitch of the exit cracks, as both require taking gloves off. My strategy is totally selfish, but, in my own mind, totally sound.

I warn Chris again about the loose rock on the Brittle Crack just as he sets off. I have the impression that I have annoyed him and he does not reply. He tests the holds. One meets with his disapproval. He deftly pulls a brick-sized piece of loose rock from the crack and tosses it over his shoulder. The debris bounces once on the ice below and launches out into the void, accelerating like a missile with sickening speed. I imagine it arriving like a meteorite at the base of the face with devastating impact.

With the offending item disposed of Chris finishes the crack and belays at the start of the Traverse of the Gods. He evidently has the same feeling all climbers do at this point. The climb is not steep there but the drops below overlap in such a way that one is awed by the situation.

'Bloody hell!'

He takes in the ropes, staring out at the face below.

We have not climbed far today but are tired, hungry and dehydrated. In this state, even more care must be taken than usual on the thin veneer of ice and snow that overlays shattered and unreliable rock. I am relieved when we are both across safely. I am even more relieved to see the big ice ledge in the White Spider is still there, 150 feet above and to my right. I set out to reach it quickly, as the sun dips below the horizon. When Chris arrives on the ledge it is dark, but there is not a breath of wind or a cloud in the sky. This is lucky indeed;

the ice ledge is directly below the exit cracks that lead from the White Spider to the summit ice field and thus in the fall line of any avalanche or spindrift. In the still night we can get the stove going for hot sugary drinks and a meal.

Once we have placed anchors to secure ourselves and our equipment we can relax a little. Chris looks exhausted and while I am brewing up he falls asleep sitting in his sleeping bag. I have to wake him up to pass him his share of hot soup.

The night is bitterly cold. I can feel the air burning on my face but the rest of me is warm enough, wrapped up in many layers of pile, down and Gore-Tex. Chris is sound asleep so I am alone with my thoughts. What a wonderful thing to be doing, making this climb. We are totally committed but I don't believe we can be stopped now. A decade of wondering and dreaming about this monster is about to come to an end: tomorrow we will be on the summit.

The dawn light provides an alarming wake-up call. I open my eyes to the startling view that reminds me that that I am sitting on the edge of a 5,000-foot drop. I had not forgotten where I was but all of the other bivouacs had felt safer or enclosed in some way. Sitting out in the middle of the White Spider feels totally exposed.

We allow ourselves just one big brew. Climbing out of our sleeping bags is a shock; the cold is bitter and contact between any metal equipment and exposed skin causes the metal and human elements to stick together immediately. After an age of packing and fitting crampons with stiff fingers we are finally ready to go and I hook my picks into the plate-glass ice and step off the ledge on to the ice slope. I have crossed into new territory for the first time. It's a new high point but I am tired. Even though the angle is not steep I find it hard work and the ice is like concrete. I belay at the top of the ice field below the steep rocky gully that marks the beginning of the exit cracks. The next difficult pitch has Chris's name on it.

He knows it too. We had discussed this pitch in our planning. Leaving his pack with me, he takes only the rack of hardware and launches himself up the steep rocky corner, long legs spread wide. There is no talking. I can do nothing to help him and if I speak it will be a distraction. I pay out the rope sparingly, no less nor more than he needs. There is a crux move to be made that will allow Chris to overcome the steep rock and gain the easier mixed ground beyond. I cannot imagine how he will do it but he surprises me with a bridging move so wide he almost does the splits. So elegant and determined, he has found his unique way to pass the problem.

We are free of the Spider and everything is going well. There is no point in rushing. We will not make it back down to Kleine Scheidegg today, so it is better that we take our time and enjoy the last of this amazing climb. We are climbing in the afternoon sunshine for the first time and the snow and ice have softened a little over the crumbling rocks beneath. The climbing is not technical but it is a little treacherous and we must concentrate.

Below us a sea of clouds has formed at about 7,000 feet, just above the ski resort, and the sun is reflecting off it. For the first time I feel warm and it is pleasant to turn my face to the sun and relax on each belay.

The rocky gullies give way to a field of ice and eventually snow. The strain on our calves from four days of front pointing is eased. The angle relents all the while and Chris and I swing leads slowly towards the summit ridge. The scene is incredible to behold: all of Europe to the north-west is hidden beneath the clouds and only the two of us are allowed to sunbathe, because we have climbed the north face of the Eiger. The shadows are lengthening but we take the time to chop out a seat in the snow so we can sit together and take in the view.

The sun will soon set but it does not matter: the weather is not a threat today. We will bivvy somewhere safe when we have passed the summit. It will be very cold but all of our down equipment is still dry so we will be fine.

Chris seems pretty happy with what we have done. I am not sure how I feel. This climb has been constantly in some part of my imagination since I was a kid.

Chris is the first on the summit ridge and I ask him to pause on the summit and raise his axes above his head in a victory salute. This had been the last scene in Leo Dickinson's film of the ascent and I wanted to have a photo like that.

He is also laughing at something. I cannot tell what it is until I join him on the very summit. He can see my perplexed expression and he simply gestures at the snow in front of him:

'Bedroom, thanks lads!'

Stevie and Victor have chopped out a big hole in the summit for a bivouac; all we have to do is climb into it and get comfortable. The little wind that there is will not trouble us. A bit of sleep is a good idea before we climb down the west flank.

As the sun sets I feel that this is the most incredible Alpine scene I have ever witnessed. All of the Alps to the east are laid out before us in the crystal-clear night air against a purple sky. It is bitterly cold and I give up on trying to start the stove, but it does not matter now.

Neither of us will move in the morning until the sun is on us and even then it is still too cold to get the stove going. Chris is on a mission to get down and I give him a lot of advice he does not really want to hear: 'Take your time, this is when accidents happen.' He does not acknowledge me and I think I am annoying him. I have been a control freak on the climb but I considered that to be my place.

The snow on the west flank is knee deep and easy to wade in. Chris is below me and I follow. It is a surreal feeling. Nowhere else in the Alps is like this: normally after a big climb there is a snowy descent, followed by a very long walk on a glacier and rocky paths as you descend into the tree line. The transition from mountain to civilisation is gradual. Here at the Eiger the transition is abrupt. Four hours after leaving the summit we walk on to a piste and are greeted by friendly skiers as we trudge along.

As we get closer to the village I can see a man walking up the slope towards us. This is unusual. Why trudge up through the snow when you could take a train or a ski-lift? It is also obvious that he is coming to meet us: if we track left or right so does he. I begin to get an uneasy feeling. Chris and I had been squatting in the hotel property one way or another and I am having a premonition that we are about to get a bill.

As we get close I can see that the middle-aged man is smartly dressed with a shirt and tie under a heavy black overcoat with double-breasted lapels. We stop where we are and wait as he takes the last few steps until we can engage in conversation. He is a little out of breath and there is a pause before he begins to address us in a strong Bernese accent:

'Congratulations on your climb (gasp), I have the pleasure of inviting you to dinner at our fine hotel (gasp), Frau von Almen would like you to join her, if you are available.'

Chris turns to me with a smile:

'Grand!'

The hotelier looks confused and searches for the meaning. I come to his rescue:

'We would be delighted.'

And then I think of our physical condition:

'But we have been on the mountain for several days and I fear we are not ... presentable.'

The gentleman assures us that we can shower and change at the hotel.

Chris and I exchange glances of disbelief. The culture shock is immense – last night we were still swept up in an adventure of a lifetime and bivouacked on the summit of the most notorious mountain in Europe. This afternoon we are being invited into one of the most famous Alpine hotels at the behest of the owner herself.

When we arrive there is a complicated moment while we remove our crampons and axes from the outside of our packs so that they don't damage other

Chris, delighted, on the summit of the Eiger.

people's luggage. We are surrounded, not by a gaggle of ghouls, but by a crowd of skiers and well-heeled tourists, all smiling.

We are entertainment for the residents of Kleine Scheidegg. I have no doubt that we have been invited to the hotel for reasons other than just kindness. We are today's fleeting celebrities, entertainers in the Alpine circus that is entrenched in the dramatic history of this place.

I am so hungry I don't care.

Our weapons are duly stored by the bellboy and we enter a wooden reception steeped in decades of family hotel tradition. No need to fill in a form or pay any money, we are asked simply for our first names and we are presented with a single key to a double room which we reach by climbing creaking wooden stairs. The architecture is the kind of ornate chalet style that I associate with very expensive old Swiss hotels, everything lovingly carved from timber.

Joy of joys there is a hot shower; it must be fed by melted snow. We peel off our smelly thermal layers to reveal two very skinny humans. We are not reduced to the same level of debilitation that Jack and I were on Huntington but we are surely lean; we have shivered ourselves thin.

We manage not to be late for dinner and as we approach the salon it is the same gentleman that met us on the snow who intercepts us in the lobby. I see now that without his overcoat he is dressed in a formal suit with a gold pin in the lapel. It is the symbol of two crossed keys; he is the concierge. He bids us to follow him as he sweeps sinuously through narrow spaces between the diners in the busy restaurant. Our entry immediately attracts attention, clearly we are under-dressed among this crowd: no smart après-ski gear for us. I see a man nod at us while talking to his wife and daughter; it seems he knows what we have been doing.

We are guided toward a table in the corner from which the sole occupant has a commanding view of the entire restaurant. Seated alone is an elegant and expensively dressed woman. She does not rise but focuses on me:

'You must be Simon and this must be Chris,' she says in perfect English with just a hint of the local Bernese accent.

The concierge bows slightly at our host and then turns to us:

'Gentlemen, it is my pleasure to introduce you to Frau von Almen.'

He leaves us by taking two steps backwards.

'Please,' she gestures to the only other two chairs at the table and we obediently sit.

I blurt out a clumsy thank you for her hospitality, which is casually dismissed.

'Well, since you have been camping in my property for a few days I thought it would only be polite to finally meet you.'

We look like two schoolboys who have just been found out to be the culprits of some prank. I can see that she is amused at our discomfort. She proffers a wry smile. We are being teased.

'Congratulations on your climb. To climb the north face in winter is truly an achievement.'

Three glasses of aperitif arrive and are placed carefully in front of us in champagne flutes. Chris looks quizzically at the red sparkling beverage – it is Kir Royale. Our glasses are raised and Frau von Almen declares a toast to our success.

She explains that her family have owned the hotel for generations and that as a girl and as a woman she has seen almost every climb, including ours apparently, through the powerful telescope on her balcony. This starts a lively conversation about the history of the north face. She is charming and hospitable but clearly the mistress of all she surveys. She sees us looking at the food being delivered to nearby tables and she summons the head waiter simply by glancing at him. He has been waiting alertly for this subtle signal to approach and present the menus to Chris and me.

I go for the dish with the largest amount of carbohydrate and with no limitations on the amount I can eat: the raclette.

Chris has found what he wants too:

'I'll have the chateaubriand, thanks.'

The waiter shuffles uncomfortably and is caught between glancing at Chris and his mistress, who offers him no help.

'Excuse me, sir, but the chateaubriand is for, err, two persons.'

Hoyland looks him in the eyes.

'Aye, I know!'

In desperation the waiter turns to his matriarch for help and she smiles.

'Give him whatever he wants.'

16
TOO LOOSE

My biggest problem was what to climb next. The underlying fascination with the Eiger had been suddenly dealt with and now I needed to really think for myself. Until this moment I had never really understood the mindset of climbers like Joe Tasker or Pete Boardman. At some point the Alps must have lost their fascination and only much bigger climbs in the Himalaya could interest them.

Alaska was the obvious destination (the challenges are similar and I could simply fly there) and Jack was the obvious partner. I decided to write him a letter to see what he had in mind for the summer of 1980. Fate took a hand before I could do so: at Alpine Sports one afternoon I received a phone call. The shop had an administrator called Angie who, amongst other things, fielded the phone calls. She was the epitome of an upper-class English upbringing in many ways, with rarefied English diction, but she fitted in easily to the rough and ready environment created by the many climbers that used the store as a social focus.

'Some bloody American is calling you.'

It is Jack. We are both delighted to be talking. What might be taken for pleasantries are more than that – I really *do* want to know what he has been doing. But when it comes to my turn he already has all the answers. He knows all about my winter of Eiger climbing.

'My spies have been keeping tabs on you, man.'

There is no slack in the conversation. It is unlike Jack to spend money on an overseas phone call and he comes straight to the point:

'Are you up for an expedition to climb the south-west face of Denali next summer?'

I do not need to think. We had looked at this face together in the ranger station in Talkeetna and I had thought about it since – still unclimbed, it was a major prize. I agree immediately and Jack is very happy. He has been anticipating my positive reply and has even decided to borrow Rob Newsom's team epithet from last year: we will be the 'Too Loose Climbing Expedition'.

Jack has procured some aerial photos of the south side of Denali from Bradford Washburn and posts me a set of copies so that we can both study the face and call each other once we have considered the possible ways up it.

Photos in hand, I begin to search for the line that will be the most direct and elegant way up the middle of the south-west face. We plan to be the first to climb a route on this face and I want it to be the best one. As on Huntington, I don't want another team coming along a year later and making the south-west face 'direct'. I intend that *we* do the direct route at the first attempt.

I draw the line of the route I have picked out on one of the photos and post it to Jack with a letter saying simply, 'What do you think?'

MAY 28, 1980

I am glad to finally be on the way to Denali and excited because my next adventure with Jack has begun. We are a little older and a little wiser but the humour between us has not changed.

Over the winter Jack has climbed the Grand Central Couloir on Mount Kitchener with Tobin Sorenson. They had a torrid and very cold time and he won't talk much about it.

We did discuss the fact that I finally dealt with the north face of the Eiger and in winter too. I feel like I have slain a demon planted in me a dozen years ago and I tell him that I now feel like a proper modern British alpinist, like one of the guys I looked up to when I was younger. The only response I get from him is a comment that 'Our ascent of Huntington's north face was better'.

I have the same feeling about climbing with Jack that I did in 1978, maybe more so. The chemistry is still powerful and we are both better than we were then. I am stronger and more disciplined. We have both been training relentlessly for months and I think we can climb anything if we want to. We have decided that the south-west face of Denali should have a new route with our names on it. The new project is twice the size of our Huntington climb but I am in the same mood I was in 1978: we will just go and climb it.

The process of flying to Seattle and then to Anchorage is beset with annoying checking and queuing and waiting. I am impatient every minute, despite the fact that we land in Anchorage at a timely 12.15 p.m. It is early in the day and my blood is up; I want to be on the way to Talkeetna as soon as possible.

As always, Jack is more relaxed as we toil through the same domestic tasks we had last time we were here. We must find a lift, collect the airfreight and go shopping at Safeway for the last of our food. And, as with the last trip, it is all so easy. Jack seems to attract help and over lunch at Casc's he gets chatting to a friendly old gentleman whose name also turns out to be Jack. He has a pickup truck and for $50 plus gas he will be pleased to take us to Talkeetna. We accept gladly and by 4.45 p.m. are fully provisioned, fed and rolling north on Highway 3.

I am hyperactive. This is the second time I have been on this road, but I still feel I must look at everything and evaluate it all again. I wonder who owns the float planes on the lakes we pass by, what they do for a living, why they came to Alaska … What do they do in winter?

Jack is doing what he does best on road trips: dozing and sometimes sleeping deeply. I think that he has had a terrible time in the last month or so, losing two close friends in traffic accidents. He won't talk openly about any of it but I have picked up bits and pieces from conversations amongst his mom and his sister Chris. These have given me a simple understanding of two unexpected tragedies. I had never met his friend Richard but I did meet Daisy at Jack's house in 1978, a very close and lifelong friend of his. I sense that despite all the fun we have had, training and playing around Santa Monica, he is grieving and keeping it to himself.

The rain is falling lightly out of an Arctic summer night when we pull up in Talkeetna. There is mud underfoot and the smells are of rotting Douglas fir and road tar.

We will fly this year with Doug Geeting since Jim Sharp has left Talkeetna and we unload our equipment at Doug's base, the 'Fort'.

Doug welcomes us and points us at an old trailer we can use for accommodation while we are in town. It isn't much but it is ten times better than a tent and the skeets cannot get in. Heaven! He explains that the weather has been the pits for weeks but that maybe we could fly in tomorrow. It sounds like a big maybe to me.

I don't mind waiting a day or so in Talkeetna. I feel like we have finally arrived, that this is all part of the process of the climb and I am in that state of mind that always takes over whenever I am in the mountains, as opposed to driving to them. I am happy and have nothing to be impatient about because I don't mind waiting for the weather once I have arrived.

Jack has also snapped out of his introverted mood and we walk to the Fairview Inn to see what fun can be extracted from the evening. We have arrived at the sleepy little village that I fell in love with in 1978 and because I know her a little now, she is all the more beguiling this time.

I am not disappointed. As we stroll inside we are greeted to a big welcome in a southern drawl I recognise.

'Well howdy, boys!'

It is Rob Newsom. I last heard from him when he hollered at us on the north face of Huntington as he waited to be flown out of the Ruth Glacier. The two years that have passed have hardened him a little; he is more confident, strident even. His hair is just as long and he is even funnier, if that is possible. We relive the times we spent together in 1978 and swap stories. We talk and boast of what we have done since and what we will do this summer.

I am swept up in the happiness of this simple tribal moment. I have travelled halfway around the world to this tiny place at the foot of the mountains to run into a friend that I have known for only a few days on a glacier. Yet there is a bond; we know who we are and what we are capable of. We are amongst a rare group of individuals. I have little money and no career in the conventional sense, but I don't care. Climbing has given me more pride than anything else. The gladness we all feel at seeing each other, on the eve of our chosen battles, is a justification for our rejection of a conventional life.

Rob is here for the first ascent of the north buttress of Mount Hunter, a very steep and difficult mixed climb overlooking the Kahiltna Glacier. Just as Jack and I have taken another step up in our climbing ambitions this summer, so has Rob Newsom.

Rob's expedition is called 'WPOD' – White Punks on Dope. With him are Doug Klewin and two brothers, Pat and Dan McNerthney. I confess that we have borrowed his name from his 1978 trip. He thinks it's cool and we shake on it.

A couple of beers later and we have made friends with the entire bar. Rob, Doug Geeting and a few locals are all able guitar players who take turns playing and singing their favourite songs. It goes on until last call when we depart for the Fort, where we sleep like zombies in the old deserted trailer.

The last thought I can remember before losing consciousness is that I am completely content.

MAY 29

It is Jack's birthday today – he is twenty-eight (I am twenty-four and a half). I cannot do much to mark the occasion but I secretly persuade the owner of the Roadhouse to serve him an extra pancake on the side with his breakfast. It has the word 'Jack' written in a drizzle of chocolate sauce and the number 28 underneath.

It gets a laugh out of him, which is good. This summer Jack has a new facet to him that was not there before. It manifests itself in moods of introspection that I do not recall. He finds all the same things amusing and, like Rob, the passing of two seasons has toughened him. But on this trip I am often finding him deep in silent thought.

After lunch we visit the ranger station to register with the park service. We are greeted just as last time by friendly park ranger Dave Buchanan. Dave knew we were coming because Jack had written to him describing our plans and he engages us in some lively conversation about the route we have chosen.

He also reminds us the north-east fork of the Kahiltna is dangerous because of the severe avalanche risks. Its nickname 'Valley of Death' is well earned. When we describe in detail the route we have in mind we get another raised eyebrow but again he makes no attempt to talk us out of it.

When we start on the climb our plan will have to be one of speed. We will only be able to carry a week of rations at most because the difficulty of the climb dictates that we must travel light. A rapid gain in height and the sudden exposure to very thin levels of oxygen may, for unacclimatised climbers, cause altitude sickness or – worse – pulmonary oedema (fluid building up in the lungs), and you can die from that. I discover that Jack has some pills in his medical kit that make you pee to get rid of fluid, after which the victim would need to descend rapidly to lower altitudes and more oxygen in order to survive.

As we talk I stare at a huge blow-up photo of the south-west face. 'Descend rapidly' – how the hell would we do that? Once we are a day or so into our new route there could be no going down; we simply would not have enough equipment for rappel anchors. Our only plan for survival was up.

MAY 30

THE JOURNAL OF FRANCES RANDALL, KAHILTNA BASE. Two flew in to do the south-west face of Mount McKinley; they are from Los Angeles – Simon McCartney and Jack Roberts. Two flew in to do the Cassin; they are Mike Helms and Bob Kandiko.

We wake to clearing skies – a cocktail of some sun and broken clouds. Doug is not sure about flying in so soon; he is waiting for information from Frances Randall, the airstrip manager and radio operator on the glacier airstrip called Kahiltna Base.

Since we appear to have time on our hands Jack and I go into town and have hotcakes at the Roadhouse. I like Alaska. For a little money we have had a huge breakfast and been heartily welcomed by the patron. There are a few great climbers' haunts in the UK but none quite so friendly.

When we return to the Fort it is 10.45 a.m. and Doug tells us to get ready because we will go immediately. We were not expecting such a rapid decision so we are obliged to rush around like scared squirrels only to discover that we are minus some items – we will have to go with what we have.

Packing the plane would have been a panic had it been my first time, but this year I am not startled by the dramatic and sudden process of getting to Denali from the plains. Climbing in Alaska is so different to anywhere else. These are big mountains and if you wanted to savour the approach to them you could, but as a journey on foot and skis to the foot of your chosen mountain will qualify as an expedition in itself very few climbers ever do it. I found the transition between the plains and the glacier so abrupt in 1978 that it shocked me. This time it seems normal.

We should have been better organised but in truth that is not my nature or Jack's. 'Too Loose' was a name that amused us, but it described us well enough too.

The morning has one surprise: we are to be reunited with Cessna 185 November 1047 Foxtrot – Jim Sharp's old plane has been acquired by Doug. Soon everything is the same as the first trip. I sit on our equipment in the back with Jack and the pilot up front. As usual Jack and I are armed and ready with our trusty Olympus OM1 cameras.

Being in the back is the best place to be because from my high perch I can look out of all the windows and observe both Doug and Jack on the flight.

We take off into a blue sky crowded with cloud formations. Doug calls it 'five-eighths' cloud cover.

The flight starts unremarkably; we roll down the runway the same as before, climb and turn to cross the Susitna River. As we get into the mountains, however, the journey takes on a very different complexion.

The flight is mind-boggling. We have to dodge low cloud while avoiding the terrain; Doug zooms from air pocket to air pocket finding little holes of clear sky. The entire flight is masked in clouds and I am amazed at his audacity and skill as he puts the pieces of the puzzle together. I am tossed about a little but I am not alarmed by it. It makes the journey more satisfying, seeing Doug's skills tested, just as we have come here to test our own.

Very soon we can make out the glacier airstrip below us and we land uneventfully at 7,200 feet on a wide flat expanse of the south-east fork of the

Kahiltna Glacier. The gently sloping landing strip is large and wide and spectacularly overlooked by Mount Hunter (where Rob Newsom is headed), and Mount Foraker in the west. These peaks are 7,000 to 10,000 feet higher than the glacier airstrip and very impressive.

We unload quickly and soon Doug guns the engine of his Cessna and is up and gone, taking two departing climbers with him. When he lands in Talkeetna he will fetch two more to bring up.

I find that I am not ready for Kahiltna Base at all. The last time we landed on a glacier in this part of the world we were alone. Here is quite a little village and I am not sure I like it. I had enjoyed the isolation of our time on the west fork of the Ruth and I am not ready for the 'base camp' atmosphere on the Kahiltna Glacier. Stupidly I had not really connected with the obvious fact that I would have to share the glacier with dozens of climbers headed for the popular way up Denali. We have wandered on to part of the *voie normale*.

There are about a dozen tents and forty climbers at the base camp run by Frances Randall, the glacier boss who coordinates activities from her radio tent. Frances is a woman of perhaps fifty years with a shock of blond, curly hair.

I learned a little about her from ranger Dave in Talkeetna. Frances has been the Kahiltna Glacier boss every summer since 1976. She would be one of the first to arrive and the last to leave. Her summer would be spent coordinating incoming and outgoing flights, helping to organise rescues and keeping order: the local sheriff. She had some relevant experience too; she had climbed Denali herself when she was younger.

Frances is the first to greet us and although it is nice to be greeted I am allergic to anything that resembles instructions in the context of my climbing. I can live with it I suppose; there are too many climbers to let them do anything they want or chaos would ensue. I sense that Jack is even less relaxed about being organised than me.

Someone calls Jack's name then yells for a beer and walks towards us.

I have heard of Dale Bard. With him is Steve Shea, who I met in Chamonix with Jack in 1977, plus Eric Reynolds, Chas Macquarie and a host of others, all friends of Jack's. He is obviously very pleased to meet his mates, just as I would be if I had run into Smiler or Wilco.

As I listen to tall tales being exchanged, beers are passed around and I enjoy watching Jack revisit old times with his mates. Maybe the village is not so bad. It has elements of the Bar National atmosphere in Chamonix. It seems that you cannot go to the Kahiltna Glacier either without meeting climbers you know.

We have made the same mistakes as we did last time – too loose and too light. We have no base-camp tent again and we are living on the glacier in a bivouac tent. The Todd Bibler tent Jack has organised is technically brilliant, but necessarily tiny. I think Jack actually likes camping. I like arranging bivouacs because it can be an art form, but for me camping is just an unpleasant side effect of my climbing.

I am restless but Jack dozes until 4.30 in the afternoon. Obviously he needs to catch up on some sleep. New snow on the tent finally wakes him.

In the morning Jack and I decide go up the south-east fork towards Mount Hunter to try out our skis. This year we both have new, broad ski-mountaineering models with hinged and lockable safety bindings. I used something similar for a few days near the Eiger but am still a very clumsy skier; Jack is disappointed that my downhill technique has not improved, but I can plod along in the soft snow well enough and that will do. We are here to climb, not for a ski holiday.

The clouds lift for us and the north buttress of Hunter is dramatically revealed. I am transfixed by what I see and I shed my skis and stick them in the snow as a backrest so that I can sit comfortably in the new sun and study the mountain.

Now I can understand why Rob Newsom is after this climb. It is the unclimbed Eiger of the Kahiltna, standing as it does hard by the airstrip. Any attempts to climb the buttress will have an audience, just as the Eiger's north face is an alpine theatre for the tourists at Kleine Scheidegg.

I fall over several times on the way back and Jack makes fun of me on each occasion.

JACK'S JOURNAL – **JUNE 1**

We had borrowed Frances's spare tent but it seems we are too noisy. Frances comes in and says we have pushed her too far and she wants us out of her tent … Why? Maybe it was the cassette music? I don't know but it bums me out and it means digging a much bigger ice cave.

The cave is dug in a few hours and we transfer all of our equipment. I am grateful for this time to relax. I would not have wanted to go up on our route immediately.

It is a funny feeling but this route is the most serious to date that I have ever tried and I want to be prepared. That means not rushing. That means proper acclimatisation for red-cell development. I won't be happy if it continues to storm for a long time but I am grateful for this reprieve. We have bags of time, food and equipment.

Simon and I have once again fallen into the familiar roles we played before. By that I mean that most decisions made are by mutual agreement according to each other's likes and dislikes.

Simon is mellower than before but is also more forgetful. He seems more relaxed externally but the same impatient pent-up spring is there inside him still.

JUNE 2

I wake up at 7 a.m. to the sound of an aircraft overhead. I awoke sometime earlier and noticed that the snow had ceased to fall but I had no idea that the weather was that good. One poke outside confirms that the clouds are lifting and it will indeed be a good day.

Soon almost everyone is up and about. Excitement is buzzing from each tent as people begin to pack up so that they can be ready to leave when their plane arrives. We kick back to watch them scamper.

Our preparation begins casually enough with Simon and I moving gear around and stowing clothes and food, but it soon develops into a frenzied attempt at controlled packing. I get very anxious about taking too much gear while Simon is trying his best to stay out of my way. Every once in a while he says something to quiet me down.

At about 2.30 we leave the airstrip. Everyone wishes us the best of luck and so on.

And so we ski down on to the Kahiltna under the blue skies above, the sun blazing its heat on to us – it is really hot! We are stripped down to just Fila pants we are so warm.

Simon is developing blisters and has to stop frequently so I go on ahead and stop at the top of the hill where it seems the north-east fork meets the main Kahiltna. This is as good a place as any to cache our gear and camp for the night.

Our neighbours are two Japanese that wish to attempt the West Buttress. They are friendly fellows and they naturally enquire as to our goals and methods. They speak enough English so that I can understand them and they me.

JUNE 3

It is snowing so we do not leave our pits until late in the morning. Jack decides that today he will ski towards the south-west face and attempt to break a trail all the way. I will ski to the airstrip to pick up the extra food we will need if we are to hang out here.

We both take a rest for a few hours before I set off back to Kahiltna Base. I am looking forward to the feeling of solitude. Much as I enjoy Jack's company there is something interesting about being alone in such big mountains. The fact that it is snowing just adds to the drama.

JACK'S JOURNAL

I leave for the north-east fork.

The visibility is poor, perhaps fifty feet, and I just follow the path made by [the] Japanese Cassin Ridge team [the Tokyo Unyro-Kai expedition] that are ahead of us and go kicking steps with my Nordic skis, slipping now and then. It isn't much fun but I go at it until I am exhausted.

I could almost puke; my lungs seem unsuited as if I cannot get enough oxygen in me. My stomach is aching for food since I have not eaten yet today so I turn back after three or four miles before something serious develops.

By now my vision is restricted to twenty feet, it is practically raining; I am soaked to the skin with perspiration.

Back in camp, I brew-up lots of hot grape juice and make up some tuna sandwiches. I get in my pit and eat and drink and take eight aspirins and pass out until two and a half hours later when Simon arrives at about 8.30.

He had a good time down below and he has carried a lot of supplies with him so now we have tons of food. Later we have a dinner of beef stroganoff followed by science fiction time; Simon grew up as an addict of the works of Isaac Asimov and I like them too so we carry on like a couple of geeks discussing the meaning in the books.

JUNE 4

I woke to good weather this morning; I slept soundly and woke early. I played cat and mouse with Simon as we did not want to get up but knew that we eventually would.

We then begin to slowly sort out our gear. It seems we have too much of everything but it is hard to know where to draw the line. Wrestling with decisions, we add and subtract, throwing away gear we don't or won't need, anticipating setting up a high camp, hanging out for a few days and then going for it.

By 12.30 we are heavily laden under ninety pounds each, with blue skies above. It is far too warm and we swelter in the oppressive heat.

We follow the tracks made by the three Japanese and two Americans who are all heading for the Cassin Ridge.

By 3 p.m. we have caught up with everyone and by 5.30 p.m. we have stopped at the 9,600 foot level. We will camp here tonight, rest up then go to the final base camp tomorrow, perhaps two to three hours distant.

Simon and I are about to start our next adventure.

17
THE VALLEY OF DEATH

The weather is looking really good, earlier on there were ominous lenticular clouds but that only means moisture high up. Now it is clear with only scattered cirrus clouds, should be good tomorrow and maybe the next day? I hope so, I am really up for this route, I want it to be great; I want the weather to be perfect, cold and clear.

It is windy over the summit, perhaps sixty miles an hour. The face is icier even than I had hoped; good conditions.

I feel strong, very strong, I feel warm and my spirits are high. We enjoy a filling meal of chicken salad, beef ramon, tea, fruit juice, Tucker bars and coffee all served by chef Simon.

We camp next to Bob Kandiko and his climbing partner Mike Helms; they are both from Washington State – Bob from Everett and Mike from Tacoma. Good companions these, good talkers; they hardly know each other actually, they met on the Ruth Glacier during a period of such bad weather that their own climbing plans were derailed. Their partners went home and they teamed up for the Cassin Ridge. That is a big climb to commit to when you are with somebody you don't know so well!

The three Japanese of the Tokyo Unyro-Kai expedition also headed for the Cassin stopped near to us but went back after dumping loads, leaving just the four of us together.

Simon is sorting through his equipment yet another time, adding and subtracting and then testing the weight of his pack again and again. There must be a way to eliminate the weight; you cannot climb with that much weight on your back. Most of it is food and clothing. If it is really cold I will want every clothing item I have so I am reluctant to leave any of it. Food, well we can double on meals or jettison if we are confident we can survive on less.

We could cut down on the hardware but not much; a couple of screws or pins or nuts could make a difference. We decide to leave the final decision until the last minute. Tonight we will read more science fiction and then sleep the sleep of the just.

JUNE 5

I woke up at 6 a.m. and got up at 7; the weather is still good where we are but ominous grey clouds have been building up against McKinley's summit. This is probably a sign that we have less than twenty-four hours of good weather left. It is crispy cold outside the tent, just a slight breeze.

Simon brings over eggs and coffee and inside the tent we eat breakfast over the maps when we hear the usual 'Crack, crash, bang' of a sérac falling off, only this time it sounds much louder than usual, like sixteen- or twenty-foot breakers hitting the wedge. Peering outside I cannot see the avalanche but the noise of it grows every second.

I suddenly think 'Holy shit it's going to hit us'. I look outside and Mike looks like he has seen the rising of the devil and all his archangels of darkness; he'd seen the smirking grin of Satan himself, all the while running facing backwards. Bob is well ahead.

I look out of the front door just long enough to know that we are being avalanched by the cloud of silvery dust that has overtaken us. Oh Lord, not again!

Suddenly the tent goes dark and shudders twice, we can hear the cloud pass over us and then all is quiet.

BOB KANDIKO'S JOURNAL – JUNE 5. We woke up to clear skies at our camp on the north-east fork of the Kahiltna Glacier, which Mike refers to as 'the Valley of Death'.

I was melting snow when I heard an ominous **crack** from the face of Kahiltna Peak. My eyes shot to the top where two huge séracs were beginning to tumble off their precipitous perches. Two huge towers resembling the decaying columns of the acropolis were falling down towards our camp.

Without hesitation I was up and running, bounding through knee-deep snow. Mike could only see my ass and was chuckling until he too glanced upward to appreciate the magnitude of the avalanche zeroing in on us. Then he was following my lead across the glacier.

Our campsite so nearly buried by the avalanche in 'the Valley of Death'.

Jack and Simon were ignorant of the immediate danger as they sat enclosed in their tent. Simon looked out of the door opening enough to see the wall of snow approaching and zipped the door up tight.

The snow dust was 150 feet high as it passed over the tents and enveloped Mike and me. Snow dust is harmless enough like a swirling white tornado. As it cleared Simon and Jack were laughing at the two scared jackrabbits huddling out on the glacier, but a look in the other direction sobered them up and quietened the two comedians.

JACK'S JOURNAL

When it is all over we both laugh hysterically, why I am not sure but it could be from the joy of surviving the avalanche – crazy climbers! Outside everything appears like a frozen Siberia. One minute everything is warm and sunny, the next everything is covered in a layer of snow. My sleeping bag is blown 100 yards down the glacier, soaking wet.

Bob and Mike have taken on the appearance of snowmen, frosted all over. If we are alive I will know it by pinching myself. If we are dead we will know it when we see six naked women skiing up the glacier, all of them beautiful if this is heaven, all of them ugly if this is hell.

The blocks of ice stopped two feet from our tent; if we had camped six feet closer to the hill our tent would have been annihilated and we would have been buried. The blocks are as big as Honda Civics and as small as marbles. The Japanese will get a chuckle when they see the debris covering their tracks.

'Ah crazy Yankee dawgs!'

So the day begins eventfully! Everyone takes a shit and talks about our near demise. We are all sensitive to any sound, but slowly everything resumes its normal state of affairs.

BOB KANDIKO. Later, when we have dried out our equipment, we packed up to continue our journey up the Valley of Death. I lead out with my sled in tow and Mike following on the rope. Half a mile on and we worked our way through a messy icefall and took a break sitting on some recent avalanche debris.

Jack and Simon travelling unroped follow us thirty minutes behind, nonchalantly travelling solo, their ropes on top of their packs. It seems unreasonable to travel unroped in this area no matter how confident one is of their climbing abilities. All it takes is one collapse of a snow bridge and serious injury or death will result.

Each to his own!

We negotiate another icefall which is made more difficult because the sleds are pulling us downhill as we side-step thirty-degree slopes. Finally we eat lunch at the 10,700-foot level in a flat spot across from the West Rib. The wind is blowing now and we set off to find a camp spot in the next bowl at 11,200 feet. I have been breaking trail all day and I am weary and sore. It seems like I am doing the entire trail braking, all of the cooking and most of the camp chores.

My weariness turns to animosity towards Mike; some of it is justified but it does not help my attitude at the moment.

Finally we reach 11,200 feet and select, very carefully, another camping spot.

We pack up and hesitatingly start to ski towards the looming icefall ahead, following Bob and Mike. It's not difficult, just good honest labour at 10,000 feet. The packs are smaller because we are wearing more of our clothes. The weather slowly degenerates from warm and slightly overcast to very windy, cold and overcast. After three hours of heartbreaking effort we arrive at 11,500 feet and we start to make three igloos, one for Jack and me and one each for Bob and Mike. We will be warmer inside the sturdy structures if it really starts to blow, and if we have to descend for more supplies we will have a permanent shelter.

There is something wonderfully primal and simple about making a home out of snow and ice; the 'Hotel California' cave Jack and I made on the Ruth in 1978 was so much fun – and satisfying too: there we were making ourselves comfortable in such a hostile place. Now we will try igloos as snow caves take too long to dig. Between the two pairs we have two snow shovels and Mike Helms has a carpenter's saw, ideal for cutting blocks of ice.

The wind is rising all the time and whipping snow into everything so there is a real and pressing need for the Inuit-style construction. Well, I am learning. Mike seems to be very good at it. We must dig deep into the heavily compacted snow where we can cut out blocks of just the right consistency.

It is cold as hell but the exertion keeps us warm. Jack and I dig and quarry large snow blocks cut to order by Mike, who has become the master bricklayer, and Bob, the bricklayer's mate.

The last igloo to be constructed is the one for Jack and me. By this time we have the hang of it and we make a really big one, large enough that we can pitch our tent inside it.

By 10 p.m. we have set up inside our igloo and are in our pits joyfully cooking our meal, tired but happy as we look forward to a good night's sleep, defended perfectly from the howling wind outside.

JACK'S JOURNAL – JUNE 6

Today is more or less a rest day. It has stopped snowing but the wind is still gusting to fifty miles an hour down here on the glacier and ripping into our route on McKinley. Plumes of snow are whistling off the mountain at eighty to a hundred miles per hour, maybe more.

After a leisurely start we break down the Bibler and set it down outside to dry, which it does almost instantly. We also take the packs outside to make more room in the igloo and brew a quart of tea each. I woke up hungry and thirsty last night and this morning it occurs to me that I am no longer eating for convenience's sake, but to survive. We are now eating three Tucks, one dinner and two quarts of liquid each per day, perhaps 1,500 calories?

The weather is hard to figure out; it looks as if a cold front may be arriving but really it is anyone's guess. The weather could be good or bad so we have to watch and wait. If it is good tomorrow we will set off on the climb. If it is bad we will ski down to fetch more supplies. A long ski down but an ever longer trudge back up.

By 5 p.m. I can't stand it any longer, we have to eat a meal. I had a Tuckerman but it won't do. So we go into the igloo and cook a shrimp creole. That is good but not enough so we eat an apple cheese cake and that fills the empty spaces.

Some reading and writing, packing the Bibler for tomorrow and bedtime arrives. Simon has enlarged the interior some (how he loves snow-mining) so we are not so cramped and it seems nicer without the tent in here. More room I suppose.

JUNE 7

We are up at 6 a.m. sorting out the food; we settle on the following for the six to seven days we expect to be on the climb:

6 full meals (four 2-man and two 4-man)

15 Tucks each

Our igloo camp at the head of the north-east fork of the Kahiltna Glacier ▶
with the arête of the Cassin Ridge top right in the background.

3 salads
1 eight-ounce salami bar
1 pound of boiled sweets
1 banana cream cake
1 pound of Cadbury chocolate
4 protein bars each
4 quarts of gas.

We have a breakfast of tea, one Tuck each and a two-man meal of chicken stew. The weather is the best yet: cold, windy but clear. We will go for it today.

I have the jitters.

Right now, just before a big route, my cowardice is at its high point. I try to reach within for strength and renewed faith, to cast out doubts and regain my courage. Slowly it happens but I am still anxious, the best thing now is to start the climb as soon as possible.

18
THE FISSURE McCARTNEY

BOB KANDIKO'S JOURNAL – JUNE 7. Jack and Simon were up at 6 a.m. and away by 8.30 for their attempt on the south-west face. Mike is still crashed out at 8.30 as the fog sat in the valley immediately below us, but above we are in clear skies. So we pack up while deciding between the West Rib and the Cassin. The rib would take less time and contains an easy exit. The Cassin is more difficult and difficult to escape. But as the wind abated and the bluest skies we have seen in three weeks emerge, the Cassin Ridge is the choice.

Jack and Simon's footsteps were a blessing to follow for a while until our paths diverge, as we climb 1,000 feet to the base of the Japanese Couloir.

We are both deep in our own thoughts this morning and we say very little to each other on the thousand feet of step kicking that takes us to the bergschrund. The best way for me to cope with the enormity of what we are doing is to break it down into small pieces and think only of a few pitches at a time. We have chosen our line up the middle of this vast face and now we have to make it work by finding the line of least resistance, threading our way around the parts that are just too difficult. We are climbing into unknown territory. This is classic alpinism and we should feel proud, but my mind is overloaded and I have no room for such stray thoughts.

The starting point was obvious: we began where the tongue of ice that intrudes into the rocks reaches highest so that we could gain as much height as we could on easy ground, and do so as quickly as possible. We solo as far as we dare and eventually rope up at 11 a.m. for the first five pitches, which are simple fifty-degree slopes of granulated ice. Simple, but heartbreaking work. The air is thin and

I pant for breath whenever I climb. The most concerning thing is the weight of my pack; I have never set off on a climb with so much equipment. We agonised over every item and yet could not see a way to attack the mountain with less. We might be out for ten days and planned rations for only seven as it is – we know we will go hungry. There is nothing new about this strategy.

The rock band rears up to vertical in front of us and we are forced diagonally leftwards into a system of ramps and mixed ground for pitches six to nine. On the belays I stare nervously at the huge vertical walls to the right of our line. Everything here is of a scale that is beyond my experience.

The climbing itself is not difficult but the face around us is awe-inspiring. To my right, towering walls of granite overhang in a way that reminds me of Yosemite – except Yosemite is not as big. To our left is a massive buttress with huge blank walls and overhanging crack systems. I estimate that it is similar to the Nose of El Capitan in size and yet here it reaches halfway up the rock band.

This climb is like no other I have done. Everything is a surprise. When I climbed the Eiger I already knew everything about it and, significant and magnificent as it was, it was no psychological preparation for this adventure.

When we made the first ascent of the north face of Mount Huntington Jack and I had plenty of time to look at it and study and plan. But here we have attacked the unclimbed south-west face of Denali just two days after we arrived at the bottom of it. I had similar feelings of concern on Huntington, but this is a different situation. On that climb it was as if the mountain itself was actually intent on killing us violently. Here on Denali I feel so insignificant that I fear that we may simply expire and fade away in the thin air.

I lead pitch nine and make a long leftward traverse, heading for what should become the crest of a vague buttress. When Jack follows he finds himself sixty feet to my right with no runners between us and he attempts to lead through and go straight up without coming to my stance. I talk him out of it because, from my wider perspective, I can see that it is not the way – he cannot see the steep blank ground above him as well as I can.

He joins me where I am belayed to a large block sticking out of the ice. I have been studying the rocky ground above, which steepens with little ice, just rock and snow, and will be time consuming.

Jack sets off and gets the first hard pitch. He is forced to climb almost all of it with his gloves off – 150 feet of rock climbing in crampons. I hope there will not be so much climbing in this way because it is slow; thank God I am standing in the sun throughout my long wait, inching out the rope. When it is my turn to follow I decide to climb rather than use my jumars because I think it will be just as quick with a tight rope from Jack. Soon I think I have made a mistake; the pitch is harder than it looks and poorly protected too.

'Well done, man.'

The eleventh pitch is no easier. We had not expected to find this level of difficulty so soon and it dawns on me that the terrain is steeper than it looks on our Washburn photograph. If we have made a mistake about the angle here, does this mean that the angle of what we supposed to be the crux of the climb, the dihedral above the big boulder, is also steeper? If it is then we may be in trouble.

The day grinds on. There is more of the same; not desperate, but consistently hard mixed climbing. By pitch sixteen we are searching for somewhere we can cut a ledge for the tent; it is 9 p.m. and we are cold and tired. Jack says his feet are hurting too. I am 100 feet into the pitch when the angle relents and I find a patch of snow. I decide to bring Jack up immediately because I think this snow slope will be as good as anything we will find today and we are both exhausted. Jack agrees that we must take a break, but it soon becomes apparent that we cannot cut a platform for the Bibler tent because there is no depth in the ice. We are actually on a snowdrift set on sloping rocks and will have to spend the night sitting out in the open. This is not unusual; if we had bivouac bags it would be fine, but we are not carrying them because we have brought the tent. The extra warmth and protection of a tent only works if you can find somewhere to pitch it, and if we cannot have the tent then we cannot use our sleeping bags because they will get wet. We must not allow that to happen at any cost or we will freeze later on this climb.

The one positive thing is that there is no wind – if we put all of our clothes on we can pass the night out in the open. It will be cold and uncomfortable but we have no choice.

We chop out a bench. I slump on one end and Jack on the other with the stove between us. And so we spend the night brewing, eating and dozing. We drink five quarts of tea between us and eat one four-man beef stroganoff meal. At least we are fed and hydrated.

We promise ourselves that tomorrow night we will be more comfortable. I think to myself that we will need to be; it is too early on such a big climb to be undergoing this sort of hardship and we will weaken quickly if we cannot look after ourselves. Jack says he is so tired he is beginning to hallucinate and his honesty allows me to confess that I feel a little the same. I think the altitude is affecting us both.

I am glad I spent the money on the best down parka that I could buy, a beautiful 'Redline' from Mountain Equipment in the UK. Jack has a parka filled with something called 'Thinsulate'. It may be the latest clothing technology but it does not look as warm as my Redline. Jack is a gadget freak at heart and will always try the latest thing. I suspect he got a deal on the jacket and that is why he brought it. I hope he is warm enough.

We have climbed about 1,600 feet today. Not bad, not great. If we can keep that pace we will spend only three days in the rock band. My worry is that we won't keep the pace because the photo tells me that it will get steeper as the air gets thinner.

JACK'S JOURNAL – JUNE 8

We had a fitful bivouac; I eventually put on my Thinsulate parka, down leggings and got into my vapour barrier liner. I managed to remain in a dream state until 4 a.m. We were up and going when it got warm at about 7 a.m. The weather is still looking brilliant, blue skies bordered with white cirrus clouds.

We're really getting some gobsmacking views of Mount Hunter, Foraker and most of Alaska.

The first two pitches were the most desperate.

There is snow in the back of a bent crack that overhangs two ways. Simon leads and almost falls off. I jumar; it must have been a scary lead since the protection is shitty at best. We alternate leads from there on, snow and rock pitches, really sustained hard rock climbing.

We traverse around and go up left diagonally again, hard desperate work at 14,000 feet. I am feeling weak; my feet are warm but they are killing me. They hurt worse than my back, which hurts worse than my left shoulder, which hurts worse than my brain. The heels of my feet are bleeding, blisters torn from my flesh; it is hard to front point, that is for certain. I wish I had a better head for this mixed stuff but I don't seem to be able to concentrate. Fortunately Simon has his head on.

My mind wanders continually back to **Daisy**. I don't know why I miss her now; just at this very moment it is hard to believe she is dead.

Then I think about Richard dying on his cycle. I suppose it is because I am terrified of this face and what could happen to us should a big storm hit that I am so obsessed with the dead. Man, I am scared shitless, I don't want to die, not here, somewhere else. Simon feels it too and somehow sharing this fear with each other makes it easier to bear.

Perhaps it is the mind's way of distracting me from what is really happening, because if I sat down and calmly thought about what we are doing, the size of the face, bad weather potential etc., I would freak out and not do it. So in order

Jack and I spend our first bivouac in the open, so far so good. ▶

to cope with the potential seriousness of actually freaking out badly, the mind creates distractions.

I am glad Simon is here with me; since Huntington there is no one else I could go this far out on a limb with.

Now we are in an area that should be easy, but somehow the dragon turns its arse in our direction and farts.

The next and last full pitch of the day is Simon's and really discouraging: mixed rock, ice and snow around the corner to the base of a snow-choked chimney which overhangs at the top. I watch him make truly frightening gains, screaming in wildly controlled desperation mixed with the agile body of a gymnast and the look of a crazed wildman on this 5.9 overhanging nightmare in his double boots, crampons and his pack!

It was beautiful to behold him climbing but terrible to follow!

The jumars are frozen up and slip with me attached to them, but the cord from one of them jams in a crack, stopping my plummet into the frozen depths below. It leaves me suspended in frozen animation some ten feet off the deck, hanging from my Swami belt which is slowly but surely cutting off my circulation.

Swinging into a small ledge enables me to get my weight off the rope and to restore some semblance of normal breathing. Then, after a rest, I get Simon to lower me down to regain the ropes and tie in normally. After much thrashing, grunting, pulling and heaving myself up the crack I do get up and collapse on the belay.

Gotta bivvy!

Simon goes another eighty feet and sees a ledge and up I come. We can see glimpses of our ice-filled dihedral from here and it is much steeper than we had thought.

Tonight will be another open-air bivvy but this time at least there is a ledge and it is dry. We cannot pitch the tent but this time we can use it as a bivouac bag at least so we can get into our sleeping bags and be warm.

We have an evening meal and I am settled into the pit. We decide to call the pitch 'the Fissure McCartney' before we say goodnight.

My hand is beginning to freeze, so tightly do I have it jammed in the crack. I am losing sensation and fear I will let go accidentally. My hand is also bleeding from the abrasion of the sharp granite and my blood is acting as a lubricant; unless I solve this next move very soon I will fall and be smashed on the rocks below. I am too far from my last protection now. I must not fall.

The points of my crampons grind and move on the small footholds and my pack pushes me out of the chimney, which is now overhanging. I scream, scream from adrenaline, scream in fear, and scream at the mountain: 'Let me pass!'

There is a ledge above me. It's my only hope but I cannot reach it. In desperation I pull my ice axe from the holster on my waist and toss it so I can let go of the head and catch it again at the base of the shaft. With the axe my arm is two feet longer and I reach up with one hooked steel finger towards the ledge.

With a metallic sound I hook the pick over the lip and test the grip. The axe wobbles on its point but does not slip when I pull gently. Time to move. All my options will be over in seconds if I do not.

I pull hard. The crampon on my right foot twists and loses purchase and skates off the rock. Almost all of my weight is hanging off the tenuous grip I have on the shaft of my axe.

I scream. And then nothing.

Am I dead?

Something is holding me tightly, squeezing me with a powerful grip. I open my eyes searching for my captor.

'Easy, man, you're OK, it's OK.'

I seem to know the voice and slowly the veil of confusion subsides as I recognise that it is Jack who grips my arms. My chest is heaving; my pulse is racing. I have awoken from a nightmare but I am not back in Kansas. I have exchanged one bad dream for the same in reality. There is a bloody bandage around my right hand, evidence of my journey.

I sleep fitfully and wake often with a bad headache. It feels like a terrible hangover and I am a little nauseous too. It is the feeling that I had once when I climbed Mont Blanc unacclimatised, so I guess my ailment is altitude-related. I hope I get over it: we have a long way to go and we have still not reached the halfway point of the technical section, or the crux where the big boulder is.

That overhanging chimney could have been the end of me. I nearly fell twice today. This is insanity. I never allow myself to get out of control like that, but what choice do we have? It is too late now: we cannot get down and if we cannot climb the rock band we are dead men.

19
MIXED FEELINGS

Unlike Simon I slept pretty well last night for most of twelve hours. We stayed in our bags so long so we could totally recuperate from the last forty-eight hours.

Soon the sun hits us and we get up and packed, leaving the ledge at 10.30 after a quick brew.

My feet really hurt badly and I can hardly walk. It is really only bearable when my heels are pointed downwards, any other way is too painful and that makes it very difficult to lead.

I lead the first two pitches of simple fifty-five-degree ice as Jack is having trouble. When he follows, it is obvious he cannot climb normally. I press him about it and he says that the blisters on his feet have torn off and are now bleeding inside his boots. He cannot climb well or even marginally competently until he can do something to dress his wounds. I agree; he cannot go for long like this. We need a good spot for the tent, which means we will not get far today and this is bad news; we are supposed to be 'fast and light'. So far we seem to be slow and not so light.

I have a theory about the cause of his problem. We are both using the same type of boot, the Galibier Hivernale. It is the best double boot around but, because it is a boot within a boot, there is a little movement between the felt inner and the leather outer. I found this out on the Eiger last winter and it is very disconcerting to have any upward movement of your heel inside the boot when you are front pointing. I could not tolerate it and spent days adjusting my boots and crampon straps until I eliminated the movement. The crampon straps were a big part of solving the problem.

◄ Our camp under the big boulder, an amazing place. Like the Apollo 11 landing site, nobody will ever go there again.

205

Jack is climbing with 'Foot Fangs', a one-piece crampon that uses a toe clip and heel clamp to attach the crampon to the boot, a bit like the way a ski binding clamps a ski boot to a ski. All of the straps that would wrap around the climbing boot have been eliminated except for one round the ankle. I feel sure he has used this crampon to avoid putting any pressure on his feet, since I have discovered he got a little frostbite last winter while climbing with Tobin on Mount Kitchener. I would like to have known that before now. I had assumed that his obsessive attention to his socks, boots and crampons was because of his ugly feet. I know now that he kept a secret.

He has recently frost-damaged ugly feet and we are forcing a new route on Denali.

Jack has too much movement in the boot and two days of climbing has caused terrible blisters. We have trained like athletes, but we have not practised and this unforeseen problem is the result.

I lead another pitch of fifty-five-degree ice and find myself on the ice field below the big boulder, with nothing but easy ground between it and us. It looms above me, much bigger than I thought, and overhanging at its base.

Another pitch and I can see all the way to the bottom of the boulder where it meets the ice. When an ice field runs up under an overhang, an ice ledge often forms and it looks like that has happened here. This is great news.

One more short pitch and I can stand on a large, almost-flat ledge of ice and snow under the biggest singular rock I have ever seen. We could pitch several tents here if we wanted to. Jack slowly limps up to join me, stopping just below so that he can take in the magnificent situation of what must surely be the best bivvy site on the planet.

'Will this do?' I ask.

I get the first weak smile out of him for two days.

Sadly, the situation is tempered by the sobering view of our dihedral above and to the right of the boulder, the supposed line of our chosen route. It is much steeper than the photo suggested and we do not have the equipment or the time to even think of climbing it. We will have to find another way, otherwise we have climbed into a fatal cul de sac.

Our progress up the mountain has been worryingly slow, but there is no need for a debate. Pushing on with Jack in his wounded state would not be profitable or kind. Or safe. And anyway the weather appears to be deteriorating; a little light snow has begun to fall out of a desultory sky.

We set about chopping out a perfect platform for the Bibler tent. It even has a slight fall to the inside so that any slipping will be into the rock, not towards

36 Our journey begins, towing heavy sleds under a hot sun. We make friends with a Japanese team bound for the West Buttress; we eat, and drink a little sake while listening to their portable stereo and my favourite Crusaders album, *Street Life*.

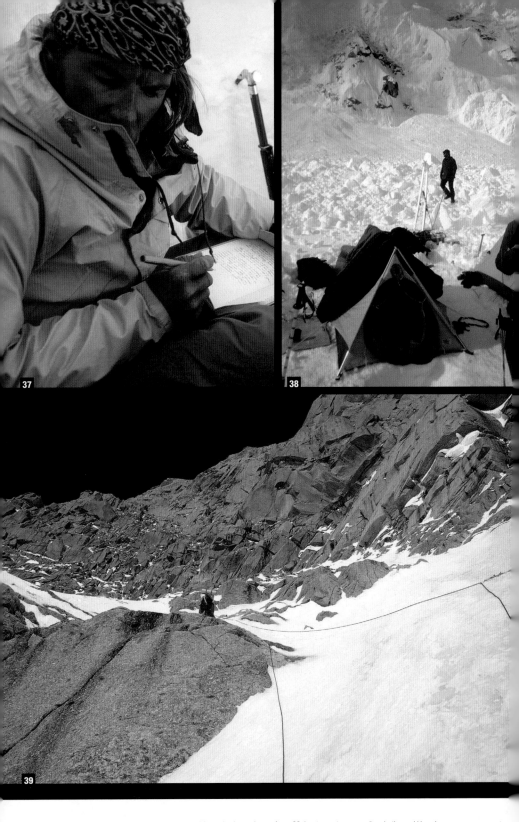

37 Jack wrote in his journal every day, seen here inside our super igloo under the south-west face. **38** In retrospect our campsite selection could have been sharper – the avalanche came to a stop, touching the tent. **39** Early in the morning of the first day, searching for a way to postpone the hostilities with those steep rocks. **Photo:** Jack Roberts.

A few pitches higher and looking back. **Photo:** Jack Roberts.

41 Day two reveals that we will spend most of our time rock climbing in crampons with our packs weighing us down. **42** A rare lucky break – the opportunity to make use of a diagonal break to buy some cheap progress. **Photo**: Jack Roberts. **43** High on the face on day six, the strain is beginning to tell – I am not well. **Photo**: Jack Roberts.

44 Rock climbing on day seven – will the difficulties never end? **45** I traverse past the 'big boulder' and look up into the couloir behind it in the hope we can get up that way. I hang my head, there is no way for us there. **Photo:** Jack Roberts.

46 All of the Alaska Range lies below Mike and Bob's camp at 18,000 feet. Only Denali is higher now. **47** We belay all the way as I feel so unsteady, and in truth swinging leads allows one of us to rest. Mount Foraker stands behind. **48** Jack traversing under the big boulder on day six.

49 We are finally out of the rocks on the sixth day; I am skirting the big sérac in the hanging glacier above the rock band. Photo: Jack Roberts. **50** A happy Mike Helms: he has found the fuel cache at 18,300 feet and the pressure has been reduced. Photo: Bob Kandiko. **51** Back at our igloo camp at the head of the north-east fork of the Kahiltna, Bob and I retrieve our skis. He is cooking his Nordic ski-boots to thaw them out. The Freaks followed us down in the night and set their box tent next to us.

52 The traverse of the mountain took three weeks: Jack and I started our ascent of the south-west face on June 7 carrying seven days' food. I made it back to Kahiltna Base (with a lot of help) on June 30. Our line is in magenta, the Cassin line is in cyan. The circles denote Bob and Mike's camps.

53 Bob has borrowed some sunglasses from the Freaks. L–R: John Rosenfield, Mike Pantelich and Bob at the 14,100 feet camp. **54** The weather is smiling and so is a very skinny Bob Kandiko – lunch is on the way to our camp at 14,100 feet courtesy of the National Park Service.

55 Ranger Dave Buchanan (left) gets his man as the posse looks on. We are just waiting for Doug Geeting to come and fly me to hospital, where I belong. Photo: Bob Kandiko. **56** A big hug from the queen of the Kahiltna. Frances Randall has overseen my rescue and she is as happy as I am. Photo: Bob Kandiko.

57 Glacier pilot Doug Geeting (standing) tells me the plan: we will fly directly to Anchorage. He has been swept up in the Too Loose drama but for him it is all in a day's work. I smell bad so we will fly with the windows open. Photo: Bob Kandiko. **58** The last bivouac of the Too Loose expedition is the Burns Unit of Providence Hospital in Anchorage.
59 Modern climbers at Kahiltna Base. R–L: Mark Westman, Lisa Roderick – today's Kahiltna boss – and Eamonn Walsh, Mark's climbing partner. Photo: Mark Westman.

60

61

60 The lighting of Studio City Macau is typical of our company's design build activity in Asia – calculated risks all. **61** I am reunited with the little Cessna that Jim Sharp flew in 1978 and Doug Geeting in 1980. In 2014 I found N1047F, parked more or less where I last saw it, fifty metres from Jim Sharp's log cabin (now extended, but still the base for Talkeetna Air Taxi). **Photo:** Pam Roberts.

62 Happy Bob Kandiko en route to Denali in 2014 aboard a Talkeetna Air Taxi Turbine Otter. **Photo**: Pam Roberts. **63** Close-proximity flying, Cessna-185 style. Talkeetna Air Taxi boss Paul Roderick allows me to look straight down the north face of Mount Huntington one more time in 2014.

64 On the west fork of the Ruth again in 2014 after an absence of approximately thirty-six years. Standing directly in front of the north face of Mount Huntington is (L–R) me, Pam Roberts, Bob Kandiko and Karen Neubauer. **65** I meet Mike Helms for the first time since 1980 at the 2015 American Alpine Club benefit dinner in Washington DC – a joyous occasion. L–R: Mike Helms, me and Pam Roberts. The photo was taken by Mike's wife, Chancellor.

Jack in Patagonia, 2009. **Photo**: Pam Roberts.

the void. Anchors are set, our home perfectly pitched and all of our equipment carefully stowed as we settle down in the best bivvy of our climbing careers. To be in such magnificent solitude, on such a vast and difficult face, and yet be so comfortable is an amazing feeling. It feels like the alpine equivalent of Apollo 11 in Tranquillity Base, totally alone and completely at risk and yet perversely cosy. Having landed on our moon we must now get off it again. Just not today.

We pile in and set to work on our chores. I help Jack tend to his feet and then I make an Italian dinner.

JACK'S JOURNAL

By the time we get sorted out inside it is 5 p.m. and now it [bivvying] seems like the natural thing to do. Pints of hot tea and lasagne make it nice. Our route will go left from this ice field; the dihedral is obviously too hard, so it is back under the séracs again for us.

We talk some. About women, other climbs, the Eiger and the possibility of a trip together to the Alps in winter for skiing and climbing. It could be fun and I'd like to go …

The tent seems drier up here, less moisture in the air I suppose. I finish Asimov's book, *The Gods Themselves*, and we each take a Seconal to help us sleep. We would like to leave early in the morning to get to the main ice field which is about 1,800 vertical feet above us.

We should be able to do it even though it means climbing directly under the séracs above; hopefully they are all as stable as they appear.

Well, one pill doesn't do it so I take another and I am out cold. The next thing I remember is Simon trying to wake me up at 6 a.m. but I am so far gone that I can hardly get up. I am so out of it that we decide to stay here.

By 9 a.m. Simon tries to awaken me again but I am even more seriously gone than before; the drugs have really affected me. My whole body seems laden with lead, I can't think clearly at all and I cannot move well either.

The weather has dropped out on us so it isn't too bad to bear here; we can easily justify it, but what a bummer I am having.

I dream again, I am in Tommy's in Van Nuys. I order a triple burger because I have never had one. I take a bite out of it and instantly begin to choke. I run out of the door to get help. The next moment I am awake and terrified with my right arm outstretched as if trying to knock a door open. Yelling 'Tommy, Tommy, Tommy!'

Simon quiets me down as I realise it was just a bad dream.

BOB KANDIKO – JUNE 9 [Kandiko and Mike Helms are on the Cassin Ridge above the hanging glacier]. We are up at 9.30 with the sun streaming in. We load up the gear. It has become a routine as we know where every item fits into our packs.

Mike leads up 800 feet of ice and snow at the beginning of the rock band. Very similar to Mount Rainier snow climbing. I lead up a mixed gully of ice and rock and around the corner, all the while looking for a ledge for a break but few, if any, exist. Finally, after leading out too far on meagre protection I find two fixed pitons and quit. Mike follows through and finds a big ledge just twenty feet above me. We eat nuts and brew a drink before Mike leads off and up a rocky corner. I struggle behind and when I reach his belay he leads another difficult [pitch].

All we want is a camp spot but it takes three more exhausting leads before we arrive at something that resembles one. Mike agrees that this place looks as good as any and we start chopping out a platform in the ice and snow. The sun is setting at 11.30 p.m. and we are barely able to move as we set up the tent and crawl inside.

I start the stove but I have a severe headache and a general malaise sends me to my bag. Mike serves soup and tea and we call it quits.

JACK'S JOURNAL – JUNE 10

It must be exhaustion; it must be the total accumulation of three weeks of happenings prior to the trip. I am weak from climbing, emotional upsets, doubts, stress and high altitude, lack of proper sleep and lack of proper nourishment. The pills have just broken down my defences to where I begin to cry over Daisy and Richard. Mostly Daisy though, she was so much to me, we did so much together.

Simon tries to comfort me by just listening and grabbing my arms. Perhaps if I let it all out of my system here I will feel better. I hope so.

By now it is 1.30 p.m. and I am feeling the effects wear off. I should be normal in a few hours. Whew!

My pulse is eighty beats per minute, normal for this altitude (15,000 feet). My breathing is not as laboured now either. We can use this period to get acclimatized and hopefully when we leave the weather will have improved.

It is cold, windy and snowing outside. Here in the Bibler we are warm and dry, very secure – like being a foetus in the womb.

I wonder how Ruth is. In the short period that we have known each other I feel like I almost love her. Whether or not that is true I don't know. She is not as outdoorsy as Jane I think but she is very intelligent and outgoing and practically beautiful. Very lovely and very attractive, the one woman in a long time (long line?) that I may just flip out over. We will see how it goes when I get back. I'd like to spend lots of time with her this summer. I want to get to know her better. I believe I am ready for that.

By 6 p.m. it is definite that I am over the bad spell, completely recovered. I am glad about that! Simon is especially glad about that.

We will leave in the morning if conditions permit.

The remaining food as of today is:

3 meals (two 2-man and one 4-man)

2 salads

6 candy bars

1 banana pudding

9 Tucks

8 ounces of Cadbury chocolate

2 four-ounce bars of salami

12 tea bags

3 quarts of dried milk

Some boiled sweets

2 1/2 quarts of gas for the stove.

Enough for five days I think.

The remainder of the day is spent in our pits, sucking on sweets talking about climbs to do; probably we will leave Alaska after this one.

What would top this route? Maybe do the Rooster Comb but doubtful. I want to hike and climb in the Sierras and Yosemite. Hike with Ruth and scope out a job for the fall. For me, I want a warm bed.

I would like to organise all my slides into three shows, throw out the old ones and get organised to do some writing. I also want to redesign the Bibler; there will be many improvements.

Dinner tonight was clams mixed in a tuna salad with some potatoes thrown in, best meal yet.

BOB KANDIKO – JUNE 10. Today is a rest day and I need it. The weather has also deteriorated. Three colossal hard days of climbing have exhausted me mentally. My headache is large and I feel ill but I will force some liquids and food down and try to think of bright thoughts.

This climb is mentally fatiguing in that no easy escape route exists. From here it is easier to go up and over than retrace our steps. **I think about this a lot and quite emotionally** since the consequences can be severe. Not really the kind of route I enjoy but had to learn by experience. What lies ahead is technically easy to moderate climbing, so as long as I hold together against the cold and altitude I will make it.

I consumed a lot of food and liquids today, so I am ready for the push.

We feel perversely safe in the camp under the 'big boulder'; we make product-placement pictures to pass the time.

20
THE ROBERTS TRAVERSE

JUNE 11

The weather is neither good nor bad. Sometimes we are in cloud, sometimes not. At least it is not windy. We must make our move. I suspect that we both regret leaving such a comfortable bivouac but it is time to put some distance behind us. As usual I am sure we are going to run out of food before the mountain is done with us. At least our packs are lighter and all of our personal equipment is dry.

The first four pitches are traverses, leaving the bivouac spot and following the edge of the boulder leftwards around its junction with the ice field below. The climbing is on very simple ground at first and I am glad to see Jack properly back on his feet. We are climbing ice of perhaps forty-five to fifty-five degrees and sometimes just walking along a ledge of snow. This is an encouraging start to the day, but my breathing is laboured and my head hurts again. Sitting still in the Bibler tent for almost two days I had felt better. I guess that when sitting quietly I am not using much oxygen and the thin air is not so noticeable; now that I am exerting myself I feel bad again.

At the end of the second pitch I can look up into the massive chimney behind the left-hand side of the boulder. It is hideous, a huge overhanging chasm. There is no way we can climb up there. At the bottom of the chimney I stop to place an ice screw to give me the security to look around and consider our options. Jack can see me but he cannot see what I am looking at. My face must have partially told him the story, but he asks, 'Can we get up there?'

'No way, mate, way too rowdy in there.'

There is a long pause. This is not good for morale. We will be forced to continue on what looks like a long traverse that starts by going down and left on easy-looking mixed ground. Easier ground it may be, but we are burning up time and resources and not gaining any height.

The decision is easily taken because we have no choice and, like a crab, I set off across the tongue of ice and out on to snow-covered rocks below a steep wall. I belay and, while Jack picks his way carefully across, I look for the earliest opportunity to break through the band of rocks above. The climbing is not so difficult, but traverses are much more dangerous than pitches that go straight up because if the second climber falls he will take a huge swing and, on this terrain, will be smashed against the rocks on that terrible pendulum journey.

We have a quick chat on the belay and both agree that we cannot climb the chasm beside the boulder. When he was following this pitch Jack had stopped below it and stared at the chimney for perhaps ten seconds before he too dismissed it. He just removed the ice screw and carefully clawed his way sideways to me. I tell him to keep going on the traverse for one more pitch. I have been staring at the steep rock wall above and it looks too hard. Another traverse pitch and the ground above seems to relent, giving us some options for upward movement.

I am delighted to see that, towards the end of his lead, Jack starts to gain height up snowy steps between a huge block and some shattered ground. I hope that our 'wandering around' will now end and we can start to improve our score in vertical feet.

Jack has a smile when I join him on his stance and he points me up a snowy corner which is heading in the right direction: straight up and maybe a little to the right.

He looks good but I feel terrible. The headache is worse and I have to stop sometimes to concentrate on not vomiting. I cannot afford to lose any nutrients or liquids – we have so little of them to spare.

I manage to fight my way up the steep snow-filled rock corner and I emerge on a little ice field that I follow left again to the bottom of a rightward-trending icy ramp. At last we have found a feature that we can follow for a while and which leads the way we want to go – directly towards the summit.

The only downer, apart from my nausea, is that we are now directly under the monster séracs at the bottom edge of the large ice field that will make up the second half of our climb. This had not been our plan. We had never intended to place ourselves in harm's way like this, but we had misjudged the 'safer' climbing line when we looked at the photos. We should have bought a few more of Washburn's pictures; some taken from different perspectives might have revealed the true steepness of the face. The picture I bought was really expensive, hence my only ordering that one. I would gladly go back in time and reverse that decision now. Still, not knowing what is coming next is a grand adventure and when Jack and I get down we can enjoy telling the tale.

My goodness ... are we really about to put up the biggest route in North America?

Jack is first into the ramp and we follow it for several pitches, soon zigzagging up below a steep wall and passing more huge boulders. We swing leads up a left-trending ramp and Jack belays just below the top of it. As I approach him I can see that we are about to arrive at a crest.

When I reach his belay I almost vomit, again. I have swung leads with him all day and this one makes our total ten so far, but Jack has picked up the load for the hard ones. I apologise for my condition but he shrugs it off.

'I still have the shivers over your lead in the Fissure McCartney, man.'

I manage to lead our eleventh pitch of the day, a nasty mixed affair out of the ramp and on to snow, but I cannot escape an overhanging rock that has an off-width crack splitting it, so I belay and bring Jack up. Looking at the crack above me I am very worried that we may be totally blocked.

Jack is feeling feistier than me, but the crack looks to be 5.9 in the Yosemite decimal system. Jack and I both climb 5.11, so a pitch of 5.9 in Yosemite or some other climber's paradise would be merely entertaining – but to come up on difficulties like this at over 15,000 feet, in big heavy boots and in the freezing cold was a horrendous prospect. This was completely new ground and very dangerous. A fall in Yosemite would result in a small loss of pride. On Denali the loss of our lives was more likely.

Jack thinks he can climb the crack, but we have no protection for it so it is dangerous to try. He then surprises me by not only dumping his pack but also taking off his crampons and overboots as well as his shell-clothing and gloves – stripping down to the bare essentials. I am glad there is no wind and that we are in full sunlight. He takes all the rock gear and sets out to find a way around the problem.

He finds a diagonal stratum in an eighty-degree face which has formed a little ramp just big enough for the toes of his boots, between one and two inches wide. He oozes diagonally up on this rising traverse, using small face-holds on the steep slab above for balance and traction. I turn blue just watching this display of agility. Jack places a nut for a runner and I pray that it is solid. If he comes off and it fails he will really swing a long way ...

Jack continues to slide further to the right on his traverse. He takes it very carefully, giving me lots of time to worry. Another fifteen feet and he meets a vertical crack in which he can place a Friend for protection. I had been cursing the weight of the rack when we started this climb but I am now so grateful we brought the Friends.

Jack lowers himself down so that the strata he used for his feet is now a hand traverse. He follows this with powerful movements until he reaches a hand-sized crack in a corner, where he can place some decent protection and climb upwards by jamming and laybacking until he reaches the top of the rock and a belay on a little ledge. Magnificent!

As Jack has only used one of the two ropes to protect himself, I can use the other to send him his pack with his overboots and shell clothes inside by lowering it out on a tail and letting him haul it up hand over hand. Hauling me up proves to be quite another matter. I have to wear my pack and even on jumars it takes me three times as long to follow as it did for him to lead. When I manage to struggle to his first runner I have to stop to vomit.

Jack throws me the end of the second rope so I can tie into it. He can both belay me and pull me upwards while I jumar diagonally. This is no time for pride.

When I arrive exhausted at his stance I am content to just hang panting in my harness while Jack puts all of his clothing and crampons back on. Mercifully, the next pitch is easy, and also spectacular: an airy traverse that leads to a ledge where we labour to cut out a spot for the tent by removing ice, mud and rock.

JACK'S JOURNAL

The traverse shall be called the 'Roberts Traverse' of course, what else?

We spend hours trying to construct a ledge big enough to accommodate the tent and its occupants comfortably. Bashing, banging and lots of heavy right hooks do a barely satisfactory job. It keeps us warm I suppose. The weather is colder here on this still day.

After the tent is erected and home is made for the night we pass the time brewing up and talking of how we must get out of the rocks tomorrow regardless how much time and effort is involved. It is simply taking too much out of us: every day there is a 5.8 or 5.9 pitch.

Today we have done fourteen pitches, none of them easy, and we have had to wander around some. There have been very few straight up pitches that are either possible for us to climb or that would keep us on route.

The food is OK if no emergencies arise; if they do we are short.

I seem to imagine that we are not alone, like there are two other people with us. Maybe it is to relieve the pressure of being with Simon and no one else.

Is the pressure too great?

I'm not sure that I need climbs like this any more. When I get out I will probably work more on a good woman, a job and less-risky climbs.

The toe is no better, but no worse. I find myself looking more and more forward to the high school tenth reunion. Hoping I am alive and well enough to enjoy it.

21
HYPOXIA

The brain craves oxygen. Nearly a quart of blood pumps through the brain every minute to supply it. When threatened by low oxygen, brain blood vessels dilate to provide even more blood, stretching the blood vessels and causing a headache. As climbers adjust to the altitude, blood flow drops and headache resolves. But if a climber doesn't adjust and continues upwards despite the telltale headache, disaster looms. The brain continues to swell from engorgement with blood, pressure builds in the capillaries and they leak plasma, like an over-pressurized hose springs leaks. This fluid escaping into the brain tissue amplifies the brain swelling and the brain is pushed against the rigid bones of the skull, with no way for the pressure to be released. Without oxygen or descent, the pressure inside the head will eventually squeeze the brainstem, resulting in coma and then death.

DR PETER HACKETT, DIRECTOR OF THE INSTITUTE FOR
ALTITUDE MEDICINE, TELLURIDE, COLORADO

BOB KANDIKO – JUNE 11. The weather is still poor so we sleep and eat the hours away. Mike eats a two-man dinner in one sitting while I doze and dream of having the comfort of more climbers being near to us at this time. The 'third person syndrome' seems almost real to me because whenever I doze off I dream of communicating with others.

The memories of my illness on Mount Logan haunt me and I am nervous about a serious sickness developing again. This time the consequence may be far more severe.

Will this headache never leave me? Aspirin seems to have no helpful effect at all and makes my constant nausea worse. I should be acclimatised by now, surely. We have been at high altitude for many days and we have not been ascending very fast at all, considering all the rests we have had.

I don't understand why I am not doing better. When I have climbed on the Brenva face of Mont Blanc it is normal to go all the way from the valley to the summit in twenty-four hours or so and that never affected me like this. We are only at an altitude similar to Mont Blanc now and we have taken a week to get here!

Something else worries me. I notice that my physical agility is not the same. At times I am dizzy and I really have to concentrate hard until the feeling passes. I have never felt this before, but I keep it to myself.

JACK'S JOURNAL

I'm still writing on my side. I turned and turned all night. It was cramped but warm, dry and sheltered. I feel somewhat rested but the weather is still fitful. It might clear up but then again it may still be snowing; either way we will have to leave and go for the snowfield above.

I close my eyes and our situation fades from my consciousness, like a helium balloon disappearing in the heavens above, becoming insignificant until you almost forget that it even exists.

I dream about Ruth. I want to be with her again so I must survive this ordeal.

I think about a job that pays well and keeps me satisfied. I might even welcome some relaxation of a less hazardous nature. I let my mind wander over to Mom and Chris, how much they mean to me, how much I love them. How much their hearts will break if anything happens to me.

Finally it begins to clear up outside and we start breakfast with a banana cream pudding for lots of energy to get us through the day. A Tuck each and two and a half quarts of tea and away we go.

One hour later it is snowing again, shit!

We get off at twelve noon, late I suppose but only because it will mean setting up camp at the end of the day when it is cold and everything will be frozen.

The first few pitches are straightforward ice, not much mixed climbing. Then we get into the hard stuff; ice and snow in rocks, stemming on the outside of chimneys. It's all very exhausting but they go straight up mostly and the angle seems to be less than before.

The grand finale is Simon's fine lead on mixed steep rock to a belay just short of exiting the rock band.

My next lead takes us over and through the rocks on to the battered bowl where the monster sérac hangs above our heads, waiting to come crashing down on us.

Momentary relief sets in. We are over the crux of the climb: no more rocks to be climbed. No more imagined dread of being lost in a world filled with nothing but rocks, ice and the deceit of illusion. We need to rest!

We have been averaging one hour per rope lead, not too bad really, and now it is 6.30 p.m. and I want a brew.

Simon wants to bivouac so we decide to continue climbing until a suitable site is found and on we go; one, two, three … six, seven leads later we climb above the séracs and Simon finds a hole to bivouac in. Well, not exactly a hole but an area where blocks have iced up with snow giving the impression that a ledge of ice is buried here. We chop some of it away and make a nice platform where the tent is erected: another home away from home.

Fifteen pitches today. We waste no time and get in with all our gear. Simon looks (and feels) exhausted. The thin air!

I check out my feet and I discover to my dismay that my right big toe is swollen and blistered with frostbite. This puts a different tone on our climb now! How to deal with this complication? No radio. No rescue.

My other toes do not seem affected but I am sure that they are, just not to the same extent; it is just that I cannot tell. Upon closer examination it appears that the blistered area is OK apart from the outer two layers of skin tissue. The toe itself is red with purple colouring the affected region.

We'll go for the top. We are at an altitude somewhere in-between 16,200 feet and 16,400 feet. Tomorrow we will go up to 17,500 feet and rest, and then go for the summit. On the way down I will try to get some emergency care or even evacuation as I'm sure the frostbite will be worse by then. We should be fully acclimatised by now.

Dinner does not exist tonight as we're too tired, a single Tuck and a Musketeer bar will have to do. We brew four quarts of tea instead, probably more important to our health than a Richmoor meal.

We will ditch all unnecessary gear here I guess: rock pins I hope, some biners etc. and my broken Charlet Moser, all dead weight. Just as well I brought a spare ice hammer.

Now more than ever I feel the pressure to finish. In the rock band you could only go as fast as each individual pitch will let you go. Here on the open ice we should be able to move much faster. Really only two more days if we have good or even marginal weather; I want to be rid of this monkey on my back, I want it to be over.

The weather once again seems to be deteriorating. Is it always like this? Must I always do big serious routes in poor weather? It seems so.

BOB KANDIKO – JUNE 12. We leave our residence of two nights and move up a steep rock and ice ridge. The remnants of a previous campsite look like something out of the *Book of Revelation*: twisted metal poles and mangled cord and wire. The rock climbing becomes more serious and Mike leads.

My sense of balance is screwy and I make many mental mistakes and lapses. I slip often and I am not even tied into the rope correctly! Mike notices a few of the mistakes and asks if everything is OK. I can barely shake my head as I know the altitude is taking its toll.

I request that every move be belayed and he agrees. The remainder of the day is one of nervous climbing, but Mike does an admirable job. I lead one ice pitch that ends in a blank rock wall with two pitons in it. Mike attempts to free climb it but to no avail. He then tries to aid it and falls flat on his back. He eventually aids it without his pack and then hauls me and the packs over the lip. This little obstacle has cost us over two hours and much energy. Fortunately just 200 feet further ahead is a good camp spot at 16,600 feet. The fatigue is heavy as we carve out a platform for the tent and crawl inside to cook and try to replenish our bodies.

JACK'S JOURNAL – **JUNE 13**

The weather is bad outside and conditions inside not much better. I feel rested but I am having a hard time breathing, much laboured.

Simon is in a poor mood. He has a bad headache and generally feels really terrible.

By noon, nothing is better so I declare a rest day. It seems to take twenty-four hours to recover from two hard days of climbing. I hope this day off will not affect us badly as food is low. If we rest here we can go to 18,200 feet or 18,400 feet and bivouac and then go for the top the next day.

Today will be another day to acclimatise. My toes are the same, not as bad, however, as I had imagined they would be. I feel clear in the mind but it is difficult to get enough oxygen to do anything I must do.

The only physical complaints I have other than the blisters and the frostbite are my cramped muscles in my back, legs and shoulder.

I want to go home. I want this bad dream to end. I just hope that I will be able to enjoy the rest of the summer. I don't want the frostbite to keep me in a bed. I'm also hungry, hard to ignore that.

BOB KANDIKO – JUNE 13. Today will be a day in camp as the wind is strong and the visibility poor. I have bad headaches and feel nauseous. Mike and I play gin rummy with a pack of cards displaying fifty-two gorgeous women with smiles and big tits. It is amazing how soon one only notices the numbers!

JACK'S JOURNAL – **JUNE 14**

We left the campsite at 12.30 p.m. under pretty good weather conditions. Very soon we're into knee-deep snow, kicking steps up the forty-five-degree slope. The weather cleared up here and all day we are treated to fantastic views of Alaska.

Pitch after pitch we climb, each one resembling the last. The big couloir that leads to the Cassin Ridge is looking large and we are usually guessing wrongly as to how far away it is.

It is hard work and I usually take twenty steps, rest and then take another twenty, put in an ice screw and belay Simon up to me. He goes up the same way. We repeat this ten times each before we have a brew.

Breathtaking sights to be seen, especially with all the hard work we are putting in; we average thirty minutes per pitch which seems fast.

After the tea I feel good but Simon looks worse and he goes slower with each pitch. By number fourteen it is obvious that we won't go for the top despite the good weather. Simon would never make it, he really looks beat.

I lead the next five pitches to a bivouac spot at 17,650 feet. Not as high as I would like but it is as high as we are going today.

A ledge is chopped, the tent erected and I jump in and pull off all my boots to check out my feet. They are really cold but not much worse on the right foot except for the big toe which is really blistered. Otherwise all are OK.

Simon slowly creeps in and pulls off his boots in the now traditional way. We get the Ensolite pads laid out and a brew is established.

Hard day; twenty leads of climbing is the best day yet and gets us to about 17,700 feet.

Simon doesn't really say much these days; he complains a lot and moans. He looks at me with those big moon bloodhound eyes of his and drops the corners of his mouth. He throws up just before dinner, in fact we didn't eat dinner either as he is too sick to eat. We just drink.

I am concerned because we are down to our last two meals and one and a half quarts of gas. I cannot get mad because how can I? I wish he were as fit as I seem to be, so we could take advantage of the good weather. We will see, perhaps tomorrow he will be stronger and the weather good.

I want to sleep but I can't, not in the true sense; I nap a lot, but not sleep.

I am letting the side down. I know it, but this is all I can do. I plod and wheeze slowly along, like an unsteady old man. I actually need to use the shafts of my axes for balance on a forty-five-degree snow slope, which is pathetic. It is not just the lack of oxygen; breathing is difficult, but I have had this headache for four days now. No, it is as if I am a soul trapped inside the body of a drunk, a stupid clumsy person.

I cannot think clearly. I try to talk to Jack because I should. I see him fretting over his frostbitten feet and I try to think of something to say to support him. I try to form a sentence in my mind because I seem to have difficulty in just talking. I am not an imbecile, I can talk as fast as I can think, but now … I try and practise what I will say and … I have forgotten where I started and stay mute. All I can do is look at him and hope he can hear me thinking.

He gives me tea, which is nice, but I spill it on myself and it hurts. Now Jack is just looking at me; his eyes are very unhappy.

JACK'S JOURNAL – **JUNE 15**
Simon is extremely sick. We stay in the tent all day. The weather is crappy, snowy, windy, cold and damp.

I try to ask Simon about what he thinks is wrong with him; he can hardly compose a sentence, almost as if he is drugged and confused, he has no idea. Altitude I think. Acute mountain sickness coupled with what he now tells me might be sunstroke from yesterday's bright light. I don't know.

He hiccups a lot and does not want to drink much, so he is dehydrated too I say. He just caves in and won't try to understand the nature of his illness. Plus partial weakness from climbing without much food, but I don't think he has ever become used to thin air. I try and try to find out just how sick he is but it does not work.

For lunch we have beef stroganoff but I save Simon's because he can't eat more than a few teaspoons of it.

Gradually during the day he regains some of his lost strength. We talk, the weather has cleared and we are packed and ready to leave at noon but the wind picks up and it's already -30. Who needs a chill factor? We sleep until 6 p.m., for me the second-best sleep of the trip thus far.

JUNE 16

This is day nine on the climb. By 7.30 a.m. we decide to split. It is still muggy out so we come back into the tent and then leave by 10 a.m. By this time the sun is around and thawing out the tent.

We had the tomato lasagne last night so we set out today totally barren of food. Foodless Day One begins.

I am not optimistic of reaching the summit from here in twenty-four hours. Simon's entry on to the ice is poor; this and the way he doesn't really seem to know what he is doing sometimes leads me to wonder about his climbing capacity. This morning he seemed much stronger, but how long can he maintain it at these high and rarefied atmospheres? Maybe we should have traversed off to the west? We should have brought a radio, it might save our lives!

So even after showing him on the map where to go, he asks me again. The first few leads are uneventful step kicking but tiring. Our progress is the same as before, about thirty minutes per pitch, but by pitch five it has slowed and I am drifting off into hazy afternoon dreams while resting after every twenty steps.

I recover fine from each pitch, it just takes longer, that's all. The day is once again a magnificent summit day with blue cloudless skies. Despite the sunshine I am wearing everything I own except the mitts, scarf and Thinsulate jacket.

We lead up to the Cassin Ridge where at 18,400 feet the altitude is really having an effect on performance. Both of us are hanging our heads at the belays and rest stops. Encouraging words are shared, and 'live forever' Christmas card shots are taken, the best views I have ever seen in the mountains.

It is hard going through knee-deep 'cornflakes' snow on a fifty-degree surface. Every second step breaks through to the one below but finally Simon hits the Cassin Ridge on the tenth lead. Now, more than ever before, the Alaskan range explodes into view. Mount Huntington, the Ruth Gorge Amphitheatre and Mount Dickey, every one of them slowly sleeping below us in the sunlight.

It is 8 p.m. as we walk along the crest of the Cassin Ridge. I feel better now than a few hours ago. Simon on the other hand says his knees and legs have turned to jelly and he can hardly walk, so I lead for the remainder of the night. I don't really mind but sometimes and more and more often I think he talks himself into one of these ailments. Maybe his legs are really weak but mentally he should be able to do it anyway.

After a couple of leads the temperature drops as the sun sinks behind Denali, leaving a shadow across the country. There are so many beautiful sights that I want to stop and admire them and snap pictures, but at the moment I have my hands full with Simon who is staggering, falling and generally having a very bad time …

Before we were looking for a spot to brew some tea, but now it is getting colder and colder and our exhaustion (especially Simon's) is so apparent that the necessity of a bivouac is all too obvious. So I lead and look and look. Seven rope lengths above the point where we hit the Cassin Ridge I make out a snow slope that might be a suitable place to hack out a ledge.

Simon is now worse than useless; he seems hardly to understand what I say. He trips a lot when he is following me, something I find frightening. I yell at him, shout, anything to get him to act and move better. It does not work – it only upsets him. He doesn't know what he is doing.

So we stop here, somewhere above 19,000 feet, and I chop out a ledge while Simon tends to brewing tea. Snow and ice chips fly everywhere, I am a blur of motion and I am in a frenzy of activity. I am doing it to keep warm and because Si is incoherent and cannot do it. I want to check out my toes because they feel awful cold in those ice traps I wear on my feet.

It's a ledge big enough for the Bibler and maybe not enough but I am beat and doing all the work so I say it is done.

By the time both of us have collapsed in the tent and thrown in the sleeping gear, I realise it is too small. But we are only going to sleep until daytime when we would split, just eight hours away, so it doesn't matter terribly much.

The stove is running and the third quart is spilled by me. I start spacing out and the gas fumes don't help much.

It is soon also apparent that Si is so burnt out and probably will not be able to go for the summit tomorrow.

Shit!

22
THE DILEMMA

The transition from simple mountain sickness to high altitude cerebral edema can be subtle. Few brains rapidly exposed to eighteen-thousand feet are functioning normally. Most climbers in such thin air have headaches, fatigue and fitful sleep. The onset of slight impairment in coordination may be written off as unimportant, and minor mental confusion attributed to exhaustion. The victim's partners are often upset with what appears to be laziness and unwillingness to help with team efforts, but in reality it is the higher brain functions [that] are starting to shut down. The lassitude becomes incapacitating; the climber can't get up and about, can't help with basic survival needs, stays in the sleeping bag and drifts in and out of consciousness. If he does try to get up, he stumbles as if drunk, and can wreak havoc in a tent or snow cave, knocking over stoves, damaging equipment and falling off the side of the mountain or in a crevasse if left unattended. By the time it becomes obvious this is cerebral edema rather than a lesser altitude problem, it may be too late, with coma and death rapidly ensuing. Climbers that continue to ascend after contracting HACE usually die.

DR PETER HACKETT, DIRECTOR OF THE INSTITUTE FOR
ALTITUDE MEDICINE, TELLURIDE, COLORADO

The darkness comes and goes. Sometimes I can see, sometimes I must wait for the light. I have no choice; I am trapped inside a body and brain over which I have no control. When it awakes I can feel its awful pain. I begin to prefer the dark times, when at least I can sleep. The hope of waking is becoming less important.

JACK'S JOURNAL
I try to sleep outside Simon's bag, leaving mine stuffed so at least it will stay dry. I keep the stove going most of the night brewing tea.

The night is a hungry one.

Just another dozen Tuckerman bars each would have made this situation entirely different. Why did we run out? Was it the unexpected delay in Simon's acclimatisation, or the initial difficulty of our route? We took all the gear and supplies I thought we could have carried. I should have stuffed my pockets, should have eaten more before the climb. We should have taken more anyway.

'Seven days stretchable to ten,' I told Frances. I sure hope they are thinking about us down below, wondering if we will be all right.

I am so hungry and have been heading this way for so long that it seems easy to ignore. I cannot get any more food so why worry. My real concern is when we run out of gas for melting water.

It bothers me also that Simon does not even try to help. He just lies there in the corner, slumped over, eyes closed, sleeping while I do everything. Plus for the last three to four days he really does not talk so there is no company in his company. The biggest mountain bummer I have ever been on. But who knows, we may get to the top of Denali tomorrow. The alternative is too terrible to consider.

BOB KANDIKO – JUNE 16. Mike and I are frankly nervous and scared. We have designated this day as a 'can't wait day' instead of either starting down, traversing the CLOD Face (named after Bugs McKeith's trip in 1977, 'Canadians Lost On Denali') or going over the top and escaping via the West Buttress.

Analysis of the options:
1) Starting down – the ridge is precipitous and would require rappelling and belaying all the way down. We only have one 165-foot rope, three pitons and seven ice screws. We could hope to scrounge some pitons on the way and maybe excavate some of the fixed lines for rappels. The process would be very time consuming and dangerous. The Japanese are 3,000 feet below but the ground between them and us is difficult.

2) Traversing the CLOD Face – the terrain is unknown, fairly steep and exposed. It would lead us on to the West Rib or the main basin of the West Buttress. The rock buttresses should be negotiable. We would be staying at 16,000 to 17,000 feet for a long time.

3) We continue, up and over the top – ahead of us are various snow slopes with the occasional rock band to cross. We must allow eight to twelve hours

minimum for the ascent. We will have light packs with just spare clothing, tent, bags, stove and what is left of the food. The option to camp half way is always open, but with changeable weather and my deteriorating physical condition, personally I think that one push is important. Once over the crest, an hour or two of stumbling down the West Buttress route would take us to 17,000 feet and hopefully contact with other climbers. The big question here is about my physical capabilities. I have been plagued by headaches since 16,000 feet with periods of nausea. Whether or not the additional 3,000 feet will be severely incapacitating or fatal is an uncertainty, one that sits heavily with me.

JACK'S JOURNAL

The tenth day on Denali, the second without food.

The interior of the tent is depressing; it's cold (even with all my clothes on), it is damp, wet, small – enough said.

The stove is purring cheerfully, doing its thing, turning snow into H2O. The weather looks OK so I tell Simon to get ready to leave in two hours, at 7 a.m. He grunts a reply but does nothing. This goes on for one to two hours and it really pisses me off that he won't even communicate. Maybe he is that sick but I think he is really more interested in sleep than going on, or I should say, getting out of this mess.

Well, finally the weather does crap out and it is almost completely white outside with lots of snow falling.

I am concerned that after a few more days of not eating we may be in no condition to tackle the summit and get down the West Buttress. I am also worried that we will be so weak we will need a rescue. If anyone even knows where we are and if they had that information could they fly that high, 19,500 feet? I don't know.

In the meantime I am OK mentally so maybe when my physical self is almost gone my mental self will kick in.

I wish that the tent wouldn't ice up each night, it's like an ice palace in here. Frozen stalactites of water crystal hang in white plumage from the rafters of the tent. What is depressing is the way the ice falls everywhere whenever anything touches the sides of the tent.

My right toe burst last night and there seems to be a larger frostbitten area, but I won't at this point worry, I can feel the tip and the sides.

I may quit climbing at this extreme, I mean this; if I survive this mountain and get back to California I am going to unload all that equipment except that which I need for 'fun' big walls.

The experiment with altitude is interesting but is limiting and exhausting also. Every breath can be an effort.

I really would like to concentrate on other things in life, learn a language – Spanish or Japanese – have a stable house with the best woman I can find, dress up more and see more nightclubs. Find a good steady income and pile it away. Drink margaritas at night after a hot meal of Spanish omelette, refried beans, chilli and brown rice. Ei Chiwawa!

It seems strange to be here with Simon. It seems my mind has been busy creating diversionary tactics to keep me from thinking about all of the real dangers involved, by conjuring up from my memory floods of easily recognisable friendly faces and placing them on parties of climbers who are constantly in sight, although I never talk to directly or confront these figures personally.

However, as the twilight of my youth arrives with this dramatic conclusion and the peril that we have placed ourselves in looms larger and larger with every dawning day, the images that concern me most are of friends who I want to see at the high school reunion in August: Richard, Charles, Pat, Marcia and others.

I will cherish my toes, no more hard ice climbing (extended that is).

Route Description:

Names; pick one:

a) South-West Face Direct

b) California Direct

c) Sheldon Route

d) White Knights' Route

e) White Punks' Route

f) Tuckerman's Route.

Well, the hours are creeping by, I have been napping some, sleep, wake up for one hour, sleep for two and so on.

Simon is his usual catatonic self, won't or can't talk or joke or anything. It is almost 5 p.m. and the tent has gone from warm and humid to chilly and damp.

Simon just took a pee. His thinking is bad. He takes the pee bottle but then takes it outside, almost falling as he tries to step through the doorway. He stares into the snow until I ask him what he is doing. He then pees into the snow and leaves the bottle outside. He then tries to get inside by bracing himself against the tent which would have broken had I not grabbed him and helped him in. He is extremely unsteady, what will I do? Must I leave him and go for the top myself to try and find help? Go together and possibly not make it, have to leave him and go for the top and try to get to a radio and rescue? I am torn between

Mike Helms makes a wonderful discovery, a cache of white gasoline.
Photo: Bob Kandiko.

personal survival and helping Si who is too far gone to do anything for himself.

If this is a prolonged storm it looks very sorry because if I cannot or do not possess enough energy to get to the top in a snow storm, then what? I guess I'll wait and see myself. I'll know when the decision is made.

Silence everywhere.

This is the closest I have ever come to dying, even more than Huntington in a way. It is almost like 'controlled death' because so many little decisions go into one big mistake. Little things I have had to do like stop when the weather was good because Simon was too tired or too sick to go. We had to stop because he just couldn't go on. Well, we are paying the price; I hope it is not too great.

While at 19,400 feet I have a terrible headache and I gotta make some water to drink.

BOB KANDIKO – JUNE 17. It is such an effort to write these thoughts. Sitting at 18,300 feet as the snow filters down, it is evident that option three was the one chosen. We go up for the summit.

We have dehydrated food and drink mixes, however with no fuel this food is mostly useless.

I break the trail through a foot of fresh snow to see how my body is functioning. I develop a rhythm of four steps **and a break and a stop** to regain energy with deep breathing.

I keep thinking that Mike will volunteer to go first because I am the weaker, but no such luck.

The mental contest rages, to continue on instead of collapsing. **Four steps**, **rest**; a too short stop and then not resume, but then the inner willpower reveals the futility of quitting here. 'Up' is 'off' this mountain.

We find a comfortable spot and give ourselves a five-minute breather. Then onward and upward again but soon Mike stops by a huge boulder and is laughing as he lies in the snow. The reason is soon obvious to me; he has found two full gallon cans of gas left by some previous climbers. Our last remaining worry seems to have been alleviated. Our karma must be good.

Now feeling that our bodies and minds are healthy and strong, we have copious quantities of fuel and enough food for the two of us for a week if necessary; with easier climbing ahead, the pressure is lifted from our thoughts.

Mike roams behind the boulder only to discover three pitons left two years ago by close friends of his. Their initials are scratched into the steel. In such a large world, on such an immense mountain, friendships are still a strong bond.

JACK'S JOURNAL – **JUNE 18**

Day eleven on the mountain, third day without food.

Simon woke me up at 10.45 a.m. because he could not stand that I was sleeping and he was not.

The weather outside has got worse, or at least not become any better, snow is steadily falling outside. The wind is still blowing, not much, gusts of twenty-five only.

My condition is not better; I have a constant headache due more to lack of H_2O and nourishment than anything else. My kidneys hurt and my stomach is eating into itself it seems. My head is very light, my thinking dazed but clear. My back hurts from lying on cold ice so much. My body has the scent of urine to it and my feet stink.

The spindrift outside is really bad; our tent in just thirty-two hours has shrunk, the snow has gathered between the slope and the tent. I should have made more of a cave with a lip on it but at the time the weather was perfect and we only planned to be here eight hours.

That was before Simon caved in. Then the weather got bad. I never meant this to be permanent.

Well, it has to be done, I will have to try to dig out the slope and repitch the tent with Simon inside. I am bummed going out, why me? Why does everything from day six on this climb rely on me? I am so much more energetic that I can do more than he can. I think he is physically able but he just won't. So I have trusted my life to the wrong person, never again will we do a serious route together. When we climb together again it will be on some fun route. I just pray to Jesus that I live through this epic.

Anyhow, I managed to get in some anchors and stretch out the floor space some but it takes too much energy to chop out a better platform, energy best spent elsewhere. So I tie us down level as best I can and get back in. One and a half hour's work.

Simon is completely helpless, he cannot even tell the difference between push my sleeves or pull my sleeves.

I hate to berate him but this is a pure survival situation and I have to survive for both of us as he can't do anything. It is not fair. Why am I always the stronger and my partner the weaker?

On Huntington we complemented each other, but then I looked after him on the Tokositna Glacier. On the entire descent I looked after Dale on Polar Circus. Who looks after Jack? I want to live!

Never have I felt so helpless, I can do nothing. I am not certain I can make it on my own, especially after my little exercise a while ago. I am slightly dizzy and beyond being hungry, always thirsty and panting for breath. But I can make it out I am sure.

I'll have to stay with Simon and I pray that God sends us a rescue when the weather gets better.

The weather is definitely much worse now; even after one hour the snow is building up against the wall of the tent. I kick it every so often because it's not nice to have that happen.

Simon does not even try; I shake him to try to bring him out of it but to no avail. He has given up and just wants to die. Just waiting now is all he is doing.

The wind is up and batters our small tent all day, eighty-five miles an hour with stronger gusts. The wind sounds like the distant horn of a railway car.

JUNE 19

The weather is beginning to clear. I hope that today I can see a few planes that we can signal to and even get picked up. Between 9 and 11 a.m. there are a few but they are so low, below 17,000 feet and they won't see us.

The few times I get out the wind blows spindrift inside and I can see that the weather is closing in again and no further landings will be made today.

Simon is not noticeably worse but does try less to do anything. The only thing left to do is for me to climb out solo and get down on the West Buttress and get some help. So I brew some tea and tell Simon my decision. He accepts it. I wish it wasn't this way.

I pack all of my bivouac gear and clothing and my camera. I leave him the stove, a rope and other equipment.

In my heart I know the chances that we will both survive are becoming unlikely. I make a list of Simon's immediate family and loved ones, many of which I know.

Judi Barnes
McCartney family
Garrett family

Smiler Cuthbertson
Ian Nicholson
Dave Wilkinson
Nipper Harrison.

I am standing outside the tent packed and ready to leave, looking at my feet; unable to take the first step.

23
THE CHOICE

BOB KANDIKO – JUNE 19. The wind abated during the night, calming through the morning hours. The silence seemed to keep me awake like a child waiting on Saint Nicholas. I tossed and turned, getting little sleep as I awaited an appropriate hour to see if the day in fact would be clear and climbable.

Finally at 3.45 a.m. I asked Mike to check out the tunnel entrance for the forecast. Hooray! There is low cloud at 8,000 feet but all is clear above.

I jumped out into the -20 calm and snapped some pictures. Now we must wait for the sun to reach the tent and warm up the air to prevent frostbite.

As the sun came around the ridge so did the wind. This is quite common in big mountains. As the sun warms the surface air the cold night air rushes down due to its denser and heavier weight. But today the wind was to stay with us until the afternoon. I was more than frustrated as Mike cuddled up in his bivvy sac, seeming to ignore the fact that we had only two dinners left and should another storm hit us, we would be in a considerably more serious situation.

Finally I broached his quiet state with some rational and some emotional considerations about getting up and off the mountain no matter how windy it appeared. It was only three to six hours to the crest and it felt better to move than to sit here waiting for further calamity. He got a bit concerned with my emotional pleas and conceded to give it a go. So we went.

We continued with our rhythmic step, slow but we would make it with this pace.

◀ Bob Kandiko and me in the Too Loose tent at 19,400 feet on the Cassin Ridge.

241

Then, as we approached 19,000 feet, I thought I heard a voice from above. I glanced back at Mike but he had said nothing.

One hears a lot of odd noises so I passed it off, but it returned a few moments later and there, on a rock outcrop 200 feet above me, was a puppet-like form in a yellow jacket, jumping up and down.

A few more minutes of rationalising passed before I could discern that it was Jack Roberts, but it took another twenty minutes to bring me to him.

When I reached him I learnt that Simon and he had completed the difficult technical section of their climb but their rapid ascent had resulted in frostbitten feet for Jack and acute high-altitude sickness for Simon, who had buckled to his knees and lay semi-conscious inside the tent. By now they'd had no food for the last four days and Simon had actually been too sick to eat for some time before that.

I cooked one of our remaining two meals. I measured Simon's temperature at 96° Fahrenheit, so apart from his altitude-related problems he has hypothermia as well. So now for a powwow.

Simon cannot stand up and Jack has not eaten for four days. Simon needs evacuation but we have no radios. Jack wants to follow us over the crest and then return to their camp with assistance, food etc. from the camp at 17,000 feet on the other side. That is totally unrealistic; leaving Simon alone would be a death sentence and even if Jack's plan was possible it would take too long. We held a hurried council of war to decide our best course of action. What could we do? There are other groups on the easier side of the mountain who might be able to help if we could reach them.

Mike has been on that side of the mountain before. He knows the West Buttress descent route and the logistics of resources, so he was the logical choice to continue. Jack could not remain at this altitude without losing his toes, so he would accompany Mike. The plan for the rescue was that Mike and Jack would go over the crest and find a party with a radio and signal to the park service that Simon needed evacuation as well as food and fuel immediately. Then they would climb back over with whatever food they could borrow ...

The inner good in me saw that I should volunteer to stay with Simon, if he was to have a chance at life. It was a difficult decision to remain behind, but otherwise Simon would not live. What about my own life?

I unloaded my gear and moved in next to Simon in the small tent. From the small doorway I solemnly watched Jack and Mike as they walked over the ridge, leaving only their footprints. Suddenly all is silent.

JACK'S JOURNAL

Bob writes a quick message to his mother in my journal:

'To Mom Kandiko, alive and well and matter of fact I am implementing the rescue of a stricken climber. I will call when it is all over. Love Bob.'

Mike and I will go and get help.

The weather clears and we hope to return with help tomorrow.

It turns out that we are at the 19,500-foot level so it takes just three and a half hours of moving together to gain the summit of Mount McKinley.

We pass ice-encrusted towers of rock. The ice has been plastered against the rock and the wind has turned them into grotesque gargoyles. The views are nice but a big front from the south can be seen overtaking and overlapping the cumulus clouds below it.

Eventually we reach the summit and my first thought is that I wish Simon had made it here with me. He had lucid moments and catatonic spells, but he told me to 'finish it'.

Down we go, descending the West Buttress. The wind drops and it warms up immediately. The weather is coming in fast so we too must move out quickly. It is three hours of staggering until we hit a camp of mountaineers at 18,200 who adopt us, feed us and let us bed down beside them.

It is really cold and extremely windy all night; I cannot sleep because I'm worrying about the boys up top. My bag is wet and I am soaked but I am safe. It makes me realise how tough it is up there. I hope we can rescue them. I write of my observations of Simon's health problems as I remember them:

'Altitude problems developed at 14,500 feet with hiccups combined with gargling in the upper chest. Next morning the pulse rate is eighty beats per minute. Still hiccups but no more gargling, but now dizziness and general weakness.

'Bivouac at 15,300 for thirty hours. Hiccups continued, weakness and threw up food.

'Bivouac at 16,200 for twenty-four hours, hiccups but kept down food but very tired. After twenty-four hours OK.

'Climb to 17,500 feet, threw up less and could take only tea and milk, could not climb well for the last twelve pitches, he is exhausted.

'Bivouac at 17,500 feet – thirty-five hours. Threw up turkey meal and hiccups continued. Liquid intake only one pint, last meal.

'Climb to 19,400 feet, exhaustion, legs go to rubber, pulse goes up to ninety.

'Bivouac at 19,400 feet, three days, average liquid intake a day: three cups.

'He has complained of terrible headaches since 14,500 feet.'

BOB KANDIKO. As the first night descended, the temperature dropped to -20°. I woke Simon every hour to serve him a cup of hot tea or soup, while I took only meagre sips. I curled my body next to his to transfer heat while Simon was unconscious. At 4.30 he awoke and pleaded for more warmth. I lit the stove and made some soup and then at 6.30 I treated Simon with the last Swiss Miss, which delighted him like a child with candy; he saw that there were little marshmallows in the drink and he studied each one before devouring them.

We then began the long vigil, waiting for our rescuers. No noise from either plane or people. The remaining pot of tea was accidentally kicked over so now we only had water to fill our stomachs. On the bright side, Simon's temperature had returned to normal and he was more coherent. We spent the long hours either sleeping or talking and becoming acquainted. The highest place in America is an odd place to begin a friendship.

A very kind person has come to camp with me, I have been able to talk with him today, and he gave me a wonderful hot drink. I have only just been able to remember his name; it is Bob. I had to pretend that I knew it all along because it is rude not to remember people's names, my father told me.

The stupid person I am trapped inside seems to be getting better, but he gets tired too easily and sometimes the darkness comes before I am done talking. This stupid body makes me angry. It is so nice talking to Bob, who tells me that we will be rescued and soon be back in the warm sun in Talkeetna where we can eat and drink and get better.

JACK'S JOURNAL – **JUNE 20**, WEST BUTTRESS

I wake up often after one hour of sleep in the snow and wind storm. The Gore-Tex 'Bomb Shelter' ices up inside just like the Bibler, and when the wind hits, it snows inside. Very miserable. Very cold.

I hoped for good weather but the winds are sixty miles per hour, too cold. I go into the main cook tent where there is warmth and room to sit comfortably and I stay there all day. It is too cold to go down for help. I hope they survive their ordeal.

I am cold all day due to the lack of food; even though they (Vick and Mick) share their food generously with Mike and I, it is not enough; I am so worn out that I require huge amounts of food.

I am so tired that I just want to die in a warm corner while I am asleep. I am sure Simon wishes his trial would end.

We will go down tomorrow if the weather allows to 17,200 feet where we can radio for help, advice and spiritual assistance.

JUNE 21

We got down to 17,200 feet yesterday afternoon; there is good weather down here. We alerted everyone to the situation and began preparations for a rescue. Radio messages bounced back and forth until, at 7 p.m., we had a complete rescue plan, equipment and personnel assembled. Eighteen people, a winch, 1,200 feet of rope, one litter and we are ready.

NATIONAL PARK RANGER DAVE BUCHANAN'S REPORT – JUNE 21. On 6/21, the National Park Service was notified by radio of the situation. At 17.40 Helms contacted the NPS with a plan to rescue McCartney using the climbers available at the high camp and requested an airdrop of food, fuel and other equipment.

FRANCES RANDALL, KAHILTNA BASE. One person of the McCartney-Roberts group is sick on the mountain (transmission by clicks from the transmission button only as the signal is bad). I switched to Channel 1 then back to 19. I called Cliff about the sick person on the mountain; communication with 18,000 is very poor. I can only hear that there is a problem with this person. Mike Helms is at 17,200 on the West Buttress. Simon McCartney is at 19,300 feet. Bob Kandiko is with him.

Mike Helms travelled with Roberts over the top and down the West Buttress to relay a message outside.

Helms can get McCartney down to 14,000 feet. In an urgent call to contact Cliff by relay to Talkeetna, I tried to get KES7604 and was overheard by a pilot over an island near Kodiak Inlet. I talked to Mike Helms; there is no radio on the Cassin.

He has a rescue plan but he did not see Kenya 80, the Scottish team or the Freaks below on the Cassin. The Japanese have a radio.

Mike has an equipment list for the rescue, needs food and fuel and wants to talk to the NPS directly. Cliff called and wanted to know if McCartney could stand up. I advised that I would ask at 6 p.m. I also advised that a group is getting ready to help.

Mike called. Mountain Trip Traverse are at 18,000 feet and Mike Helms is at 17,200 feet. Mike Helms advised that:

1) Mountain Trip Traverse needs batteries and is willing to help in the rescue.
2) Must understand the gravity of the situation.
3) They request a flyover of Kandiko and McCartney.
4) They plan to bring them up over the ridge (about 800 feet), rather than down-climb the Cassin.
5) They request a weather report.
6) Weather is clear at 17,200 feet, winds calm. At 18,000 feet the winds have died down to forty-fifty knots.
7) They need a 6.30 p.m. contact and then one every fifteen minutes.

Mike says McCartney is in very serious shape and we should try to get him and Kandiko to move up the ridge. NPS advised that Peter Habeler and Michl Meirer are willing to come back to help.

BOB KANDIKO. As I sat there two days later the decision to stay rested heavily, as heavily as it ever had! At the moment there seemed little option unless I just felt selfish and so I hoped for the best for Simon's rescue. So I pushed my own safety (my life) to the back cupboards and I crawled in the tent with destitute Simon, who could not sit up or clothe himself. At least he is a little better now.

I had to constantly dig out the tent because of the constant bombardment from the slope above.

I boiled out the residue from the Mountain House meals to make a very weak soup and more diluted tea. Simon accidentally kicked the tea over and I screamed bloody murder about him not being able to care for himself, a point that is proven when he pisses in the tent because he is too unsteady to hit the opening in the piss bottle. At least he is not hypothermic: his temperature is back to normal at 98.6, from 96° Fahrenheit, but he is clearly still very ill.

After three days of waiting the despair became intolerable. The longer we remained at this elevation the weaker we became and there was no rescue in sight. I got psyched up to attempt to climb out. In our enfeebled condition it took more than four hours to put on our frozen boots and pack the tent.

When preparing to leave for our attempt to go up to the summit ridge we discovered all the climbing hardware in Simon's pack. We threw the (expensive) gear down the slope as it was useless weight. We found humour watching such costly gear being thrown away.

We would attempt to climb to the crest and descend the West Buttress.

As we were packing two climbers came by heading towards the summit: Rob Milne and Scotsman Brian Sprunt. They gave us some Kendal mint cake. I told them that we would be right behind them and they were gone before I realised I had made a terrible mistake: I should have told them that Simon was ill. I had given them no reason to wait. We had an entire camp to pack, so why would they wait in the cold? My brain had gone soft, I should have asked for help.

We left at 2 p.m. and Simon immediately slipped on a thirty-degree step. He could not stand up for more than three steps at a time without falling to his knees. He moaned and he would cry like a child as he struggled to regain his balance, only to fall again a few steps further.

The footsteps up were quickly drifting in and he was unable to stand or follow so I pulled the rope tight and screamed at him to get up and continue. I was frustrated and frightened that he could not follow. In my frustration I looked at the rope and considered untying the knot and continuing up by myself. In a sense I realised that I was not brave enough or strong enough to go up alone with that burden. I was demoralised to turn around and re-erect the tent. Simon was unaware of my possible action as he was bent over on his knees, incapacitated by his illness.

My feet were beginning to freeze and we had gained only about 200 vertical feet before I realised the hopelessness of our endeavour.

We returned to the campsite, which looked like an empty sports arena after a championship loss, with all the surplus gear and trash scattered to the winds.

In a howling wind I set up the tent and put Simon inside before regrouping our essentials. Then I went inside and warmed up the tent with the stove, for hours.

A deep depression set in, but it was tempered by a feeling of triumph because we had a least made an attempt to climb out. We now knew that we could not go over the top. The only way was down. Our only chance to live was to descend the difficult ridge. The prospect intimidated us but the desire to survive conquered our apprehension.

At night my toes started to get so cold that I put hot water into a water bottle and placed it between my thighs in the sleeping bag to increase blood heat and circulation.

FRANCES RANDALL, KAHILTNA BASE – JUNE 22. NPS advised that all of the Chinook helicopters are grounded, no high-altitude capability available. The highest capability is 14,000 feet.

Wolfgang (three) was with Mountain Trip Traverse last night, but did not see McCartney or Kandiko.

I have advised Helms the Chinooks are grounded. Doug Geeting will do a flyover of the Cassin for NPS with ranger Roger Robinson on board.

BOB KANDIKO. All night the tent shook as it was pelted with chunks of snow and ice. Our sleeping bags were soaked with frozen condensation. It was a miserable morning with nothing to heat for breakfast except water. My mind was scrambled by the effects of altitude and the lack of food.

I had deep, fond thoughts of my family and how tragic the scene would be to die in these frozen heights without seeing them again. Why was I here? I could go over the top by myself and leave Simon but my humanity wouldn't allow it. He was a dead man unless we got some assistance. Is it courageous to choose to die?

I was still strong enough to make it over the top, but Simon would not survive without me. If I remained with Simon, we might both die. Was I selfish in wanting to continue my life?

I shuddered at the thought of my parents hearing of my death. They would never understand the circumstances which forced me to stay behind to help a total stranger, but if I left now and survived I would always have Simon's death on my conscience. If I stayed with him we both had a chance to live.

The wind and the bombardment were less and we decided to head down in the hope of meeting someone, maybe the Japanese. At 19,300 feet we were deteriorating in mind and body and the absence of food forfeited any acclimatisation for another summit bid or any hope of help on the West Buttress.

Where was our rescue food? I had no idea. We could only hope that Jack and Mike made it safely over, but I realised that they would be too exhausted to make a return trip. I also doubted that any other climbers would be in shape at altitude to make the journey over from 17,200 feet. So we packed our wet gear. I gave Simon only his personal gear to carry and down we started.

Bob has some special medicine, I don't understand what it is but he has a joke name for it: 'black bombers'. I get two and Bob takes just one. I feel much better not long after as I am sitting in the hazy sunshine. I have all my clothes on and I don't feel cold but my legs still won't support me. My balance is still ruined.

BOB KANDIKO. Simon was cooperative and wanted to descend but his balance had gone and he had to glissade on the seat of his pants. I anchored and belayed him down on his slides, then he would anchor himself, I would trot down and we would repeat the process, 150 feet at a time. We made slow but convincing progress through broken clouds. For Simon it was the fastest way to travel and the safest.

As we approached the snow arête at 18,500 feet I heard a plane. Maybe it was a search plane looking for us! I urged Simon to hustle out of the rocks so we could be more easily spotted on the snow arête. He had no energy so

I went first, making rhythmic steps, hoping that he could keep up. He was like a drunken man, full of stumbles and falls. I shouted for him to follow. The engine roared downslope; a sense of panic filled me as I dragged Simon down the arête.

DAVE BUCHANAN. Ranger Roger Robinson is on board in Talkeetna Air Taxi Cessna 185 N1047F, piloted by Doug Geeting. At 13.45 they spot two climbers on the Cassin Ridge below the campsite.

The first person on the rope waved to the plane.

McCartney and Kandiko are identified as descending the ridge when the plane spotted them at 18,400 feet. Helms reported that he and Roberts could descend out to the landing site and did not require a rescue.

Bob is really happy that we have been seen by the plane. So am I but can they really come and get us here? I help Bob set up one of our ropes in the shape of a cross in the snow to help mark the spot where we are.

I can only crawl about on my hands and knees, but my headache has improved a bit and I am no longer a victim to my body, which has stopped just shutting me down whether I like it or not. For the first time in many days I have some say in whether I am conscious or not.

Sitting in the sun is pleasant and I drift and doze through the day until the temperature starts to drop.

No sign of any helicopter.

BOB KANDIKO. Disappointed, we continued with the descent, each rope length a battle against exhaustion and hunger. After five gruelling hours we could go no further. At the 18,000-foot campsite Mike and I had used, Simon and I now struggled with the tent and crawled into its psychological shelter.

To improve our hot-water diet we decided to add toothpaste to the pot, thinking that this would help with the lack of electrolytes in our intake. Our subsequent indigestion revealed why 'toothpaste stew' was not a common 'soupe du jour'.

At 3 a.m. I awoke too cold to sleep and started the stove in the tent door for warmth and hot water. The shadow of McKinley drifted over the rosy dawn

Bob and I hear the sound of a light aircraft high on the Cassin Ridge. We lay out the rope

light on the range. I simply listened to the 'ping' of the pot over the stove. I had a deep sense of serenity as dawn arrived on the peaks below.

JUNE 23. We had to descend a steep 700-foot exposed snow slope to the east. Simon was able to stand now and contribute, but I still belayed each rope length as we did not want any mishaps.

The first highlight of the day was finding and collecting the second gallon can of white gas we had left at 'Gasoline Alley'. Mike and I had left the second can for future climbers that might be in trouble. At the time I had not expected that Simon and I would be those climbers in peril, just a week later. At least we would have plenty of hot water.

We used all our energy to move slowly and deliberately on that section. By the time we arrived at the top of the higher rock band we were exhausted and the speed had worn off.

It took a ridiculous amount of time to set up the Bibler tent as we were on our knees. We could not have started down through the rock bands in that condition with only one rope.

Later in the afternoon I crawled up the slope to cut a section of fixed rope to add to ours. At that piton anchor I discovered two coils of climbing rope, plus some Hanes underwear and two poly bottles containing what looked to be food residue. When I triumphantly returned to our tent with these treasures Simon immediately scooped some of the residue (jam?) and swallowed it. I watched for his reaction; there was a thoughtful pause while he analysed the flavour, then he turned to me with the face of a happy child. We put the sweet stuff in boiled water to make a sort of slurry of liquid to drink, both of us staring at the brew like kids in a candy store.

The stove and extra gas will be our salvation on the descent.

I am no longer imprisoned in a body of dysfunction and pain. My sense of balance has returned, although I am pitifully weak. I can help Bob with the chores; I can set up anchors, tie knots. I have no strength but my technical skills are the same.

It seems that I have forgotten or I am unaware of much of what has transpired over the last four days. Bob mentions a few things about how he looked after me and they are a revelation. I have to ask him to explain where Jack and Mike are and his answers start to open doors in my clouded memory. He tells me how he and Mike had found Jack and how they decided that Jack and Mike would go up and over and Bob would stay to look after me.

Until this moment I have been drifting along, trying to do whatever I am told, whatever Bob suggests, like a child following a parent. I now hear the details of the truth and it shocks me. I am like an alcoholic suddenly sober, awakening to survey the awful damage done to my body. There is one fact that overwhelms me with emotion: Bob chose to stay and look after me. We hardly know each other.

We may still not survive, this much is clear. We may yet just fade away on this mountain. Tears well in my eyes as Bob recounts the parts I cannot remember. Then there is shame too. Apparently in my incoherent state I tried to take a piss and managed to urinate over Bob, myself and the floor of the tent. I try to apologise but he tells me there is no need – I can buy all the beer if we get down alive.

JUNE 24

I wake at 2 a.m., freezing cold. My movement disturbs Bob and he lights the stove to warm us and make hot water. Glancing outside the tent to check the weather, Bob sees something he says I must see too and I stick my head out beside his.

The vista is amazing, the most spectacular view I have ever seen in the mountains. The sun is rising north of the summit and has created a pyramid shadow of Denali that stretches to the southern horizon. Each peak in the range is brought to life, one by one, as the shadow of the vast mountain retreats. I do not know many of their names, but I can see Mount Huntington become brilliantly illuminated, like a shark's tooth, far below. I remember looking at Denali from there in 1978. It was a view of Denali that played a part in why I am here at this moment. We are spellbound, and for a short while we forget our predicament. A new day has begun.

We had hot water for dinner and now hot water for breakfast. Every little exertion makes us light headed. Bob looks as I feel, exhausted by the simple act of packing the tent and yet we have barely moved.

Some little pride has returned to me. I was a liability to Jack, and then, for the last six days, a liability to Bob. We might yet all die because of my illness.

I don't know why I have been so badly affected, but my head is clearer now. I am only alive because of the bond between climbers, and now that I am free of my stupidity and the random descent of darkness, I must take my share of the load as best I can.

We can only endure four hours of movement before collapsing on the old tent platform Bob and Mike constructed at 17,000 feet. It takes us an age to erect the tent because we are too weak to stand up.

BOB KANDIKO. The third highlight was my finding the used tea bags that Mike and I had left on our ascent. The subsequent tea, lukewarm and barely coloured was the best we had ever tasted.

We had spent six days higher than the summit of Mount Rainier without a single meal. Simon had endured four days of starvation prior to that.

By now I feared that the park ranger service may have notified our next of kin that we were missing or worse. I crawled deeper into the insensitive cocoon; which was my sleeping bag, while Simon stared blankly at the doorway.

We had come a long way in the last three days but the lack of food would soon end our chances for survival. The weather had been merciful but a storm was approaching from the south. Almost delirious we fell asleep.

24
THE FREAKS

BOB KANDIKO – JUNE 25. The wind tore the fabric of the tent. Simon and I lay motionless, hoping that the seams would not rip. Each blast of wind hurled the nylon fabric of the tent into my face. As the snow piled up I pushed with all my might to prevent the wall from collapsing. Mercifully at noon the wind ceased and sunshine bathed the tent. Quickly we packed our bags and started down. We had to get off this mountain.

Exhausted to the point of tears we climbed and rappelled down the steep ground of the upper rock band. We struggled to remain upright, one slip here will result in a certain and quick death. At times it almost seemed preferable to let go but thoughts of my family brought back my desire to survive. To make matters worse I had dropped my sunglasses and was feeling the effects of snow blindness set in.

I must be very careful; I am struggling as much mentally as physically; my exhaustion is affecting my brain's function. I forget what I am doing from one moment to the next and I am afraid that I will forget to clip into an anchor or, my worst fear, that I will accidentally rappel off the end of the rope. So fearful am I that I stop on the next good foothold, pull up the fifty feet of rope under me and tie a figure-of-eight knot including both tails and then cast the rope out below me again. If I forget about how long the rope is, the knot will jam in the crossed karabiners I am using for a rappel brake and halt my descent.

The thought of my karabiners brings another jolt of anxiety. Are they the correct way around? Making a brake out of karabiners means that you don't have to carry a piece of equipment specially for rappelling, but it is not

◀ The arête should have been child's play, but despite the fixed lined from the Tokyo team every step was a trial. **Photo**: Bob Kandiko.

257

foolproof and at this moment I have the head of a fool. If I have the gates on the wrong side I may accidentally unclip myself and fall to my death. I freeze and stare at them for about a minute until I am convinced that I have arranged everything correctly.

The day is long and complicated. Rappelling in this rock band is problematic because the terrain is not steep enough for clean rope retrievals. When the ropes are pulled down they tend to snag because there are so many medium-angled and less-than-vertical features on which the ropes can – and do – catch. This happens many times and on two such depressing occasions the pulled rope jams and we are too exhausted to climb back up and free them, forcing us to cut the ropes. If Bob had not found the stash of rope we would be dead men by now.

The nightmare Jack and I had on the descent of Mount Huntington is being relived, this time with Bob. The same game is afoot: a first ascent, followed by a descent of a classic route. I am seeing a lot of quality Alaskan climbing in spontaneous disasters.

Because I am getting to know Bob in a nightmare, we become close to each other very quickly. We are facing the possibility of our deaths and in such circumstances every layer of human affectation is stripped away, nothing can be hidden and each of us can see the soul of the other. I am seeing into the soul of a selfless and very brave man. Bob is an experienced climber, he is highly intelligent and he thinks about everything in his life, more than I do. When Jack and I attacked the south-west face I just thought to myself that if the going got tough we would deal with it. Bob analyses things and thinks about all the 'what if' stuff that I don't. Or used not to. Maybe I have been too confident, or maybe I put up a screen to avoid the imponderables so I can get on with a climb. Or maybe I am just a bit slow. It doesn't matter now.

Bob is the person who is saving my life. The incredible thing is that he knew what he was doing when he made the decision to stay with me. He was nearly home free on the Cassin and yet he chose to put himself in great peril to nurse a cripple towards a chance of life. How lucky am I to have met Bob?

Bob told me that he and Mike had considered climbing the West Rib instead of the Cassin Ridge. If they had done that we would never have crossed paths and maybe the McCartney-Roberts team would have become a statistic. What a trap Jack and I set for ourselves this time. We are immortal no more.

I help Bob rig one more rappel using recycled pitons that I found above a little ledge. How we wish that we had not thrown my rack of Friends and chocks away at 19,400 feet, thinking back then that we had no need of them; I could have made cunning use of them now.

I tie another knot in the end of the doubled rope and start down. I make a bad job of walking backwards down over the rocks, losing my balance several times and twisting on the rope as I lose my footing, crashing into the rock face-first and banging my head. I stay motionless until I can regain composure and then arrange my feet and continue, but only go eighty feet before I near the knot. I know we have no anchors left and wonder if we will be able to make another rappel or if we will simply fade away, unable to get past the rock band. My life will surely end soon. I hear a voice. I cannot understand what it is saying. I glance up at Bob.

'What?'

He shakes his head. He has not spoken and I continue to descend through the thin cloud. I can hardly see Bob now as the mist comes and goes.

I hear the voice again, below me. Am I dreaming or hallucinating? Bob and I are alone in the clouds, surely. I hear a voice yet again, louder this time. I really am losing my mind. Then Bob is shouting at me from above, waving and pointing, shouting for me to look down.

'Si, there, below you!'

I am confused but do as he asks and am so amazed by what I see that I have to stare for a long moment to make sure it is real. Set up on the toe of the rock band is a Whillans-type box tent, with several climbers nearby. One with a beard is calling to me. I look up at Bob and he looks very happy. This dream is convincing!

With shaky steps I stumble towards the end of the rope. The bearded climber is obviously concerned about my uncoordinated movements and climbs up from his tent with a sling and karabiner ready to attach to me for safety.

He reaches me just as I get to the end of the rope, which whips out of my enfeebled hand. I would have fallen to my death had it not been for the knot which jams in my karabiner brake.

In tears I try to explain that we need help, that we'd had a week or more without food, that I had been ill. My incoherent babbling is not necessary – he can see all he needs to see from my pitiful state. He helps me sort out the mess with the rope and guides me to a ledge cut in the ice and sits me down.

'How many of you are there?'

'Just me and Bob. Bob!'

I must call to him. I try to get up and shout but my bearded friend cuts me off: 'No need, here he comes.'

My rescuer arranges another belay for Bob, in much the same way that sober people care for deeply drunken people who are not fit to look after themselves. I am bundled into the box tent and I collapse on the floor weeping, my cramponed boots left sticking out of the sill.

We have crash-landed in a team of four climbers and our ragtag arrival has shocked them. They had been making an organised ascent of the Cassin Ridge but now have two wounded to deal with. Their afternoon has been shattered. Their ambitions and a year of planning to climb the Cassin Ridge have been turned on their heads in a moment. Without their help, we will die.

Bob is helped into the commodious box tent, a nylon and aluminium shelter of the type originally designed by Don Whillans for siege-climbing Himalayan mountains. It is as if we have been transported from hell into a tiny hotel. Bob and I curl up in each other's arms crying and laughing. Relief and elation have taken over simultaneously. We feel we are now going to live, an outcome that had seemed unlikely just an hour before.

Our hosts look on quietly and with concern at the shameless emotional display of two grown men who have realised that their expected demise has been postponed. Nothing could have prepared this team for this and I wonder what they think of us. Perhaps to them we are just two incompetent climbers, out of our depth, who have wrecked their expedition.

Yet they are generous. They are short on food but prepare a Mountain House Mexican dinner while we talk and they share it with us. It is Bob's first proper meal in a week and my first in ten days. While the feast is being prepared Bob and I take stock of our hosts.

Bob and I eat rapidly and then sadly regret it; our bodies crave the nutrients but the indigestion is severe and we both double up in discomfort after the meal. Clearly too exhausted to scrape out a flat spot on the slope for our tent, we are allowed to move into the box tent for the night. We sit up instead of lying down due to the crowding, Bob and I leaning on each other for support. The nightmare has abated; we are not home by a long way but we are not so cold and I am not so sick any more.

Only when Bob and I have composed ourselves can the introductions be properly made. The group hales from Pennsylvania and the name of their expedition is the 'Freaks'. FREAKs means 'Far out, Radical, and Environmentally Aware Klimbers'. We are in the company of Peter Carter, Michael Pantelich and John Rosenfield from Pennsylvania, and Sean Meehan from Washington State.

The Freaks took us in and shared what they had. Cramped in their tent, Bob and I begin to believe we will survive. L–R: Sean Meehan, John Rosenfield, Mike Pantelich, Bob and me. Photo by Peter Carter on either my camera or Bob's.

Bob and I take turns explaining what has happened over the last two weeks, how we had both started up our chosen climbs. How Bob and Mike had climbed the Cassin, how Jack and I had made the first ascent on the south-west face. Bob describes how he and I happened to meet at 19,400 feet, and my severe altitude illness and lack of food over ten days. There is silence amongst our hosts but many shared glances between them.

JUNE 26

The next morning there is a discussion amongst the Freaks. I don't know how I would feel if I were them. They have been planning this trip for a long time and come a long way from home. In their minds they probably thought they would make it to the summit, but they decide to abandon their ascent and stick with us so we can descend as a group.

Breakfast is provided and we have a little porridge and tea. In the process of food preparation Bob and I can see that, even without us, the Freaks don't have enough food to finish their climb, particularly at the rate they have been going. We both mention this, hoping it may help with the disappointment of abandoning their ascent, but it is not taken that way; our weasel words are clearly steeped in self-interest. If I had been in their position I would have felt annoyed too, but they did what they thought was the right thing without hesitation and I am forever grateful for this.

We all begin the descent from 15,800 feet together. We need to rappel about 700 feet down through the lower rock band. Below these rocks is the hanging glacier and a huge, almost-flat saddle on the Cassin Ridge. Bob and I both hope that we can catch up with the Japanese there. The Freaks confirm that they passed them on the way up.

Bob and I had been hoping for an easy ride, just tagging along with the Freaks, but it becomes obvious that a six-man descent is tedious. We have limited ropes and equipment and we are getting in each other's way. Bob becomes impatient and this makes relationships difficult. Not only have we wrecked their expedition, but Bob is now directing the retreat, finding the fixed gear and placing pitons. I am beginning to feel really bad about what we have done to these lads but I remind myself that only yesterday Bob and I were staring death in the face.

My head is clearer now; whatever was wrong with me has almost passed and I watch all the rigging on the way down. I think the lower altitude is doing me the world of good although I am still very weak. Bob looks better than me, but that makes sense: I have had a longer period of starvation and he looks like a bigger and stronger guy than me anyway.

It takes us until early afternoon to get down out of the rocks and I am almost in a daze when Bob does something that totally confuses me. He joins me on a snow ledge just above the bergschrund that forms at the top of the hanging glacier and then suddenly abandons the rope, jumps over the 'schrund and starts running down the snow slope below like a madman. I shout after him, asking what he is doing. He doesn't turn and all I hear is:

'Japs!'

It only takes me a moment to work out his plan. My eyes follow Bob's trajectory and looking ahead I can see his goal. There are three figures in the distance, at the edge of the hanging glacier about to start their descent on to the arête. They are all moving together on fixed lines and Bob is chasing after them to use their radio.

25
AIRDROP

FRANCES RANDALL, KAHILTNA BASE – JUNE 26. 2:15 p.m. Kandiko called to say that he and McCartney are on the way down to 14,200 feet and are with the Japanese. They are desperate for food and request an airdrop. McCartney has gone ten days without food. The Japanese are headed for the Japanese Couloir and have little food left. The cloud level is 10,000 feet and the air is clear above and calm.

Kandiko borrowed the Japanese radio to make the call. McCartney is alive. McCartney is very weak, but stable and able to walk.

3.05: The NPS will drop food and medicine at 14,100 feet on the West Buttress.

A helicopter is coming in from McGrath: Roberts wants the helicopter to drop fuel and food to Kandiko and McCartney.

Bob is in a triumphant mood when he returns from his sprint to catch the Japanese team. He tells me that lunch will arrive shortly. The park service is sending a helicopter to pick up an injured climber and they are going to drop food and fuel on the way. He is also relieved; the park will call his folks to tell them he is OK. He confides in me for the first time that his greatest fear was that his parents might have been notified that we were missing and that they would be torn by anguish.

Bob tells me that Jack and Mike made it to Kahiltna Base today too, so they are both safe. Given the great weather up here I hope that it clears below so they can fly out and Jack can get medical help for his feet. Bob also tells me that

◄ The missing component for our survival has arrived; climbing ranger Roger Robinson flies over us again; this time he will deliver breakfast, lunch and dinner.

he reported to Frances that we had no injuries so we did not require a rescue, even though this was an option. I agree with his decision. We have come this far and survived, and with food and a rest we can climb down by ourselves. The Japanese set off on their descent after Bob had finished using their radio.

We have clawed our way back from the edge of the abyss and have made it on to easy ground with food on the way. Thanks to the Japanese we will have an easier descent because of their fixed lines. I would hate to be evacuated now.

I sit in the snow, warming in the brilliant afternoon sunlight. For the first time the pressure has lifted and Bob and I are in control of our destiny again. Slowly we dig out a flat spot for the tent and a sheltered spot for the stove.

The pressure to simply survive has passed and my mind is free for the first time to wander. I am only here today because of Bob and I need to thank him. He has been alert through all of our time together while I have been helpless and semi-cognisant. Bob has had to suffer every moment of it; I sense that I have missed the worst parts.

I try to open the topic with him. I am not sure how to do this and he does not make it easy. Maybe he is uncomfortable. I should thank the Freaks too, but my consuming bond is with Bob and I leave all these thanks unsaid. My clumsy attempts are cut short by a welcome noise in the distance, the unmistakable throb of an approaching helicopter; it sounds like one of the big choppers from *Apocalypse Now*.

The sound gets louder and we all scan the horizon for the first sight of the chopper. Bob sees it first:

'There!'

Slowly climbing above the Kahiltna Glacier is a large helicopter equipped with skis. Its door is open. The feeling of happiness I have at this moment, seeing that aircraft coming to deliver food, is tempered with a new determination to get back to Base on our own steam. High on the ridge, if I could have been rescued I would have accepted it gladly, but not now. The tables have turned dramatically in our favour and I want to return to Base Camp in the manner that I departed twenty-four days ago – on my own two feet, without any more help.

I can see a figure moving about inside the helicopter as the aircraft assumes a noisy hover just below our position on the snowfield so the downdraft does not damage our campsite. The figure comes to the door and drops a khaki green duffel bag which falls the fifty feet between the helicopter and the hanging glacier below and lands harmlessly in the snow. Then there is another and, finally, a cardboard box.

The figure waves to us and we all wave back. Then the helicopter banks away,

I met this happy team from Tokyo three weeks ago in the north-east fork of the Kahiltna.
Since then Jack and I climbed the south-west face of Denali. I survived days of illness,
and Bob and I climbed down the Cassin Ridge to meet them again at 14,200 feet.
In a different mood I might have thought about the difference in our climbing styles.
But that day I was grateful for the loan of their radio.

makes a big lazy turn across the spine of the ridge and heads west on its next mercy mission, to collect an injured climber I guess.

Some happiness pervades the campsite but the happiest of all are Bob and me. There is a vast amount of dried food and fuel but also bags of nuts, dried fruit and chocolate. Bob and I briefly discuss the fact that maybe we should eat slowly in case our shrunken stomachs reject the sudden ingress of food, but the concern is soon forgotten and we gulp fruit and nuts while the stoves melt snow for the dehydrated meals.

Bob finds a copy of the Anchorage Sunday paper in the box and amuses himself reading the cartoons. The contrast with our experience of the last week could not be more extreme.

A non-stop eating feast ensues that goes on for hours under the hot and sunny Alaskan sky. Collectively, the six of us eat two 4-man dinners, two 4-man lunches and two 4-man breakfasts, along with gallons of sweet tea. The Freaks are no longer hungry for food but I can see them looking up the ridge, no doubt hungry for the dream our collision with them has destroyed.

For a moment it seems that all is well in the mountains for Bob and me and it is warm enough that we can strip off most of our disgusting soiled clothing. In the warmth and safety of life at a mere 14,200 feet there is now time to notice that we smell very bad, especially me. I have the pungent odour of sweat and, embarrassingly, urine.

Now that hunger has passed I have time to consider all the little things I can do to improve my condition. I turn my sleeping bag inside out and toast it in the sun, hopeful that I can kill some of the smell. I dry all the clothes that I am not wearing and then I turn my attention to my feet. Unlike Jack, I had no concerns about frostbite; my feet had been fine all the while and I had not taken my inner boots off at any time during the climb. I have small feet that fit easily into climbing boots and I can live easily with them on my feet for many days. On big climbs like Huntington or the Eiger, it had never occurred to me to take off my inner boots because they were warm and comfortable. But, here, it has been three weeks and it seems like a good moment to wiggle my toes and dry what must be very smelly socks.

Sitting inside the tent on my mat I take off my outer boots and put them out to dry. I then unlace the felt inners and take off my socks. At first the feeling is pleasant, tingly, as if my blood is flowing more quickly through the veins in my feet. But the nice feeling soon passes and my feet begin to swell rapidly and painfully. Bob has come over to see how I am doing and I see his face fall as he sees my swollen feet and anguished face. The swelling continues dramatically and I become racked with agony. I feel as though I'm being electrocuted through my feet and the pain is unbearable, leaving me squirming in agony on the floor.

Bob is back in kindness mode and sits with me until the fit passes. Painkillers are found and administered and for a while the pain relents, leaving me breathless and exhausted.

In the night I am awakened by a deep throbbing pain in my feet that rapidly gets worse. Soon the pain is excruciating again and I can't help but writhe for twenty minutes before the feeling of electrocution eventually starts to ease.

We wake early when another bout of agony in my feet disturbs us both. Still, we are doing OK. Bob is a new man and he sets about cooking a two-man breakfast for us while we wait for the Freaks to get ready.

Just two days ago we were crying in desperation, rappelling alone through the snow trying to save ourselves. This morning there is no haste; we have one more meal to eat and a plan. We have slept late, me especially because of the agony I had to endure from my feet during the night. I am going to have trouble walking, let alone climbing, but I know that with Bob's help I will get down.

I doze while we wait for the others. We will all descend the arête and the Japanese Couloir together. Bob has already begun to allow himself to think of his home; the expectation of our survival has become solid and the mood is that, whatever Denali might throw at us, we are close enough to our exit to make it. Tonight we will camp at the site of our igloos, back on the north-east fork of the Kahiltna. There we will rest and tomorrow head for Base Camp.

I can see the Freaks getting ready so it is time to try to put my boots on – which may take a while as both my feet are swollen. Normally there is space inside them around my toes but not now. They are splayed apart by inflammation and my usually comfortable inner boots have to be forced over a single pair of socks. The vice-like grip causes another agonising fit and that has me writhing while Bob does his best to comfort me. It's not an auspicious start to the day.

When Sean, John, Mike and Peter are ready we decide that for the tricky arête we will split the six of us into two ropes of three. Bob wants to put me between him and one of the Pennsylvanians because he is worried about how I will climb with my problem feet.

Organised in this way, we set off down the Japanese fixed lines, beautiful 9-millimetre ropes. Our progress is immediately slowed by the conditions. The arête is very exposed and, I suspect, a little awkward even at the best of times. Today it has a coat of wet snow that sloughs off in big pieces. We really have to be careful and the exposure means that not everybody is having a good time.

The group behind us has fallen back and the gap between us is growing. I just follow Bob, hoping that I do not suffer another fit with my feet while I am on the arête. I can hardly control myself when that happens and this is not a good place for that to occur.

Features like this arête are dangerous places: no matter how fit you are, or technically capable as a climber, a slip here could spell death for you and anybody on the same rope. It is not like rock climbing or pure ice climbing when all four paws are firmly attached to the mountain, here you have to stand up like a tightrope walker and balance along a knife-edge ridge of snow and ice. It is a stunt easily performed ten or twenty feet from the ground, but here – thousands of feet above the glacier – the mind uses fear to create doubts that would not normally surface.

Bob is constantly doing little things to keep my morale up; he gives me a running commentary on our progress towards the top of the Japanese Couloir. He tells me the arête is nearly over and we will shortly reach a ledge where he and Mike camped on the first night of their climb. It will be easy to get to the ledge because of the fixed lines and we will stop there and have a brew while we wait for the others.

I am in a lot of pain. The meds cannot even begin to breach the chasm between agony and comfort. I beg for the arête to end and in answer to my plea it finally fades away. When I catch up with Bob he is safely belayed to a rock anchor placed by the Japanese, God bless them. I am no fan of siege tactics and in my more normal, arrogant mood perhaps I would have been disparaging about them, but today I follow their fixed lines as if angels had laid them.

The lines go straight down the Japanese Couloir. The clouds come and go and we can see that, thanks to the three happy lads from the Tokyo Unyro-Kai expedition, we have a nylon highway back to the glacier.

I find that I can look out across the south-west face. It is important to me that I remember the details of what Jack and I did and where we climbed. We took ourselves to another dimension in our climbing and I am uncertain what will follow in my life. It feels a bizarre ending to this climb that circumstance has parted us, but there it is. In the clearer moments I can trace our route to the big boulder where we spent two nights. I can see where we traversed left, but the angle of my view does not allow me to see the detail. Higher on the face I can make out a few features, but the memorable big boulder is the anchor.

The pain in my feet is offset by the joy of our continuing escape from Denali. The Tokyo team have done a great job rigging their fixed lines. Bob and I do not take turns – we just flee. The ropes and anchors are so good that we can plummet down two pitches at a time, Bob descending on the line above and me descending on the line below. As I remove my weight from one rope and transfer it to the next, Bob is hard on my heels, zipping down the line I have just used. We take only minutes to dispense with each rope length and I have a feeling of joy now my speed and confidence are restored. After a week of clawing and crawling and sliding on my arse, I can fly a little again.

The fun is short-lived. After we cross the bergschrund there is a long walk back to the igloos and a dreaded fit arrives from my feet. Electricity pulses through my soles and I sink to my knees in the snow until it passes.

Bob waits patiently all the while and then helps me up so that I can stagger back to the igloos that we constructed more three weeks ago when we were in a mood of excitement and anticipation. Seeing them again, and the skis we abandoned still standing like scarecrows, feels like a dream. At least they are not standing as tombstones.

Tired, we set up the tent. There is no sign of the Freaks, but we will see them soon. We allow ourselves only one sweet brew before we collapse into the tent and settle into our sleeping positions. We have returned to the scene of the crime, the genesis of an amazing and unlikely adventure. Surely tomorrow or the next day – two at the most – we will be free of the snow and back in the green world of Talkeetna, where we can begin to repair the damage to our bodies and minds.

Before I can pass out the mountain sends us a message with a crack and a boom. Denali has unleashed another avalanche. We start as the sound grows and bellows before diminishing. Icy concrete debris swarms about the tent and stops. A block of ice bounces into the tent near Bob's head. All we can do is look at one another and, in that moment, I see partially suppressed desperation surface in Bob's face; he had begun to believe that we were almost home free. A glance outside tells us the avalanche would have buried us had we camped just a few metres away.

JUNE 28

The boys from Pennsylvania arrive later in the night. The noise of them setting up camp awakens me and I take a peek out of the tent. I can see that the four of them are down – good, they are all safe. Their hazy outlines are all I can see from the tent because we are in a white-out – clouds have filled the valley and it is gently snowing.

Dawn brings disappointment: the weather is the same. We will have to descend in the white-out, guessing where we are and not seeing crevasses or obstacles until we are right on top of them. We may make mistakes. But we have no choice – we have eaten all the food and we have no idea what the weather will do. The option of waiting is not even a consideration and the magnetic pull of Kahiltna Base is strong.

Bob is up before me and makes a brew that he passes to me in bed. Gratefully I drink it but am confused to hear the stove running for an inordinately long time afterwards. I begin to fantasise that there is some secret food left and crawl outside to see what he is cooking.

The disappointment is crushing. It is not food Bob is cooking but ski boots. He has found his abandoned Nordic shoes and is using the stove to thaw them out.

We are ready to roll in an hour but the Freaks are still resting so we leave alone. I feel guilty about the fact that we have wrecked their adventure. But we are alive now because we did. I don't see what else we could have done. Bob and I had no choice about asking these lads for help; we were at death's door when we met them. It makes us feel worse to have been moving faster than them – and to be about to ski away from them.

We only have one 150-foot rope left of our own and we tie on, Bob at the front and me at the back. Jack and I had not bothered with a rope on this part of the glacier on the way up but we are taking no chances now. We are both exhausted and I am a liability. Every step is painful and I cannot move well. Luckily I have my mountaineering skis back.

I do not think about where we are going – all of my efforts are concentrated on the simple task of plodding after the loop of rope that slowly snakes ahead of me. I cannot see Bob most of the time and his ski tracks and the movement of the rope are the things that convince me I am not alone.

The snake comes to a halt and I catch up with Bob and see that we have reached the icefall marking the junction of the Valley of Death with the Kahiltna Glacier proper. The terrain is steeper here and Bob has removed his skis. I must do the same and I allow myself to fall over in the snow so that I can disconnect the bindings and shed my pack. I attach my skis to the side of my pack before struggling to my feet and waiting unsteadily for the snake's instruction to move. Bob has disappeared in the white-out again.

All of a sudden there is a whack. The rope goes tight and a violent tug pulls me to the ground. I am yanked through the snow like a plough, towed by a great force and although I flail my arms it does no good.

Whack! The force that pulled me down increases and I am wrenched from the ground. I make a hard landing and a split second later I am hurled into the all-white air. I'm falling. There is darkness, a heavy impact and then nothing.

I open my eyes. I am confused. I do not know who I am. It is dark and blue and I look into the blackness of a chasm below. I am upside down in a crevasse, swinging like a victim of the hangman's noose – only the noose is not around my neck but my waist.

I remember I am a climber. But which one? What am I doing here? It does not matter now; I must not be upside down. I reach up with my right hand to grasp the rope to pull myself up but when I try to grip the line there is a searing pain in my wrist and my normally powerful fingers open uselessly, like soft fruit. I am suspended between two walls of ice, one overhanging and the other just less than vertical.

If my right wrist is broken then I must use my left. My Curver axe dangles from its leash below me, having slipped from its holster when I inverted. I gather it in with one hand and when I can grasp the shaft I swing the pick into the wall that is not overhanging and pull up. This causes my body to rotate to horizontal, but the position is still very uncomfortable and the weight of my pack is pulling me back down, head first. I need to strike higher with my axe, but if I remove it from the ice I will flip upside down again. To stop the rotation I need to stabilise myself by pulling on the rope with the other hand, but that is now useless. I wrap my forearm around the rope, pinching it in the crook of my elbow and pull as hard as I can. This is not a reliable purchase but I can quickly pull the tip of my axe out and strike again at the ice, further up. I slide my right forearm a little higher and repeat. One last strike with my axe and I pull my body into a vertical position.

The excess blood in my head begins to drain and the bulging behind my eyes relents. I know what has happened: I am a climber and I have fallen into a crevasse, a vast one, but where? There must be somebody on the other end of the rope, but who? Whoever it is has my full weight and will inevitably be pulled into the same chasm. It is only a matter of time before we both plummet to our deaths in this tomb of ice.

26
FLIGHT

JUNE 29

I awake in the very early hours. I have rolled over in my sleep, on to my shattered right arm, and the jolt of pain is like a gunshot. I have little recollection of yesterday other than that I had an accident. I have obviously been concussed but this seems to have passed, if not completely (my headache is epic), but at least enough that I can comprehend what is happening and hold a conversation.

I have another problem too: I need to take a dump and I cannot do it by myself. Bob has to hold the only good hand that I have left so that I can balance unsteadily without falling into my own leavings.

I suspect that like most of us in life, when we encounter people who are disabled in some way we try not to allow our minds to wander and analyse all of the difficulties we imagine they must endure in their lives every day. I am taken there now whether I care to be or not. There is no façade of pride, no brave face to wear and my view on life has changed. For the first time, I am humbled by all that has happened to me. All of my previous climbs had emboldened me. I do not feel very bold today.

Bob sombrely describes the events of yesterday that I cannot recall. He had been descending in front of me but behind the Tokyo team. Our skis were off, tied to our packs. The white-out had been intense and he had simply missed a turn in the footsteps and stepped over the edge of a sérac and started tumbling. The fall had pulled me off my feet and I was dragged after Bob as he somersaulted over an ice cliff.

The only thing that saved us was that Bob landed in a patch of soft dense snow and 'postholed' himself hip-deep, which stopped his fall. Unfortunately, I was catapulted past him and I fell into a deep crevasse, only coming to a halt when all of the rope between us was used up. We were left in a terrible situation, the rope between us holding my entire weight and Bob unable to move – his body was the only anchor preventing both of us from being dragged into the crevasse and the bowels of the glacier.

Minute by minute he could feel himself weakening and being dragged forward by tiny increments. My full weight was pulling his harness so tight the circulation was being cut off below his waist. It was only a matter of time before he would collapse or lose consciousness and be pulled from his hole. But we were lucky: the three lads from Tokyo were just below us when the accident occurred, and even more luckily another four-man team from Minnesota was 200 feet below and they heard the screaming and commotion that followed the fall. They rapidly climbed up to help and assisted the Japanese climbers in pulling me out. The Minnesota team were known as the 'Twin Cities Health Club Expedition' and comprised Steve Friddle, Paul Dvirnak, Tracy Holland and Rick Nelson. The West Rib of Denali was their objective.

Apparently I was totally out of it with a concussion and in the only lucid moment I had I asked one of the Twin Cities team if they had any spare food. Bob found this amusing. We had lost all pride about asking for food from strangers and it was, by this point, invariably the first thing I said to anybody I met.

They put a sling on my wrist and arm and carried me to their camp where they graciously shared some of their rations with us.

After all the fuss died down the Japanese and the Freaks continued down the north-east fork with the intention of going all the way to Kahiltna Base and alerting the park service. The Twin Cities team had a radio but reception is very sketchy from Kahiltna Base and the only messages to get through had been re-layed from a party on the West Rib.

My missing memory is dealt with but what of our retreat now? I am quite a mess today and, if broken bones were not enough, my feet are torturing me even more. I tell Bob that I am not sure I can go on without help. He has been busy: he tells me not to worry and that the park service is coming to get me tomorrow with a helicopter.

I am not sure how I feel. I am excited to dream that this ordeal will be over for us. At the same time I hate the fact that I had been winched off the Eiger last winter and, just a year later, I am to be assisted again. Still, I am not the only one suffering. Bob deserves a break as much as I do. Any lingering doubts that I have about a rescue are silenced soon after when one of the most painful attacks in my feet leaves me weeping.

After all our travails we succumbed to a simple glacier accident: I fell the full height of the icefall ▶ into a crevasse, which left me concussed and with broken bones. Hanging upside down in a crevasse made sense. It was a long while before I remembered Bob's name or my own.

PARK SERVICE. On 6/29 the weather was poor but contact was established between the Twin Cities expedition and Buchanan with a relay by a party at 16,500 feet on the West Rib. McCartney could not descend any further and wanted a helicopter. This was relayed to the NPS and plans were made for an evacuation.

Under instructions from the park service, Bob and the Twin Cities boys make a helipad of compacted snow by stamping it down with their feet. My contribution, pathetic though it is, helps me retain some pride: I crawl around on my knees and help to arrange a rope in the form of the letter 'H' to mark the landing spot. My distorted right wrist is now so tight and swollen within its bandage that I can use my forearm as an amputee might, as one single blunt digit. So long as I do not attempt to use my fingers the pain is bearable.

During the day a team of three Swiss mountain guides descends rapidly and very skilfully on skis from the West Rib where they have been acclimatising for an attempt on the Cassin. Upon sight of my pitiful condition they offer to ski me to Base on a sled. It seems that they are also a ski rescue patrol so dragging me off would be normal for them. I consider their kind offer very briefly and thank them but turn the offer down:

'It's OK, the helicopter is arranged.'

I get a big shrug of the shoulders and a look that says, 'Well, be it on your own head,' and the Swiss leave as rapidly as they had arrived.

Night has fallen and Bob has been kindly given a little more food by the Twin Cities team. Mentally I add another four thank-you messages to the ever-growing list: Bob is number one, then there's the Freaks, the Tokyo lads, Frances, the four from the Twin Cities team and now the entire park service led by ranger Dave Buchanan and including a helicopter crew.

I try to let myself be warmed by the bond climbers have when they go into the mountains but I cannot enjoy it. I am ashamed to have become such a helpless liability.

I set up with Bob for yet another night in the tiny and now very smelly Bibler tent. To my shame, I am the cause of most of the malodour, a fact that is only tempered by the thought that we will be free tomorrow and Bob can go home to visit his parents in Ohio. My last thought is of Jack. I may be able to see him again in a day or so. I hope his toes are OK.

JUNE 30

In the night the weather deteriorates with low clouds and snow. I stare at the awful reality that we are stuck here; there can be no flying today. Bob was busy on the Twin Cities radio before they left to establish their next camp and Dave Buchanan's new plan is to come and fetch me with a team of volunteers from Kahiltna Base and pull me out on a litter.

Bob and I are left alone together and all we can do is wait.

PARK SERVICE. The next day, 6/30, the weather continued to be poor. Four climbers from Base Camp volunteered to join Buchanan and Porter in a ground evacuation of McCartney. The group left at 10.00 from Base Camp and met Buchanan and Porter at 8,000 feet at 14.30. A strong group of three Swiss mountain guides, Beglenger 3, were met descending the NE fork at 8,800 feet. Two agreed to go back up and assist the ground party in the evacuation.

The day grinds painfully by; a long foodless wait and the nightmare of starvation we had endured begins to haunt us again. The entire day passes and there is no sign of help.

By evening I am dozing in the tent when I am awakened by what sounds like mock yodelling. Bob is out of the tent in a second to see who is making the noise. I can hear Bob shouting back and a conversation begins with some climbers approaching the camp. Their accent is Swiss. Then there are more voices, American and English, and a crowd of climbers arrives. Bob looks back inside the tent at my quizzical face wearing a rare smile:

'It looks like you are leaving, the cavalry has arrived.'

The next face I see belongs to the Swiss who had offered to ski me to Kahiltna Base this morning. Even though I turned him down he has come back to get me. I pay a dear price in lost pride as he makes merciless fun of my poor decision earlier.

Dave Buchanan is leading the rescue team of volunteers that includes the two climbers that passed us high on the Cassin: Rob Milne and Brian Sprunt. They must have been knackered but they have come all the way up here to help. Frances and Dave have also persuaded Billy Ireland, whom I know, and his partner Ulf to help start the rescue.

I get a big bushy-bearded smile from Dave as he explains that the Swiss are going to ski me down through the crevassed section on a litter and then the group will tow me back to the glacier airstrip during the night. I am lifted from the tent by strong hands and placed inside my sleeping bag and a bivouac sack, then on the litter, where I am securely tied down.

One of the Swiss is behind me and the other in front, attached to me by short control ropes. They are belayed by other volunteers forward and aft of them. We take off at great speed. I am the worst passenger in any kind of vehicle and so the anxiety I experience crossing snow bridges and crevasses as a helpless piece of luggage is immense.

The two Swiss are obviously experts. They skilfully use gravity to overcome the terrain, the leader skiing down aggressively into depressions or bridges so that the momentum created by the litter is enough to carry us up the other side. All I can do is look with alarm at the crevasses to my left and right.

The progress is rapid, the high jinks of the icefall are left behind and the litter surges along steadily, powered by human huskies. We stop for a rest from time to time and kind bearded faces ask me if I am OK. In one of the breaks I remember that Bob is here somewhere and become anxious – who is looking after him?

After another hour we stop again because a team of three Americans has come to help and to take a turn at lugging me along. We stop again as yet more climbers come out from Kahiltna Base to help bring me back. I am out of danger now, there are no more crevasses to worry about and I let myself accept the bliss of unconsciousness, rocked to sleep like a child to the sound of swishing snow.

We have stopped. People are talking about me as if I am an object. It must be very late in the night. I pull back the fold of the yellow nylon bivouac sack that has been protecting me from the light snow. A female voice is a shock, who can it be? A tall woman is standing over me, hands on hips.

'So I suppose you want to borrow my tent again?'

She laughs out loud watching me try to figure out where I am. It is Frances Randall and I am back at Kahiltna Base.

PARK SERVICE. At 20.00 the party left 11,000 feet with McCartney. The descent went very quickly through the icefall on the NE fork. At the base poles were attached to the litter and four skiers took it down the glacier. The three-member Aspen-Denali Expedition joined the team lower on the NE fork and provided assistance. The team grew as the evacuation proceeded down the Kahiltna Glacier. The team arrived at the junction of the NE fork and main Kahiltna Glaciers at 22.30. They left the camp at 00.15 on 7/01 and arrived at Base Camp on the SE fork at 03.15. Approximately thirty climbers from six countries participated in the operation.

The Swiss climbing team put their great ski-patrol skills to use; I am the package.

My arm is put in an inflatable splint and I am helped from the litter and placed in Frances's empty red tent. I am sat in the very same place that Jack and I stayed when we first set foot on the Kahiltna exactly one month ago. This time I am alone.

It is late and everybody wants to sleep, but Bob comes to see me before he turns in. He will not share the red tent, I suspect because I smell so bad. He has brought me a present though: some chocolate and a beer.

Once again I am left alone and determinedly force myself to stay awake long enough to drink my beer.

I am awakened by the hint of sun on the tent. I shuffle over to the entrance and unzip the flap to be driven back by the brightness outside. I have lost my sunglasses and cannot see well. I am momentarily traumatised by the fact that my good left hand is covered in some congealed brown goo that I am initially deeply suspicious of. I am delighted to find that it is only chocolate.

The sky is not yet clear, but the weather is trending that way. There is a layer of thin, overcast cloud but I can feel the sun's rays. I hear the crackle of busy radio transmissions from Frances's radio tent next door and guess that the Talkeetna pilots are arranging their taxi activities for the day, hungry for information on the local conditions up here on the south-east fork.

My first visitor of the morning is Dave Buchanan. A pair of boots crunches to a halt in front of the open tent flap and a mug of tea appears. He is very happy; like the sheriff of the glacier, he has got his man. I have been rounded up and brought back to town by his posse.

Dave sits in the snow by the door of the tent and keeps me company while I drink my hot, sweet tea. He tells me that it will clear soon and that me and a German climber with badly frostbitten feet will be the first to fly out. He also tells me that Bob is fine and still asleep.

Dave has a daysack he found in the remains of the snow cave Jack and I made. He can find no sign of our equipment but the bag has more important things in it: my wallet, credit card and passport. I want to tell him how grateful I am but whenever I attempt to do so I feel tears welling and I just let him keep talking happily, a grin in the middle of that big beard.

There is a plan for me and I listen without comment. Doug Geeting will fly in as soon as conditions allow. We will fly directly to Anchorage and land at a small airstrip where an ambulance will take us to Providence hospital. I am worried that the little insurance I have will not cover the cost of my treatment, but what choice do I have? As Dave is chattering away I look down at my swollen and distorted right wrist. It is an ugly mess and I really need to get that looked at.

A patch of blue breaks cover while we are talking and I hear Frances announcing the arrival of clear skies on the radio.

All too soon I hear the drone of an aircraft engine; the effect is like electricity in the camp. Climbers are packing and moving around in the sunshine. Bob has been awakened too and he comes to see me off as Dave's posse load me back into the litter and tow me out of the red tent. Unfortunately Bob cannot come with me, it is not his turn and anyway my flight will not go to Talkeetna.

He stays with me and takes pictures while the drone of Doug Geeting's Cessna gets louder. A minute later the little plane is spotted. I cannot see it well because the sunlight is so bright but the pointed fingers of others are enough to convince me of the reality of my escape until the familiar white and orange plane slowly sweeps up the valley and flares for a perfect landing in the snow.

As Doug unloads his two incoming passengers, I am towed over. Bob takes pictures of me with Dave and Frances, who bravely gives me a big hug. And then there is Doug standing over me with the amused demeanour of a taxi driver for lunatics.

'I saw you waving high on the Cassin.'

'Well, Doug,' I reply, 'I could still wave back then!'

I am loaded into the back of the Cessna and as we taxi for take-off Doug opens all the windows. He tells me that I smell worse than his horse's ass and so we fly all the way to Anchorage with fresh air streaming in.

As we fly I realise that my physical contact with Denali has come to an end. I hope like hell that Jack crossed the summit. I would hate it if some anorak said that our ascent of the face was not complete because of what had happened to me, because we had been parted by my illness and because neither one of us had made it to the very top.

My fellow passenger is depressed and we do not talk. He is miserable because of his injuries. He has paid a high price for his climbing holiday on the West Buttress. I guess he may lose some of his toes. I may yet lose more of my pride. The noise of the engine is mournful like a wail of pain and regret.

The cost of my broken and enfeebled body is the price I paid for a new ascent on the steepest side of Denali. I may yet count my wounds in years to come and think back on the battle and the prize. Maybe I will wear these wounds with pride, maybe with shame. One thing is certain: I am not the same person I was just one month ago. The mountain remains as it was but my attitude has changed.

Jack and I have not been playing the game of chance we played on Huntington. Serious as that climb was, here we have embraced a new strata of suffering and deprivation in which we have exposed ourselves totally to the mountain, higher and for longer, giving it new ways to wear us down. My illness nearly killed both of us, and Bob.

As we flew out of the Ruth Glacier after Huntington it was a thrill. Jack and I had used our arrogance as a shield and won the grand gamble: double or nothing. Today, alone, my escape is only a relief. Our new route is an extraordinary thing, I suppose, but something inside me is troubled, the mixture of emotion too complex for me to fathom. It is not fear or trauma – mountaineering has never frightened me and does not still – it is emptiness. All of my climbs have been part of a progression, each next climb a step up from the last. For the first time I cannot imagine the next step.

The most unsettling thought I have as I soar above the south-east fork in Doug's little Cessna is that I do not even know where Jack is. It was not meant to be like this.

Being in the midst of humanity again will be a jolt and as before the transition from the high glaciers to the populated world is much too abrupt in Alaska. This time it will be even more unsettling because the transition will be beyond my control, in a hospital.

Below I can see a highway and farms and float planes like seagulls waiting quietly for their turn to soar. The outskirts of Anchorage are appearing and Doug is busy on the radio. We bank this way and that and descend rapidly to a small airstrip on the edge of town, not much bigger than the strip at Talkeetna but surrounded by buildings rather than Douglas fir trees and cabins; here the environment is mostly concrete.

The little plane flares for a perfect landing and we roll down the runway, slowing until we are taxiing toward a small control building in front of which an ambulance is parked. Two paramedics are standing nearby and two stretchers have already been unloaded.

BOB KANDIKO. Due to the poor weather there was a backlog of climbers to be flown out.

When the skies cleared late in the morning, Geeting came in with the first plane and Simon was loaded into the rear. Since I was technically the last climber arriving back at the Kahiltna Glacier, I was the last to get a flight out and this did not happen until almost midnight. I was the only passenger and the quiet whine of the engine was like a song of freedom as we lifted off with the moon rising over the range. It was an eerie finale to the ordeal.

A large celebration happened in Talkeetna that night with lots of drinking. Simon's clothes and sleeping bag smelled so horrible that we had to throw them into a dumpster.

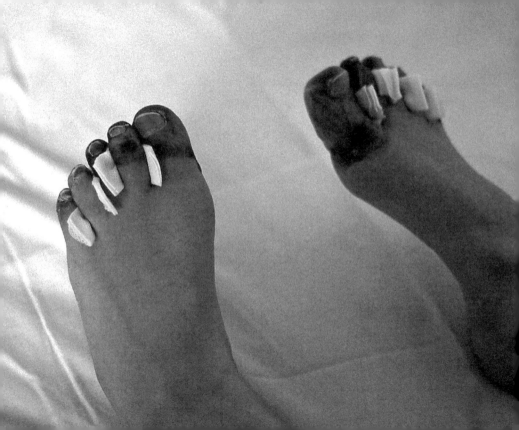

27
PROVIDENCE

JULY 1

I am swept into Providence hospital and surrounded by nurses in pastel uniforms and a middle-aged doctor who rapidly gets to the nub of my problems. My fellow passenger, the German, is dealt with first. It seems they already know his problem and there is a predetermined routine for him. Clearly he is just the latest of many such climbers to pass through.

Apparently I am more interesting because I have bone trauma and possibly cranial injuries. I try to explain that it was just a bang on the head when I fell into the crevasse but the medical team are having none of it – there will be a thorough investigation.

I am introduced to the doctor who will be responsible for my care and I feel immediately at ease with him. He makes a joke about climbers always wanting the best treatment – they may as well since they can't pay for it anyway! I tell him not to worry; I (untypically) actually *do* have insurance, with the British Mountaineering Council. I don't think he believes me.

A detailed exam follows and a lot of time is spent looking into my eyes. My wrist is obviously badly broken but that can wait – it is my head they are most interested in. I am asked many questions about what happened to me and when I start to describe my illness at high altitude I am asked to stop until another specialist doctor can come and listen to the interrogation.

During the pause a nurse describes what they will do with me. Apparently I am not 'hygienic' and I must be thoroughly cleaned up before anything else. I notice that when they don't have to, my carers do not stand close to me.

The second doctor joins us. His speciality is high-altitude medicine.

A question and answer session ensues during which I am asked to describe the onset of my altitude sickness. Very close attention is paid to the precise symptoms. When I mention the onset of my lack of coordination, knowing glances are exchanged between the two doctors. Notes are taken as I describe what happened to me next, day by day. When I describe the time I sat down to take a rest on the Cassin and then found I could not stand up again I get a bigger reaction. I have just solved a puzzle for him and he nods as if I have just confirmed some popular theory.

I must take a bath and have some X-rays; these are the next most important issues. I hope lunch might be near the top of the list too.

Charts are filled in and clipped to my little bed on wheels and I am whisked away by two nurses into the gleaming bowels of the hospital. We enter a large room that has large stainless-steel circular baths like huge cooking pots.

Apparently it is good for the problem with my feet, which is an 'immersion injury' not unlike trench foot. My rancid clothes must be removed and are cut from me quickly with rounded scissors and peeled away in pieces with forceps to be placed in plastic bags marked for disposal. Normally this would have bothered me because my Lifa and pile clothing had been expensive. Today I seem to feel no regret at seeing the back of them.

Hell, I am terribly thin. I thought that I had been skinny when I came down from Huntington but I have taken on a new level of emaciation this time. One of the nurses smiles and asks what I would like for lunch later. I am offered pizza or burgers and I choose both.

It is extremely pleasant in my bath and I can relax. Strong jets of aerated water vibrate my flesh and I am encouraged to stay put for a long while because this is actually a treatment as much as a bath: it will improve my circulation.

My long greasy hair is washed for me and my beard shaved. The nurses explain that I will be treated in the burns unit because that is the centre of speciality in the hospital most suited to dealing with frostbite and high-altitude ailments. Because of the way they treat burns, the need for hygiene is extremely important so I can expect to be in the bath for a while. I would happily stay in here all day if I were not so hungry.

The next wheeled journey is to X-ray where, rather painfully, I have to lay my arm in critical positions for the machine. The photos of my wrist are a sobering sight. Inside my grotesquely swollen paw I can see that the impact of my fall has shattered the head of both the ulna and the radius. Two half-moons of bone have been cleaved away and are floating uselessly in the middle of the joints. This shakes my confidence but the surgeon assures me he has fixed worse. I ask him if I will be able to climb when the injury has healed. While we are travelling to the ward he tells me that I have a lot of work to do but if I try hard with the physiotherapy I will regain ninety per cent of the wrist's function.

I am rolled into the burns unit feeling sorry for myself and we pause at the desk so that I can be handed over to the dedicated staff here. The paperwork takes a little while and a noise behind me arouses my curiosity: the voice of a young woman who sounds like she is playing with a child. I wrench myself up on one shoulder so I can see. The sight freezes me; I cannot move or look away.

A nurse is playing with a child, a little girl less than two years old. Terrible disfiguring burns cover half the child's face and hairless head, then, like a lava flow, the burns extend across her shoulder and torso. Despite this tragic misfortune, the little girl is laughing at the nurse who is playing with her as if she were her own.

Like some sixth sense the child feels my presence and turns suddenly to see who has been looking at her. Her face is distorted into two halves – one side perfect, the other a riot of deep red and purple burns. She smiles at me as best she can and lets out a happy little squawk. I stare, motionless. I have never seen such a terrible misfortune.

One of the nurses notices me looking; I am still frozen on my elbow. She leans close to my ear and says, 'Just smile back.'

I am ashamed of myself. I am not yet twenty-five years old, I will be fit and strong again and I will not have to go through all of my life with the burden that poor child will carry. If I was feeling sorry for myself a moment ago, I am not now.

This distraction means that I am not really paying attention when I am wheeled into a four-bed ward. I am wheeled in lying down, head first so I cannot see where I am going. The first person I see in my wake is the German as I pass by his bed and we acknowledge one another. The trolley ride continues and as I am brought to a stop the nurse says, 'I believe you two know each other.'

I shuffle around so that I can follow her gaze and I connect with a pair of blue eyes set amongst long, unkempt blond hair. Sitting on the bed opposite is Jack, his face pensive, a wan smile. It is not a surprise for him – he knew I was coming. I can see he is pleased to see me but the smile is complicated by other emotions. I know him well enough to sense a torrent of unhappy thoughts beneath the surface. For my part I am delighted to see him alive, but the spirit of the Too Loose expedition has taken a beating. I last saw him ten or eleven days ago. Since then we have had our own trials and know little of the other's journey.

Here we are together again, safe but sorry. I break the silence first:

'Did you cross the summit?'

His voice is a little broken when he replies:

'Yeah. I wish you could have been there.'

I shrug. 'Good. It's done, man, it's done. I would shake your hand but … '

He notices my swollen hand and the happiness that had begun to build in his face drains away.

'What happened? I heard you were getting down OK from 14,000. You got the food, yeah?'

'Yes, we got the food and we got down to the igloo site OK, but sometime the next day I fell into a big crevasse; the Japanese rescued me – and Bob, with help from four other guys.'

Jack is sitting up in bed, his legs covered by a sheet supported by a metal frame – so that the material does not touch his feet. For a moment I am fearful of my question but I am compelled to ask it:

'How are your toes?'

'I still have all of them,' he says quietly, and pulls back the sheet.

For the second time in a short while I am rendered silent: all of Jack's toes are frostbitten to a greater or lesser extent. The big toes are the most damaged and the right foot is the worst of course – this is the foot that had been troubling him most on the climb.

I am shuffled from the trolley and on to the bed. Any further thoughts of a conversation are banished because lunch has arrived. In seconds I am eating like an animal and Jack grins at me from his bed. He calls one of the nurses over to give me one of the beers he has stashed in his locker. I can hardly believe this: beer in a hospital! Apparently in the burns unit beer is not a sin. Beer helps to thin the blood and promotes circulation to the extremities. It keeps sick climbers quiet too.

The effect of the nourishment and the alcohol is like a massive sedative as my body sets to work doing its priority task, extracting nutrients.

My eyes are heavy as I distantly observe my broken hand being hung from the fingers by two nurses. Four metal coil springs are suspended from a shiny bracket above my head. Each of my fingers is inserted into one and when the weight of my forearm is hung from the device, the springs contract and grip each finger gently, the way that babies will grip your finger if you offer one as a toy.

In the early evening I am visited by the surgeon and the altitude sickness specialist. The prognosis from the surgeon is simple: the swelling of my wrist and hand is improving and tomorrow or the next day, when it has reduced sufficiently, he will set my broken bones and put my arm in a cast. After a few days a new, lighter cast will be applied that I can travel with, but only if the problem with my feet can be cured sufficiently that I can walk.

The altitude specialist has a more complicated message and Jack listens in intently to what he has to say. The doctor explains that he has determined that I have been suffering from 'high altitude cerebral oedema'. I tell him that I had heard of pulmonary oedema, something like pneumonia, but he says no, cerebral oedema is a related hypoxia issue that affects the brain, not the lungs, and that it is often just as fatal.

Individual characteristics among climbers and their levels of acclimatisation means that the susceptibility of individuals to this serious illness varies. The effect of the oedema itself is better understood. Lack of oxygen causes a kind of trauma in the brain, which begins to swell. Because the brain is contained within the rigid structure of the skull, it cannot freely expand and an increase in intracranial pressure results. This is very bad for you at best, and fatal if it is allowed to escalate.

He goes on to describe all of the symptoms he would expect from the initial onset to the most extreme prior to death. He has an escalating list of conditions and asks me whether I can recall any of the stages. Jack is drawn into the conversation when I look at him with an expression that says, 'You remember better than I do.' The doctor understands the dynamic between us and begins to direct his questions to both of us:

'After the headaches and the vomiting at about 16,000 feet did you become clumsy, uncoordinated?'

Jack and I look at each other and both nod in agreement.

'Were there changes in your behaviour? Introversion and lassitude are common.'

Jack explains that I went into my shell and rarely spoke when I was ill.

Step by step, the doctor follows the progression of my oedema as I continued to climb into increasingly rarefied air, the pressure on my brain steadily growing and shutting me down.

When we talk of my partial collapse on the Cassin at 19,000 feet the doctor stops and considers his next question carefully, as if we have reached some watershed in his analysis:

'What did you do then?'

Jack is very uncomfortable in explaining that, with no options left, he tried to drag me over the summit crest but I collapsed completely. Jack is in anguish and I am at a loss. I have very little recollection of what happened.

We tell of the arrival of Bob and Mike and the subsequent parting of the ways. Jack tells of his descent and desperate attempts to organise a rescue with Mike. I relate what I can remember about the descent of the upper Cassin Ridge.

Listening to our tales has a disquieting effect on our doctor. He listens intently for many minutes without speaking. When Jack and I run out of things to say there is an awkward silence.

The doctor looks at both of us in turn and I can see a troubled conclusion of emotion rise within him.

'I don't understand what drives guys like you to do what you do.'

And then to me in particular:

'Given your symptoms, you were as close to death as I consider possible without actually … well, now that I hear all of the circumstances of your oedema, I am surprised that we have met to have this conversation. Climbers with cerebral oedema who continue to ascend usually die.'

For me his explanation is a relief. I had felt I'd let Jack down and put Bob at great risk but now, for the first time, I have some understanding of what had happened to me. Jack lies back in his bed and does not speak further.

Later in the night the pain in my wrist penetrates my slumber and I open an eye to look up at it. The swelling seems lessened, so the pain is not unwelcome. In the pale illumination of the ward night lights I can see Jack is awake but unaware of me. He is staring unfocused at the ceiling, his face deep in thought and contorted with misery. He brought demons with him on to the mountain and has collected still more along the way.

So this is what has become of the happy Too Loose boys: two now-damaged souls bivouacked in a hospital, one observing the sorrow of the other and unable to talk about it.

JULY 2

I awaken early in the morning. My exhaustion has passed and the constant semi-light of Alaska has stirred me. Still there are benefits: now that I am awake I can press the button by my bed and demand to be fed. If I am awake then I should be eating.

The starched angels bring me two breakfast burritos with coffee; the day is allowed to begin only after I have eaten them both.

My next challenge is the bathroom. I cannot walk or even stand without crippling pain. I must try, but can only manage with the assistance of two nurses who I am beginning to adore. How can they possibly be so nice and so patient with a climbing brat like me when they have little burnt children to care for?

For Jack the extent of my immobility is a surprise. I can see in his face he is building an inventory of my health problems.

Yesterday we had been awkward with each other. I admit that I am a typical British male and my upbringing came with the stiff upper lip. Jack is even more reticent to talk about his feelings. In truth I now realise that he is deeply emotional but that the thoughts that truly haunt him are kept locked away. The fact that we are both alive and may become well in time is an unlikely outcome when I think about everything that has happened. Now that I understand a little about cerebral oedema I can see that I would surely have perished if any of the circumstances had been different in any detail.

I think that Jack is most deeply troubled by the events that unfolded at our high camp on the Cassin. He was presented with a terrible dilemma. I sense that the time Jack had to face alone when I was at my worst has cost him another scar that may never be soothed away. We should talk about all of this but I am not sure we will.

Any chance of a chat with Jack is swept away by the morning ministrations of doctors and nurses. My eyes are looked into, circulation-inducing exercises for my feet are prescribed and more X-rays are on the agenda. Another team come to tend to Jack's feet and we are even visited by a psychologist who is pioneering techniques whereby you use your mind's power to help heal your body. I am cynical at first but I try and, to my surprise, I become convinced that I can will the blood in my feet to circulate.

Then the crowded schedule is interrupted. We have visitors and I am asked if I am ready to see them. Of course I am, but who can they be? A wave of happiness surges through me when I recognise not only Bob Kandiko but also Frances Randall. Bob looks happy and well, if skinny. Frances is in fine form; I get a hug and a comment that I smell a whole lot better than when she last saw me. She then makes fun of Jack, asking him if she can use the spare bed in the ward for a while and play some loud music because she forgot to bring her tent. An hour passes easily – we talk about what happened and Bob fills in the bits I cannot recall.

Both Bob and Frances thought to bring a gift and both, sensibly, chose beer. We drink a couple together, which is a nice thing to do, yet so incongruous in a hospital. Even the quiet German gets a can.

Bob tells us that yesterday he spent all day watching planes come and go from Kahiltna Base and that he was the last to leave as the sun was setting. While he was waiting his turn, a group of four Canadians flew in and sought him out to ask advice. They were headed for the Cassin Ridge and they wanted to know about the conditions. He recounted the story of the entire Roberts, McCartney, Kandiko and Helms adventure, which helped pass a couple of hours and apparently had a sobering effect.

The conversation soon turns to the adventure that has consumed us for the past few weeks. Each of us has a piece of the story to tell and Frances describes the rangers and climbers who became involved. I am humbled as I discover the scale of the operation; I can now identify at least fifty individuals who played a part.

Frances is a lovely person, strong and deeply caring. I apologise for annoying her when we first camped at Kahiltna Base and her reply is another big hug; she is simply delighted that everybody got down alive.

Frances and Bob have planes to catch so the visit must come to an end. I am sorry to see them leave. Addresses and phone numbers are swapped and Frances does the writing for me because I cannot. I begin to say thank you to Bob, and Jack joins in but Bob tries to shrug it off:

'Don't go on with your life feeling like you owe it to me.'

Long after he has left the hospital those words resonate within me. I am alive today because a very complicated series of events and decisions passed exactly the way they did. But more than that, I count myself lucky that when Jack and I had used up all our luck, it was Bob Kandiko who collided with our disaster, not anybody else. I know that I shall never forget that.

28
AUSTRALIA

It is July 3 and Jack announces that he is checking himself out of hospital. He will be staying in Anchorage with some friends and tells me I can come and stay too when I am allowed to leave.

Jack hates being in hospital whereas I am quite content, for the moment. I am not yet over the novelty of being warm and dry and well fed. Jack is itching to get out and I know him well enough to see that it is not just the hospital that is bothering him. Under different circumstances he would be flirting with the nurses or drawing industriously in his journal. There is none of that. He is a man who is haunted. All that befell us when I collapsed must have been more awful for Jack than for me. I was semi-conscious a lot of the time, whereas he had all his faculties and could avoid none of the trauma of being marooned with a cripple while death crept inexorably closer.

I try to assure him that there was nothing else he could have done but I cannot get him to open up. Part of me thinks he wants to be away from me so that he does not have to talk about what happened. It feels odd to be separated now, but obviously he cannot just camp in hospital if he doesn't need to be here.

Seeing him pack and discharge himself troubles me greatly. It's as if we have been forced apart by sea-level reality. In spite of all that's happened I wish that we were still in high Alaska, only fit and well. He gives me a phone number for the house and brief instructions:

'Call me when you're on your feet. I'll get a lift and come and get you.'

And then he's gone.

Being alone in the ward does have the advantage of privacy. It is time to call Judi and I have been counting the hours until it is morning in Sydney, where she is staying at her father's house. My heartbeat goes up as I listen to the phone ring,

◀ Australia, I discovered, has excellent speleology, and cave diving in the Jenolan Caves in the Blue Mountains was in its infancy. First ascents were swapped for first descents: here I'm exploring new passages flooded in Imperial Cave in a place we called 'Far Country'. Photo: Judi McCartney.

hoping for the pickup. I am in luck:

'Bill Barnes here.'

'Hello Bill, it's Simon.'

I get a very quick but friendly, 'Oh, hi Simon, hang on a tick', and then he is gone to fetch Judi. Bill is such a nice person; he has immediately given priority to his daughter.

Judi's greeting is like a sweet sigh of relief, as if a month of worries have been wiped away in a second by a single word from her. We stumble through the silly questions people ask each other when dear ones talk for the first time after months of separation. But Judi has always been very sensible and direct and she comes to the point first:

'So how was it? You OK?'

The pause at my end tells her part of the answer already. Haltingly I give a very short account of the climb. We put up that ambitious new route, but no, I am not really OK, I am in hospital and will have to stay for another few days.

Judi has obviously been anticipating a number of outcomes for this climb and now that the worst of all the possibilities has been eliminated, she quickly selects the option she had prepared for a 'slightly damaged Simon' scenario. A succinct and as usual direct pronouncement follows:

'Well, you obviously can't go back to work yet so you should come to Australia. It's beautiful here – you will love it. We will organise the ticket, just tell me when you can fly.'

I am swept up in this loving fait accompli. Going to Sydney to spend time with Judi is exactly what I yearn to do. There is the whiff of adventure too – I have heard so much about the great southern land, it is time to see it for myself.

If things had been different, if Jack and I had no injuries on the climb, if we had simply walked across the summit and down the West Buttress, we might have gone back to Santa Monica and after a few days headed for Yosemite. But the consequences of the climb have already changed me. Until now it was unimaginable that I could be glad about *not* going to Yosemite, but at this moment, I am.

After another three days of treatment I make some rapid progress with my feet. They still hurt but I can hobble around like an old man. My arm is set in a more durable cast and all that remains for me to do at Providence is to find and thank everybody who has helped me. My last memory of the hospital is the smile I get from the little girl I had met in the burns unit as she cheerfully waves me on my way.

Australia is everything that I had been told it was.

Judi and her father Bill come to collect me from Kingsford-Smith in Mascot, an airport with a view of white sandy beaches and a deep-blue ocean laid out beneath a clear sky. Our reunion is wonderful; the passion of our embrace wipes away any thoughts of the pain I endured on Denali and an entirely new type of adventure has begun: the pursuit of happiness.

Judi's sister Carol has a spare car we can borrow and I can drive it because it is an automatic. Soon we are off to the Blue Mountains west of Sydney with a tent and two backpacks we have rented from an outdoor shop on George Street.

I had no concept of what the Blue Mountains were but as we wind up towards them I am treated to magnificent views of huge sandstone cliffs and deep valleys containing a stand of massive eucalypts – the Blue Gum Forest.

Judi and I go exploring the mountains and beyond. We drive up the coast from Sydney to Newcastle exploring every national park and the rugged spectacular coastline before turning inland and southbound via the wine country of the Hunter Valley. This is Paradise. All I need is a good job and we will come back and settle in Sydney or somewhere nearby.

Back in Sydney a couple of weeks later I decide to ring Bob Kandiko and Jack. Jack is not yet home in California so a postcard with a kangaroo on the front will have to do for him. Bob picks up, however; he is where he said he would be – with his folks in Ohio, eating his way back into condition. The greeting is warm. I tell him where I am and he thinks this is great. Bob asks me what I have been doing so I tell him, 'Just a little backpacking.'

I am not ready for the answer: a gale of laughter. Bob can barely contain himself:

'You, a little *backpacking*?'

Eventually the hilarity dies down and the conversation turns to more important things, such as how we are, how our families are. Before I hang up I want to make sure I thank Bob again but still he will have none of it. Instead he wants to tell me something:

'We all came back alive which was not the most likely bet. I am happy with that and you will be too.'

He continues, 'Do you remember I told you about four Canadians I met at Kahiltna Base while I was waiting to fly out? They asked me for advice on the conditions on the Cassin where they were headed. Well, Dave Buchanan called me a couple of days ago to ask if we had left any tents on the Cassin when we came down and I told him no, we took everything we had with us. When I asked him why, he told me that the Canadians had disappeared on the Cassin and have not been seen for a long time. The park service fears they are all gone; they can find no trace of them.'

I pause to consider what Bob has just told me. Before I can answer, Bob continues as if he understands exactly what I am thinking:

'Si, it has made me think again about all of what happened. Just as we barely escaped with our lives to celebrate, four more fit young hopeful guys have taken our place on the mountain and the mountain has taken them.'

The last thing he says to me before we hang up is this:

'Enjoy the rest of your life, Simon.'

29
THE KANGAROO ROUTE

AUTUMN 1981, LONDON

Judi and I have decided to spend one more ski season in Europe and then move to Australia. The plan has given us both direction and, despite the claustrophobic nature of our bedsit in Streatham in London, we are very happy. We will get married during the winter and enjoy a two-week skiing honeymoon in Val d'Isère.

Managing Britain's busiest ski and climbing shop in Kensington High Street is hard work but fun for us both. Judi enjoys the atmosphere created by an eclectic mix of Australians, Kiwis and Brits all working to earn money so that they can afford to go skiing or climbing during long holidays.

Jack and I have corresponded a little and as usual had each sent the other a copy of our photographs from the last climb so we both have a full set. I have not heard from him for a while and am surprised to receive a call out of the blue. Jack has been in Chamonix with Jim Bridwell and they are now in the UK and we arrange for the four of us to meet for dinner at an Italian restaurant in the West End. I can't wait to see Jack and to introduce Judi to the best and toughest climbing partner I have ever known.

Judi and I are the first there and I am glad of that. I have time to compose myself before Jack arrives. I am so pleased to be seeing him but the reason for doing so has changed: in the past I would have been eager to get into a huddle and plan some new first ascent, another step towards the limits of what was possible somewhere like Alaska. This time I am just happy because he is alive and well.

◀ The absence of climbing in my life left a vacuum. Canyoning, hang-gliding and cave diving were welcome distractions, but offshore yacht racing became a lifelong passion. The 1984 Sydney to Hobart race was one of those especially stormy events and we had to retire. While the owner of Southern Cross sleeps below, my friend James Judd and I contemplate the little problem that necessitated our retirement from the race.

The Americans' entrance is unmistakeable even from the very far side of the sprawling restaurant.

'That would be them over there then.'

I follow Judi's gaze and sure enough, like two tough cowboys entering the saloon, Jack and Jim cross the threshold, heavily tanned, long-haired and with the collective presence of Clint Eastwood and Chuck Norris all rolled into one.

Judi permits herself a smile.

'I see what you mean now!'

I stand up so they can see me across the crowded restaurant. The result is two big neon smiles as they wade through the tables to meet me. Jim is first and a big calloused hand arrives four feet before the rest of him.

'Hey Simon, great to finally meet you.'

The greeting is openly friendly and heart-warming.

Jack's hand is next. The grip is as firm, and the gaze as direct, but at the same time he is less confident than last summer. He notices that I have lost a lot of movement in my wrist; I can hardly turn it for a handshake. Jack nods at my arm:

'How is that coming along?'

'It hurts like hell when I exercise it but it will improve.'

Over dinner the talk is obsessively and constantly of climbing. The two Californians are full of schemes and Jim especially wants to take his next climb to another level. But there is a difference in me now and unlike Jim and Jack I have no chatter to offer about future projects and my contribution to the conversation is all reminiscence.

I find that I have to try to seem more interested than I am in the conversation and a sickening realisation dawns on me that I might have no climbing ambitions left at all. The counterpoint is painful: I am having dinner with two famous Stonemasters and I begin to wonder if Jack has brought Jim along to stir me up, to persuade me to go back into the mountains. For Jack, climbing is the force that guides his life; nothing else can divert it. He lives, as I once did, to climb obsessively, and for a few years we formed a bond that allowed us to do some remarkable things.

I need a break from the climbing talk and I turn to more mundane matters – what are the immediate travel plans of my guests? Jim is going home apparently, but Jack has no agenda, so I ask him if he wants to hang out in London for a while. Judi and I have a tiny place that won't hold three of us, but I can easily find him a place to stay and even a job if he wants – we are hiring at Alpine Sports for the busy winter season. His acceptance is immediate. Working in retail is hardly inspiring but if it is the ticket to a few months of fun in the best city in the world, so be it.

On the way home I am happy to learn from Judi that she is pleasantly surprised by Jack. She had been expecting a wild man and yet I have produced a slightly wild-looking Jack who is actually very polite. I tell her he is just on his best behaviour.

We get a lot of wealthy customers at Alpine Sports in the build-up to the ski season. Many elegant, well-heeled ladies from the better parts of west London choose to shop for expensive apparel or ski boots during the week. Jack, I discover, has become the big attraction in the clothing department. I had thought that his knowledge of equipment would have suited him in the hardware section, which it does, but I am wrong about his strongest suit. I cannot tell at first if it is the ladies that lunch who are more fascinated with him or the other way round, but no matter, the mix is good for business. He flirts with the women, calls them 'Mam' and tells them how nice they look in those tight ski pants. The girls begin to ask for the muscly blond by name.

We have fun, often eating and drinking together, but whenever the subject returns to climbing it is awkward. I suspect Jack thought if we spent time together we would eventually devise some grand new adventure. It makes us both sad that this is obviously not going to happen. I wish that I could tell him why it won't but I am still trying to understand this myself. I am not afraid of the mountains and I can rehabilitate myself in time, these are not problems. The problem is that the drive for climbing that had ruled my life from adolescence has gone. It is as if all the climbs in my life have been a logical progression, like steps on the rungs of a ladder, gradually ascending higher in difficulty. Now I cannot imagine another step up after Denali, at least not a step in risk or commitment that we would survive.

I have tried to imagine climbing easier and less-committing routes but to deliberately climb at a lesser standard than I am capable of holds no appeal at all. Tearing myself away from climbing will be difficult, but I have a life in Australia to build with Judi.

Jack has no such option. It is clear to me that he will continue his life in the mountains; for him there can be no other way. The mountains define him and he will never stop climbing. Jack is intoxicated by the tests he finds there and I fear for him. He is a creature only truly at home in a world of rock and ice. Good luck,

Jack – you are a great mountaineer. I hope like Bonatti, Cassin, Messner and Harrer you find a way to live as long and boast about your deeds in old age.

When the time comes for him to go home to California, typically and sadly neither of us can find the words to express ourselves properly. I am afraid that I may never see him again. I find myself staring at the hole in the sky where I last saw his Pan Am flight, long after it has disappeared into a cloudy English winter sky.

Judi and I stick to our plan. Happily the issue of finding a job in Australia is solved for me – a French ski-binding supplier wants me to work with their importer in Australia.

When we arrive in Sydney things are easy for us: Judi is offered a job at the same company and we have somewhere to stay in Bill's cavernous house in Lindfield. We have a double income, a company car and a place to stay until we can rent something for ourselves. We travel all over Australia for business but it feels more like a working holiday to me. We ski often and there is a party every weekend either in the mountains or on the beach.

It is a busy, happy life, although the sudden loss of climbing troubles me from time to time no matter what I do. For me, climbing is over and I have to find a way to accept it. Like a lover who has been wronged, I felt climbing had abandoned me. So, as one might at the end of an unhappy affair, I set about removing all trace of it. All my photos are put away and with them any old books or magazines, all out of sight.

30
HONG KONG

JUNE 2012

I don't get to go home to Australia often enough. Back in 1996 Judi and I bought a large rural property on the Hawkesbury River, north-west of Sydney. Our property is 250 acres of wetlands, rugged hills and hidden meadows. It is surrounded by state forest so it feels as if the property is boundless. Not a sign of human activity can be seen from the deck of our house, which is perched on the side of a steep hill overlooking the lake and almost a mile from the nearest road.

Our home is shared with many dogs and cats and the wildlife is a delight: parrots and kookaburras fly to the handrails of our balcony to demand snacks. Sea eagles regularly circle above the lake hunting for fish, while on the ground the creatures range from kangaroos and wombats to sugar gliders and native rats. Oh, and of course there are snakes.

The peace and quiet of our paradise has become the antidote to my work environment of Asia. I used to be away for a week or ten days at a time but increasingly the reverse has become true. I have little choice; Asia is where the work is.

I am still full of energy from my last trip home. It had been a mad week of chores, sawing firewood, slashing the grass and fixing gutters – simple relaxing jobs that are the opposite to my money-making chores in Hong Kong.

The business I have with my partner Peter specialises in architectural lighting and today has been one long heart attack since breakfast. First there was a site visit in Macau, then a dash back on the Hong Kong ferry to attend a meeting with an architect, followed by arguments about late payments. I have just one more meeting and I can go home to Lantau and relax, or at least go home and read another fifty emails with a glass of wine in my hand.

I like to keep all my personal emails until last. A message from Al Chambers has popped up on my smartphone but I have not yet read it. There is an attachment; perhaps he has found another obscure blues classic to share with me.

I can easily walk from my office in Wan Chai to the ferry piers where I will catch a ferry to Lantau Island. The government has finally implemented a plan to sort out the mess that has arisen out of ad-hoc reclamation of the harbour shoreline and for the first time in a century there is organised public foreshore access all the way from Wan Chai to the busy passenger piers that serve the outlying islands around Hong Kong.

Victoria Harbour is constantly abuzz with maritime traffic and the shore bustles with commuters and island children who attend school in Hong Kong. I have become inured to the hubbub. If the weather is fine I stare peacefully at the rocky islands we pass en route from Victoria Harbour to Silvermine Bay, imagining where I might go sailing at the weekend. If the weather is dull or I am behind in my work then there is always my laptop for distraction; there is always one more thing I can do to prepare for tomorrow so the ferry ride is never wasted. And so it is today as I trace through pages of email, trying to sort the urgent items from the merely important ones. Al's message is cryptic:

'Someone is looking for you, please go to this site.'

There is a hyperlink under the text. I have a little portable modem that I carry everywhere but at sea it is slow and internet links become unreliable, so I send my laptop to sleep and close my eyes. I will read his message and check the link when I get home.

Disembarked from the ferry, I exchange pleasantries with half a dozen mates and locals I know as I retrieve my bicycle from where I locked it to the railings early this morning. I take the path that follows the beach at Silvermine Bay and I'm rewarded by the sight of a dozen feral cattle ambling along the lane, headed for the beach where they like to sleep. On the way they stop to eat the roadside flowers planted by the Hong Kong Leisure and Cultural Services Department the same morning.

A few minutes later I am home. The last of the sun is streaming in from the patio windows and the line of sunset shadow is creeping up the slopes of the rolling mountains in front of my house. My helper has been shopping and there is a fresh baguette and cheese on the table. A bottle of Australian Merlot is looking at me from the kitchen.

Shoes off and shorts on I settle down on the patio with my laptop. There are a few messages from friends and family and a long list of things to discuss with Peter in the morning, but it is Al's message that gets priority. I am perplexed when the website opens.

'SuperTopo.'

At first I have no idea what I have opened, but bit by bit I begin to understand that this is some kind of climbing blog. I had no idea such things existed, but nowadays there seems to be a website for just about every obscure pastime.

I still have no idea why he has sent me here. I have clicked on some kind of forum for climbers. I have not climbed for decades, so what is this?

It is like science fiction: hundreds or thousands of climbers posting comments about mysterious issues and using assumed nicknames. I am about to abandon the site when I see a search function. Al sent me this for a reason; I should at least give it a few minutes of my time.

In the search box I type my name 'Simon McCartney' and press enter.

The screen refreshes and I am presented with a new list of pseudonyms posting and replying to posts. One post leaps off the screen. It is a message from 'RDB'. He is asking if anybody knows where I am and he mentions Jack.

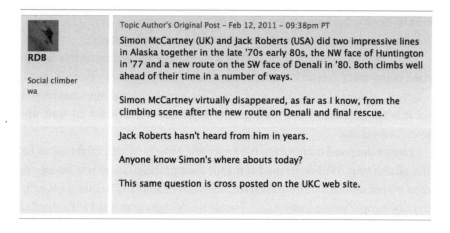

RDB

Social climber
wa

Topic Author's Original Post – Feb 12, 2011 – 09:38pm PT

Simon McCartney (UK) and Jack Roberts (USA) did two impressive lines in Alaska together in the late '70s early 80s, the NW face of Huntington in '77 and a new route on the SW face of Denali in '80. Both climbs well ahead of their time in a number of ways.

Simon McCartney virtually disappeared, as far as I know, from the climbing scene after the new route on Denali and final rescue.

Jack Roberts hasn't heard from him in years.

Anyone know Simon's where abouts today?

This same question is cross posted on the UKC web site.

My heart misses a beat. My God, Jack is alive! I had not expected that. And he has been wondering about me, it seems. But who is RDB? I notice there are historical mistakes in the message: Jack and I climbed Huntington in 1978 not 1977. It is as if an acquaintance of Jack's has posted this message based on approximate information. It was a long time ago so this in itself is not surprising.

A wave of complex emotions swells in my mind and I can feel adrenaline surging within me. I believed Jack to be dead long ago. I had no evidence to support this but the trend of our climbing was very likely to be fatal. I looked for Jack a couple of times, unsuccessfully, and then became afraid to look again for fear of receiving bad news.

I had been gloriously wrong! Jack is out there and I begin to realise that through this website I can probably reach out to him without difficulty. I get out of my chair and walk out into the garden. My mind is racing, with snippets of memories surfacing as I try to take in this amazing revelation. I can see Jack's face clearly and even hear his voice. Happy memories and frightening moments are fleetingly shown to me, each for a few seconds before my mind races on to the next and then the next without any cognisant instruction from me. I am not sure what to do.

The immensity of my discovery is almost paralysing and I stand, staring at nothing, for fifteen minutes until shaken from my reverie by the fact that the sun has set. It is now dark and my dog is staring at me, confused.

I head back to my PC and discover more leads to follow. I know now how I feel: happy at this joyous discovery, and also excited. What on earth shall I say to Jack after three decades of silence?

I read the post from RDB again. There is a box I can tick to reply and I open a dialogue box with a single click. My fingers hover over the keyboard for a minute, unmoving. I am frozen. I do not know what to say.

In the end I type the least eloquent prose I have ever written:

'Hi, It is Simon McCartney. A friend of mine stumbled onto this website when doing some research. I am alive and well living mostly in Hong Kong.'

Several glasses of wine follow as I wait for a reply. I want one immediately, but it is the middle of the night in the USA and I shall have to wait until America awakens.

I cannot sleep so I do not even try. I pace and imagine what I might say to Jack after all this time. Will he be mad at me for disappearing? There was no internet when we last saw each other and I have moved continents twice since then, telling very few people where I was going. I made no deliberate attempt at camouflage but I certainly left few tracks. Because I've had no contact with climbers for three decades, there would have been no clues to follow, nowhere to even begin to look.

I decide to read further into the climbers' forum, out of curiosity. Goodness, there seems no end of it: arguments and comments within long strings of unimportant chat. I never use social media and to see it applied to climbing is bizarre. When I was climbing there were just a few journals and a handful of magazines. I can see that climbing has exploded.

I decide to refine my search of the site and I make the obvious choice. I had learned much from searching my own name, so I type 'Jack Roberts' into the search window. I stare at it for more than a minute before I have the confidence to press enter.

The screen refreshes.

I am a speed-reader – a necessary curse in my line of work. I scan the page in a few seconds; there are many entries, but my eyes lock on to one that stops my heart:

'Jack Roberts RIP.'

No, this can't be true.

Paralysed, I stare at the screen. I tell myself there must be more than one Jack Roberts in the world. This can't be him. I push back the chair in an attempt to free myself from sudden claustrophobia. I pace the patio with wild eyes before returning to my PC. I expand my focus and I find that there are many related messages, all kind salutes to a brother who has indeed passed.

I cannot accept that what I am reading refers to my Jack Roberts until one compelling item of irrefutable evidence forces me to accept reality: a climber called Mark Westman has posted some text and a photo. He explains that he knew Jack and spent time with him in the mountains and that they had talked about Jack's climbs. He goes on to explain that Jack had told him that he thought that his proudest achievement was his ascent of the south-west face of Denali with Simon McCartney. There is an attachment, a photo of the face with the line of our climb sketched upon it.

I have to remind myself to breathe. Never have I been so swept up by a wave of melancholy. I trawl through the site with tears blurring my view. I find a picture of Jack. He is smiling at the camera, high on an ice climb somewhere. There is less hair, the face is a little rounder and the beard is gone – but there can be no mistake. It is my old friend, still with the wry grin and the swagger that was always his signature. The lightning bolt earring is still in evidence.

Cruel fate has conspired that I would find Jack unexpectedly, only to have my joy murdered by the knowledge that I was just a month too late. I have found him and lost him in the same hour.

He had been out for a climbing adventure on the frozen Bridal Veil Falls at Telluride with his friend Jon Miller. Jack had climbed the route many times before. Inexplicably he fell while leading, a long fall, sixty feet or so. Jon was able to arrest the fall, but Jack sustained a very heavy impact and major internal injuries. Jon was able to get to Jack and do all he could, the accident had been seen and a rescue was on the way.

Jack died in Jon's arms.

31
THE BOND

The circumstances of my discovery of Jack's life and death in 2012 were cruel. I doubt I will ever escape the regrets I have. The end of my life as a climber saddened me and for three decades I kidded myself that it didn't matter. I see clearly now that I was deluded.

If the timing of the internet discovery was awful, there have also been some surprising and wonderful things that have come about since and I think of them as Jack's gift to me.

I got in touch with Mark Westman immediately. A kind and generous person, he had indeed known Jack, and identified with the particular style of climbing that Jack and I favoured. 'Denali Mark', I discover, is a talented alpinist himself, a modern climber of the highest order with an encyclopaedic knowledge of all things related to Alaskan climbing. Mark is a climbing ranger with the Denali national park and lives in Talkeetna. He is even friends with Roger Robinson, one of the rangers who helped during my ordeal on the Cassin Ridge.

In a short amount of time I learn a great deal from Mark who, despite the melancholy circumstances, enjoys talking to me and discovering the missing history of my two big climbs with Jack. It seems that little was written about the climbs. Jack wrote a short article about our Huntington ascent called 'The Timeless Face' but that was it. Like a benevolent tomb raider, Mark helps me dig through the archaeology and, gradually, I begin to write about the climbs and discover something that has eluded me since 1981: pride in what Jack and I achieved.

A week or two later I get in touch with Pam Roberts. Finding her had been an objective that troubled me every day, but I waited until I felt ready. Poor Pam

◀ The beginning of our bond. Jack and I confront our first life-changing adventure as Mount Huntington stares back at us.

had no inkling of my resurrection. Jack had probably believed I was no longer alive so my email to her was a total shock. I was a dead man arriving at the most emotional instance possible – Pam was walking as a pilgrim across the Camino de Santiago de Compostela in Spain, scattering Jack's ashes as she went. I wish that I could have chosen a more peaceful time to introduce myself. Pam received my message without warning in an internet cafe.

Pam's grief, of course, is far greater than mine, but we share a strong connection. When Pam returns to Boulder we begin to talk often. I learn that Jack and Pam had discovered the love of their life in one another. Jack married Pam a few years after I last saw him and his life was blessed from then on. I also learn that Jack used to talk of me quite often.

When I knew Jack, he was totally driven by climbing and I had expected him to join the league of ghosts, climbers I had known as a young man. I learn that in fact he was far smarter than I gave him credit for: he saw the path of his demise in our style of climbing and found his own way around it so that he could continue to climb at the highest standard. Jack was happiest in the mountains and discovered a way to follow his destiny in them. He had become a mentor to younger climbers and like a sage, and the author of the ice-climbing guide to Colorado.

Pam and I have quickly and naturally become friends – through her I now have many others. It seems that I have become part of the climbing community once again.

All the while, memories from my climbs with Jack grow and grow. Back in Australia, Judi reveals boxes of photographs that I thought had been lost decades ago but which she had kept. Pam discovers still more, along with Jack's journals from 1978 and 1980. For the first time I discover what my old friend had been thinking on those climbs. Jack was very honest with himself and he wrote almost every day. Not always easily, I learn what he was thinking but not saying to me in some desperate moments.

I feel ready to make the next vitally important step and track down Bob Kandiko. I have the phone number for his home in Bellingham in Washington State. Summoning all my courage, I dial, and get the answering machine: 'Bob and Karen are out'. Breathlessly, I begin to leave a message.

'Bob, this is an old friend from the past … it is Simon McCartney … yes, *that* Simon, I hope this finds you well … '

I am lucky: the next day Bob picks up on the second ring. Somehow we manage to stumble through a joyous but halting conversation that is interrupted by waves of emotion and tears at my end.

Over the next few days we talk and laugh often.

In September 2014, I am finally able to travel to the USA for the reunion tour. I discover that I have several moving targets: old climbers keep travelling and having fun. An itinerary is strung together: I will fly to San Francisco and then Seattle and on to Bellingham where Bob Kandiko has lived for decades, by the shore, overlooked by snow-capped volcanoes. Bob and Karen are both just retired and are so much fitter than I am that it is embarrassing. While reliving old times, I observe these two spry adventurers and start to make certain plans for my own health in future.

Pam Roberts is my next target, in Boulder. Never in my life have I felt so welcome. Pam's middle name is Ranger (also her family name) and I wonder at that: Pamela Ranger Roberts. It suits her perfectly! Through Pam I gain new friends and renew old acquaintances. She asked me if I would do a slide show while I am in town, to tell the tale of those two enigmatic climbs. I love to tell stories and so I instantly agree, imagining a wine and cheese evening at Pam's house with maybe a dozen friends.

Wrong! Pam is at the epicentre of the climbing community and social media is powerful. I am to be the attraction at the social centre of the climbing scene in Boulder, Gary Neptune's cavernous climbing store and museum.

Thursday evening arrives and I am nervous as hell. Pam *has* organised a wine and cheese night, but just as a prelude to going to Neptune's. Rick Accomazzo arrives; I last saw him in Chamonix in 1977. Jack Tackle, a new friend, is in town for the event. I had reached out to him because he had climbed with my old friend.

Jeff Lowe, perhaps America's greatest technical climber, arrives with his partner Connie Self. Jeff now has a debilitating condition but he and Connie have gone to a lot of difficulty to come and hear what I have to say. I am humbled by this realisation, but I had underestimated the power of the bond between climbers. Jeff has always been curious about the two climbs I did with Jack, just as I am fascinated about his solo ascent of *Metanoia* – the hardest climb on the north face of the Eiger. I had missed his pivotal climb completely in my years of ignorance. To sit opposite Jeff and exchange anecdotes is glorious.

Pam is an excellent sleuth on social media and she found Mike Helms alive and well, living in Snohomish in Washington State. I call him. The great welcome I receive when I speak to Mike is testimony to the bond between all of us who survived Denali, half a lifetime ago.

I learn the details of their gruelling descent of the West Buttress, during which Mike and Jack had frantically tried to organise a rescue, finally making contact with a radio borrowed from the Mountain Trip guided expedition at 17,200 feet.

Shortly after, Mike received a message from pilot Doug Geeting telling him that he had seen me and Bob descending the Cassin Ridge. Mike told me that receiving this information felt like someone had plunged a knife into him; there was nothing he could do for us after that. The fact that Doug Geeting had managed to fly over us at more than 18,500 feet on the Cassin Ridge is in itself remarkable because the ceiling altitude for a Cessna 185 is about 1,500 feet lower than that altitude. In Alaska, aviation seems to have more flexible limits than elsewhere. The little bird was totally stripped of all non-essential equipment with only pilot Geeting and climbing ranger Roger Robinson on board. Mike remembers that they had also borrowed an oxygen bottle from a local dentist.

'Just as well they did not take the laughing gas by mistake.'

Mike was filled with anxiety for us throughout his and Jack's own hellish descent, during which they had to beg and scrounge whatever food they could from other climbers. On the way they even helped to evacuate a climber with a blood clot.

Mike cannot recall how long it took to get back to Kahiltna Base, but he does vividly remember his hallucinations as he and Jack slowly limped in. He thought he was leading a horse along a dusty street lined with houses. People were looking out at him. A blonde girl greeted him, saying, 'You sure look like you could use a drink'.

The swing doors of the saloon were parted and he stepped inside to sit down.

Actually it was Frances Randall's tent and the 'saloon doors' were the tent flaps.

Mike and Jack did get their whiskey.

Mike apologised for not being at Base Camp when Bob and I got down. It bothers him to this day. Once he was told that we were on the way down to the Kahiltna Glacier he allowed himself to fly out. He has nothing to apologise for: Mike was utterly spent, physically, mentally and emotionally, and we would never have expected him to wait.

In the happiest possible reunion, I met Mike Helms in the flesh for the first time since last I saw him on the Cassin Ridge in 1980. Mike and his wife Chancellor attended the 2016 American Alpine Club annual benefit dinner in Washington DC. Mike Helms and Bob Kandiko were the co-recipients of the David Sowles award for heroism, for their selfless and instant assistance to Jack and me, without any regard to their own safety.

Through Pam, I learn much about Jack's life and compare it to my own. He followed his dreams and I admire him immensely for that. She tells me he thought I was the strongest and best climbing partner he ever had.

'I feel the same,' I reply.
'Pity you couldn't tell him yourself,' she says.
All I can do is say it now, Jack.

POSTSCRIPT: A RETURN TO THE SCENE OF THE CRIME

I am riding in the co-pilot's seat of our Talkeetna Air Taxi ski-plane, camera in hand, spare lenses in my lap. We have barnstormed Denali at 17,000 feet, flown close to and stared down at the south-west face and the Cassin Ridge, the scene of a life-changing adventure. To come here was Bob Kandiko's idea – just a week ago he sent me a mischievous email:

> 'Karen and I are driving through the Yukon and when we get to Talkeetna we have booked a flight over Denali, I don't suppose you could pop over?'

Of course I 'popped' over. What was I going to do, pass up a bucket-list trip and let him piss me off by sending photos of the spectacle afterwards? No way.

We loop around Mount Huntington, passing the west face where I can easily see the route Jack and I took down to the Tokositna Glacier and across the north-west ridge. It is very different today, dry and rocky on the west side where it was all snow before. We pass the north face and make a loop into the great gorge of the Ruth before heading back into the canyon of the west fork, just as we had done in 1978. The same startling views unfold.

We pass the Rooster Comb at one third of its height and slide past the base of the north face of Huntington, gently flaring for a smooth landing in perfect corn snow. The prop whines to a halt and the plane is sensibly parked on the north side of the glacier, furthest away from Huntington's threatening séracs.

For the first time in thirty-six years, a Roberts and a McCartney set foot together on the west fork of the Ruth Glacier under the only-once-climbed north face of Mount Huntington. Pam Roberts is with me and there is a little of Jack here too; Pam has brought some of his ashes with her.

The four of us stand in the snow and talk a little. I point out the line of the Roberts-McCartney route up the north face. I am shell-shocked to be here again, bombarded by memories this time, not avalanches.

We watch silently as Pam scatters Jack's ashes. There is a slight breeze, enough to carry them shoulder-high towards the very base of the climb. I cannot speak for several minutes but I talk to the mountain in my mind. I stare up at the jagged shark's tooth, a shriek of ice in the sky. The Timeless Face glowers back at me as only it can.

'Do you remember us?' I ask.

I will the mountain to let loose a sérac avalanche in reply but it defies me, as of course it would. Perhaps we are just out of range.

The flight out, like everything else we had encountered, was overwhelming. Yet nothing had changed except my point of view, myself. The face had not changed; it would be forever the same: timeless.
JACK ROBERTS, 1978

ACKNOWLEDGEMENTS

I had eschewed all contact with the world of climbing for three decades.

Like a coma patient I was jolted awake to discover what had transpired during my long episode of deliberate unconsciousness. Having decided to write about my climbs with Jack, I needed all the help I could get.

Many people have shown me great kindness during my research and the writing of this book. Every climber I have contacted has offered support and encouragement and many of them have been generous with their time, sharing their journals and photographs, and in one or two cases much, much more than that.

Pam Roberts was my first supporter when the notion of writing a book was first floated. Despite the awful circumstances and grief surrounding Pam when I first contacted her, she selflessly answered all my questions, hunted down Jack's journals and made hundreds of copies of his photos. From Pam I learned much about who Jack became and about their life together. I learned that Jack never forgot me and would often reminisce about our two adventures in Alaska. Inevitably Pam has become a fast friend. The world needs more folk like Pam. She is a teacher and, maybe without realising it, she has taught me many things.

The very existence of **Bob Kandiko** and **Mike Helms** is a defining factor in making this book possible. Finding both of them alive and well after three decades has been one of the most wonderful things in my life.

Without the generosity, unique knowledge and remarkable skills of **Mark Westman** this book might not have even begun, or at best it would have been a shadow of itself. Mark is a greatly talented alpinist and a passionate climbing historian with an encyclopaedic knowledge of Alaskan climbing. He is also a determined sleuth. Together, we have been able to verify the location of every photo taken by Jack or myself and it has been possible to reconstruct the precise line of our climb on the south-west face of Denali. His help with this was crucial as I was not at my best during much of that climb.

Mark has also helped me connect with climbing again after a thirty-three-year absence. It has been an amazing journey for both of us, sometimes funny, sometimes poignant. Going on a virtual alpine climb with Mark has encouraged me greatly – the spirit of alpinism in which I lived my life as a young man is alive and well.

In the long hours of conversations with Mark, amongst his incredibly accurate analysis of the climb on Denali – for Mark knows the mountain like no other – I have been lucky to relive my past. This has been a gift because it might so easily just have faded away. Mark has also helped me put what we achieved in perspective.

Some of Mark's contemporary landscape photographs of the Alaska Range have been used in this book so the reader need not suffer blurry old versions of the same perspectives taken with either Jack's camera or mine. If one of Mark's beautiful studies is clearer, we have used his shot. Luckily, most of the critical original photos on the climbs did survive, albeit with a few crinkles, and I have **Judi McCartney** to thank for that. After I put them away and tried to forget them, she kept them safe without telling me, 'just in case'.

Dane Burns was one of Jack's great friends, another alpinist and a fine person. Dane has helped me navigate a safe passage through some potentially troubled waters and he has been generous with his time in giving me advice. Throughout the early writing of *The Bond* he provided invaluable support. He has also taught me a lot about how climbing has changed during my absence and how Jack lived his life.

I have many climbers to thank, climbers who despite their own distractions helped Bob Kandiko and I when we were in dire need. My thanks are three decades overdue. Mike Helms used his knowledge of Denali to help us by desperately trying to arrange a rescue, only to have his hopes dashed when he learned that Bob and I were seen descending the Cassin Ridge. As Bob and I stumbled down, starving and on our last legs, the first people we met were **The Freaks**, the four-man team from Pennsylvania who showed us kindness, shelter and a willingness to share their meagre rations. Our collision with them would not have been easy to bear. Effectively our crash landing on their camp derailed their own climb. We were insufficiently grateful at the time.

Without the help of the three-man Japanese **Tokyo Unyro-Kai** team and their radio equipment we might have starved. Bob and I owe a debt to the boys from Tokyo and to another team we crashed into on the north-east fork: the **Twin Cities Health Club Expedition** from Minnesota.

In addition I owe a debt to the Denali climbing rangers **Roger Robinson** and **Dave Buchanan** as well as the Kahiltna Base boss, **Frances Randall**. Roger and Dave will get to read this but sadly not Frances. I was heartened to learn that a peak overlooking the site of Kahiltna Base is named after her: Mount Frances. Frances kept a diary every day. After she passed away in 1984 her logs of the seasons spent managing the Kahiltna

Base were published in *Denali Diary* and I have quoted them in the sections that refer to Jack and I, as well as Bob and Mike.

In 1978 there were other parties active on Mount Huntington. **Angus Thuermer Jr** and his friends were in Alaska to make the first ascent of the south-east spur. I was able to track Angus down. We had never met but such is the bond between old climbers that I immediately acquired another supporter who happily shared his journal and research with me.

Rob Newsom and his friends were camped nearby on the west fork of the Ruth Glacier that summer. Rob was an uncommon and entertaining fellow back then, just as he is now. I have Rob to thank for moral support and his startlingly honest and often entertaining journal. He is a great wine maker these days, he tells me. I look forward to pulling a cork with him.

I managed to get in touch with the famous glacier pilot **Doug Geeting**, thanks to a little help from Mark Westman (Mark lives in Talkeetna too). Remarkably Doug remembered me and he had seen Jack in Alaska often since we were last there together in 1980. Doug willingly helped me with some aviation facts relating to flying in the mountains.

I think that I am blessed with some fine friends and one outstanding example is **Al Chambers**. Unwittingly he provided the genesis for this book.

Professor Aldwyn Cooper gave a lot of his time as a young man, teaching teenagers to be more than they might otherwise be. A volunteer for the London-based adventure group New Horizon, 'Coops' invested a lot of time and attention in me when I was a kid. He taught me to climb and helped shape me to become determined and self-reliant. I recently had dinner with Coops in his favourite London restaurant in Baker Street. I had not seen him for thirty-five years. Coops is still shaping young people for the better; these days he is 'the big cheese', the vice chancellor and chief executive at Regent's University in London.

If one lacked any faith in the climbing community, **Agustin Castiella** would put paid to that. We have never met but Agustin got wind of my intention to write this book and immediately set about helping me with the research without even being asked. Agustin has uncommon skills in historical climbing research and has helped me make contact with some long-lost friends and answered some questions I could not have without his help.

Rick Accomazzo is, among his many talents, a climbing historian, and I have been the beneficiary of his knowledge. With his help I have been able to piece together the 1977 climbing season.

The process of researching this book has also reunited me with the American side of my family, my cousin Brendan in particular – **Captain Brendan Lally** to be precise. Brendan has provided a friendly but critical eye to my drafts. He was a climber too so his perspective has helped give me confidence.

Doctor Peter Hackett is a world-renowned expert in high-altitude medicine and I tracked him down for advice about the illness to which I succumbed, high on Denali. Peter's insights are a great benefit.

Talkeetna Air Taxi enabled us to get fantastic photographs of the Alaska Range when Pam Roberts, the Kandikos and I flew with them in 2014 in our trip down high-altitude memory lane. Pilot Dave Wiewel went out of his way for us, and owner and pilot Paul Roderick reunited me with the north face of Mount Huntington in a way I shall never forget.

I have been fortunate that **Vertebrate Publishing** took me on. Jon Barton probably gets a great many, very average submissions to read. I am sure that I served up another, but he saw something in *The Bond* and with his help I have been able to tell a story in my own words that has troubled me for more than three decades. Susie Ryder was appointed as the editor of this book and I am fortunate indeed. Patient, determined, disciplined and passionate, working with Susie has been inspiring and she has enabled me to do things that I had not realised I could. John Coefield's enthusiasm, creativity and attention to detail have been an inspiration while Nathan Ryder has shown me a vision (patiently) in design I could not have imagined.

Finally, I did not write this work alone; **Jack Roberts** has much to say for us both.

A nylon climbing rope loses its strength in a season or two, but the bond
between climbers on Denali remains unbreakable.
BOB KANDIKO

INDEX